CRETE

12/02

Second Revised Edition
1995

TABLE OF CONTENTS

FEATURES

GUIDELINES

LIST OF MAPS

Please note: in some cases the spelling of the place names on the maps is not the same as in the text, because the spelling on the maps is according to UN guidelines, whereas the common English spelling is used in the text.

Nelles Guides

... get you going.

TITLES IN PRINT

Australia
Bali / Lombok
Berlin and Potsdam
Brittany
California - *Las Vegas, Reno,*
      Baja California
Cambodia / Laos
Canada - *Ontario, Québec,*
      Atlantic Provinces
Caribbean - *The Greater Antilles*
      Bermuda, Bahamas
Caribbean - *The Lesser Antilles*
China
Crete
Cyprus
Egypt
Florida
Greece - *The Mainland*
Hawaii
Hungary
India - *Northern, Northeastern*
      and Central India
India - *Southern India*
Indonesia - *Sumatra, Java, Bali,*
      Lombok, Sulawesi
Ireland

Kenya
Malaysia
Mexico
Morocco
Moscow / St Petersburg
Munich and Surroundings
Nepal
New York *and New York State*
New Zealand
Paris
Philippines
Provence
Rome
Spain, *North*
Spain, *South*
Thailand
Turkey

IN PREPARATION

Prague – *Czech Republic*
England / Wales
Israel
South Africa
Tuscany
U.S.A. - *The West, Rockies and Texas*
U.S.A. - *The East, Midwest and South*
Vietnam

CRETE
© Nelles Verlag GmbH, 80935 München
  All rights reserved

Second revised edition 1995
ISBN 3-88618-042-5
Printed in Slovenia

Publisher:	Günter Nelles	**Cartography:**	Nelles Verlag GmbH
Project Editor:	Michèle Macrakis	**Color**	
Editor:	Wolfgang Josing,	**Separation:**	Priegnitz, München
	Marton Radkai	**Printed by:**	Gorenjski Tisk

- 04 -

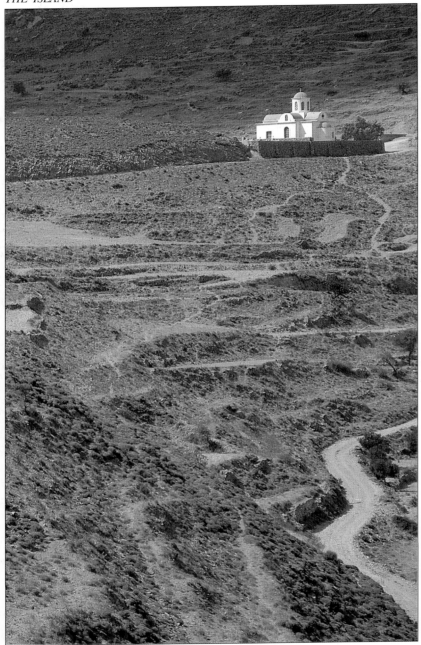

THE ISLAND

A portrait of Crete

Geography

Crete is Greece's largest island with a total surface area of 8261 square kilometers. It is also the fifth largest in the Mediterranean after Sicily, Sardinia, Corsika and Cyprus.

To megalonisi, or the great island as the Greeks call it, lies between the 35 and 36th parallel north, which places it on par with the central part of Tunisia, North Africa. The island lies like some part of an ancient ford that might once have served to conect two great continents. It is nearly 260 km long from west to east, and its width varies between 12 and 61 km. It is around 100 km from the southernmost section of mainland Europe, the Peloponnese, and 200 km separate it from the Anatolian coast of Asia. The distance to Africa, specifically to Kyrenaika on the Libyan coast, is about 300 km. This remarkable central location has earned Crete a nickname: The "little continent." While it officially belongs to Europe, it is nevertheless an isolated appendix in many ways, geographically independent and with its own very special historical evolution.

Crete's coastline measures approximately 1000 km. Access to the sea on the northern half is by and large open. Gently rolling hills and flood plains mark the landscape here. The southern coast is quite different. Crete's mountains plunge steeply and forbiddingly into the sea.

Preceding pages: A soapstone statue of the bull rhyton from the Little Palace, Knossos. Typical old Cretan. Sea and sun. The picturesque port of Iraklio. Left: Inland mountain landscape.

Some of these mountains are almost 2500 m high: Lefka Ori (White Mountains) in the west reaches 2453 m; the Psiloritis, which used to ba called Ida, in the middle of the island is 2456 m; and the Dikti chain in the east reaches 2148 m.

One of the peculiarities of Crete's landscape are the great abysses that penetrate deep into the mountains especially in the western part of the island, and lead all the way down to the southern coast. The most famous of these abysses (it is the longest of Europe), is that of Samaria. From its cradle in the White Mountains to the sea, it is a full 18 km long.

Another peculiarity are the almost perfectly round, drainless upland wolds. The Lassithi Plain, at 815 m, is the most impressive one of the lot. It is best known for its windmills that stretch thousands of canvas arms into the sun and wind. As opposed to the Lassithi Plain, which is basically a ravine in the karstic highlands, the Omalos Plain (1050 m) and the Nidha Plain (1355 m) are in fact dried out lakes and not nearly as fertile.

Running Crete

The mountainous landscape of Crete means that intensive farming can only be practiced in limited fashion. The largest agricultural region of the island is the Messara Plain south of the prefecture of Iraklio, followed by the smaller valleys along the northern coast. The olive tree used to be by far the most important economic buttress for the farmers of the Messara Plain, but thanks to technology, modern means of irrigation, greenhouses and clement winters, they have become major suppliers of early vegetables. Still, olives and wine have maintained their supremacy as the most important agricultural product on the island. Olive trees occupy about 42 per cent of the arable area. The olives themselves are for the most part pressed into oil.

As for grapes, which take up about 14

CRETE IN THE MEDITERRANEAN SEA

per cent of the arable land and are mainly concentrated around the prefecture of Iraklio, they are sold primarily as table fruit, then dried to raisins, and finally pressed to make wine. All types of vegetables are grown on Crete, and there is a great deal of fruit, especially citrus, and even, albeit in limited quantity, bananas.

The mountainous interior of the island has found a role for itself as a pastureland. During the warm seasons large herds of sheep and goats frequently roam around the highland regions.

There are no industrial areas on Crete to speak of. The largest business undertakings are the ones involved in the production of foodstuffs, be that the making of raisins, making and bottling wine, pressing olives.

Craftspeople, on the other hand, are very active in countless small operations. The most important trade center on the island is the port of Iraklio followed by Hania, a distant second.

Besides agriculture, the most important source of income is the "white industry," that is tourism. It not only provides thousands of direct jobs, but also gives great support to the building industry and retail.

The most important means of transportation is shipping to and from Crete. Ferries and ships connect Iraklio and Hania daily with Athens' great harbor Piraeus. Depending on the season and the weather, ships also run regular routes from Kastelli Kissamou to Githio on the Peloponnese, from Agios Nikolaos and Sitia over Karpathos to Rhodos, and finally from Iraklio through the Cyclades to Piraeus. Furthermore, many of the ferries connecting Adriatic ports with Egypt, Turkey and Israel, make a stopover in Iraklio. That is where Crete's international airport is situated. The second airport on the island is in Hania, but it is only used during the high tourist season by charter aircraft from abroad.

Right: Dusk as it has fallen for millenia upon the shores and mountains of Crete.

16

Crete's roads are for the most part in good shape, especially along the main northern artery. The forks toward the south are also well-tended, but the by-ways in the south are something of a problem.

Crete is one of ten Greek regions. The island itself is divided up into four pre-fectures (known as *nomi* in Greek, singular is *nomos*): Hania, Rethimno, Iraklio and Lassithi (the capital is Agios Niko-laos). The prefect of each (*nomarchis*), who is at the top of the administrative py-ramid, is nominated from Athens, as is typical for the centralized Greek system. The island is further subdivided into 20 districts, but this is only of minor statistical interest. The island consists in all of 578 urban and rural comunities with a total of 1450 townships.

Climate

Nowhere is the Mediterranean climate as well exemplified as on the island of Crete. The summers are hot and ex-tremely dry, and it seldom rains between April and September. Winter along the coast is by and large mild with abundant precipitation in January and February, falling as snow in the upper regions of the island. Cretans distinguish mainly sum-mer and winter, and refer to spring as a brief interlude. Nevertheless, April, May and June are without a doubt the best months to travel. At this time, the island looks like a beautiful, blooming garden.

Water temperature in July, August and September is around 25°C, the air is on average 30° C during the day and rarely drops below 20° C at night. The *meltemi*, a wind that blows along the northern coast, sometimes brings a little relief from the heat.

In the south, however, desert winds blowing in from Africa frequently turn the island into an oven from the wee hours on. But it is the proximity of Africa that makes the autumn days so pleasantly warm. December afternoons in the south of Crete can recall those halcyon summer days of the middle of Europe.

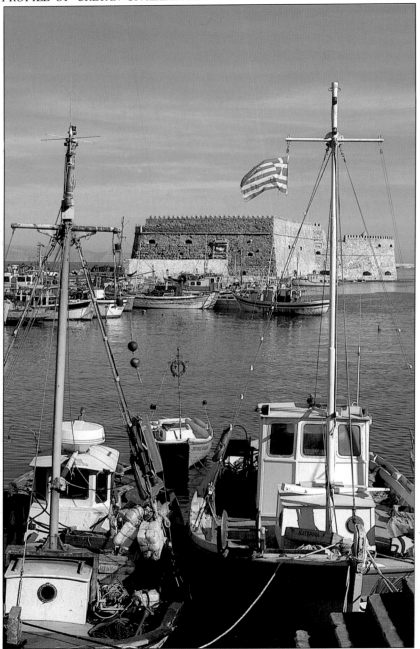

PROFILE OF CRETAN CIVILIZATION

"There is a kind of flame in Crete – let us call it soul – something more powerful than either life or death. There is pride, obstinacy, valor, and together with these something else inexpressible and imponderable, something which makes you rejoice that you are a human being, and at the same time tremble."

(Nikos Kazantzakis, *Report to Greco*)

Much has been said and written about Crete and the Cretans over the millenia: Crete is the cradle of all greek islands, it is the sixth continent of planet Earth. The Cretans are all liars, or so thought apostle Paul, they are lazy bones and nasty beasts. On the other hand, there are those who say that the Cretans have always been on the barricades for freedom, that they have resisted all attempts to suppress them with virtually anarchistic energy...Whatever the case, one thing is sure: There is something very special about this island and its people.

Obviously, Crete is not just another Greek island. Situated in the center of the eastern Mediterranean, halfway between Europe, Africa and Asia, it was considered in ancient times as being at the center of the world. In such a position, Crete could not escape contact with the foreign cultures of East and West. On the contrary, each new influence was first assimilated and then adapted to suit the needs of Crete itself, thus creating a unique culture.

The peculiarities of Crete – its exposed geographic position, the succession of foreign domination and revolts – created their own mood, not found in other is-

Left: The Koules fortress built by the Venetians stands in the port of Iraklio.

lands in the area. Its climate, people, and ways of life belong to the Aegean Archipelago, Greece, and Mediterranean Europe. Its civilization is part of that of Greece and Asia Minor. Its people came from all cardinal points in the world to settle on the island. Lying between the last promontory of the Peloponnese and Cnidos in southwest Asia Minor, and framed in the north by the islands of Kithira, Karpathos and Rhodos, it forms the southernmost bridge of the Aegean Sea between Greece and Anatolia, the link uniting continental Greece to Asia. "Crete is like a leviathan, pushed up by successive geological explosions," wrote Lawrence Durrell. "It is also like the buckle in a slender belt of islands which shelter the inner Cyclades from the force of the deep sea..."

Crete has gone through the same upheavals as Greece and has witnessed the arrival of the same waves of peoples while serving as a contact between the Near Eastern and the Greek world. It influenced the Mycenaean civilization, and during the classical period it was the source of numerous legends. Its people traveled to Egypt, Anatolia and Syria, propelled by the winds of the summer, and brought back exquisite objects made of ivory, steatite, and semi-precious stones together with exotic foodstuffs that had all been traded for their own distinctive handicrafts.

Positioned between the Orient, Egypt and Greece, Crete eventually worked out a mode of survival. Throughout different periods the island was to play an individual role of paramount importance in the Mediterranean world.

Notwithstanding all the successive foreign occupations, the distinctive character of Crete has not changed much throughout the ages. For 4000 years, despite all the invasions and oppressions, Crete has jealously guarded its special identity. High in the White Mountains, ancient institutions and a love of tradition can still be found among its blue-eyed, blond-haired people who speak an archaic Greek and, at times, look like the "golden Dorians." Rich in tradition and Homeric in its sense of hospitality, Crete, like Mani in southern Greece, has a sense of honor and a deep and abiding passion for independence. These are common traits in the two regions.

The Cretans have experienced the disappearance of the Minoan Empire, the rise of Venice, Turkish Islamization, Nazi brutality, and present-day tourism. Under the Romans, the Venetians and the Turks they rose in revolt, led by their chieftans – the famous *kapetaneï*. During the early phases of the Second World War, nowhere in Europe did one see such fierce fighting as in Crete and nowhere were there more martyrs to the cause of freedom or more widows left to lament.

The human element is rich in Crete. In the small villages, old women still weave,

Above: Romantic moods on the southern coast. Right: Mountainous splendors.

men of all ages work silently on their farms, wearing their traditional high-boots, black shirts and baggy pants. One feels in the presence of an ancient and noble people, who have descended in a straight line from an unknown past, with minimal changes on the way; "eventually the grandeur of the place is forgotten; it only supports a background in whose foreground a huge Cretan stares at you." (Raymond Matton, *La Crète au Cours des Siecles*).

The Poets' Crete

And yet it is this "background" that helps to explain Crete and its people.

Crete, "the great island" as it is called, appears still larger, with tall mountains and deep valleys that dominate the countryside. Over the last three centuries these mountains have been immortalized by poets and songwriters, who in their moving Cretan songs – *mandinades* and *rezitika* – tell us of revolts of the chieftains of the island against the Turkish yoke. They have also inspired foreign artists, like Captain Spratt, who have tried to capture the shimmering light of the mountain tops in the morning, or the change of the pastel hues after sunset.

"...I sat watching its play of pink, purple, and golden hues, tinting the mountain tops or lower landscape as the light faded, with intense admiration and pleasure, until... the bright tints vanished, and all was gray..." (Captain T.A.B. Spratt, *Travels and Researches in Crete*).

The mountains are omnipresent in Crete's history, geography, and its art: "...The mountains of Lassithi and the rock of Sfakia and between them Psiloritis – the tallest, like a giant patriarch – hold, engraved on their sides, their plateaus, their peaks, and hidden among the densely forested slopes, many centuries of vicissitudes, of lessons, and accounts of man's fate," sang the Greek poet, Kostis Palamas.

It is in the isolation of these forbidding mountains and wind-haunted valleys that the Cretans became so self-sufficient, proud, and unique. It is in this island with its stretches of rolling hills and fertile soil, extravagant flora, and rich culture, that the people felt and still feel that they are Cretans first, Greeks second.

Who today would react any differently to the extraordinary landscape than did Spratt: "...I was captivated by this brilliant effect, and sketched the panoramic view of hill and dale, coastline and bays, ... as seen from my aerial position on Ida...".

The mountains rise "ironbound from the deep sea on the southern coast like great walls against which the sea pounds." Deep caves have also been found in most of the mountains; the one at Ida is believed to have been the birthplace of Zeus, while the Dikteon cave is where the god was hidden and cared for as a child. And the sea determined the development of Crete and the character of the people as much as the mountains. The slim silhouette of Crete is sandwiched between the angry Cretan Sea in the north and the vast, empty Sea of Libya in the south.

The Cretan coastline is irregular. From west to east there are many gulfs: Kastelli, Hania, Alimirou, Mirabello, Sitia, with long stretches of beaches in between. In the south lie the unique Bay of Messara and the three capes: Krios, Lithino and Goudouras. There are deep gulfs in the north and narrow beachheads in the south, but the finest of them all is the Bay of Souda, the largest natural bay in the Mediterranean, a gulf of great beauty which captivated Spratt with "the intensity of its ultramarine blue, as it combines the azure reflected from the firmament above, with the blue hues arising from its own crystal-clear transparency and profundity beneath."

With natural ports such as these it is no wonder the Cretans became good seafarers and explorers early on, even in the third millenium crossing the Aegean Sea to the north, to Sicily in the west and to

21

Egypt in the south, spreading their culture around the Mediterranean as they went. Homer mentioned the richness of the island with its hundred cities and palaces. Its influence was so great that it could survive without any fortifications. But natural forces were stronger and more able to destroy fortifications than any human endeavor, although what remains of Minoan civilization will still impress today's visitor.

Digging up the Past

Europe's first civilization arose on Crete. It reached its high point about 3500 years ago, at about the same time as riverine communities began to grow on the lands between the Tigris and the Euphrates. Around the turn of this century a swarm of archeologists invaded Crete to attempt to determine what mysteries lay

Above: Piecemeal past – archaeologist Sinclair Hood at work. Right: A copy of the bull jumping fresco from Knossos.

behind the origins of this people. Among the first was Heinrich Schliemann, the excavator of Troy and Mycenae. He made his way to Knossos but had to give up after differences with the owners of the properties he intended to dig up. His successor, Arthur Evans, ultimately revealed the artifacts of this past world to the present. Evans, in fact, had turned to archaeology later in life, after a successful career as a journalist, curator and antiquarian. He had a passion for the Balkan peninsula, but above all Crete attracted his attention. He was certain that in Crete he would find a rich, prehistoric civilization, as reflected in the Homeric lines:

"Out in the dark blue sea lies a land called Crete, a rich and lovely land, washed by the waves on every side, densely peopled and boasting ninety cities... One of the ninety towns is a great city called **Knossos**, and there, for nine years, King Minos ruled and enjoyed the friendship of almighty Zeus."

Evans was familiar with the legends about Crete. He knew how Rhea, the mother of Zeus and wife of Cronos, had saved her son from his murderously jealous father by hiding him in a cave on Crete where he grew up among the Corybantes and the Curetes. These ancient people were the masters of fire, and were the first to forge bronze weapons and armour. He had also read *Apollodorus* and knew the story of Theseus and the Minotaur. As lord of the Aegean, King Minos demanded tribute from the state of Athens once every nine years. This tribute took the form of seven noble Athenian boys and seven maidens whom he then sacrificed to the Minotaur, the monstrous offspring of his wife Pasiphae and a bull (a passion some say was spawned by Neptune). Some say that the Labyrinth the Minotaur lived in was the Palace of **Knossos** with its long corridors and complicated access.

Theseus, the son of the king of Athens, Aegeus, decided to liberate his city from this heavy tribute. He sailed for Crete where he met the daughter of King Minos, Ariadne, who fell in love with him. Ariadne gave him a spool of thread to roll out behind him so that he could find his way out of the labyrinth after killing the Minotaur. Theseus succeeded in his task, and sailed back to Athens. Unfortunately, in the heat of excitement, he forgot to give the prearranged signal of victory – white sails instead of black. His father, Aegeus, waited impatiently at Cape Sounion, and thinking his son dead, flung himself into the sea in grief. That is how the Aegean Sea got its name.

In March 1900, Evans started digging in Crete and found the "labyrinth" of Knossos. The legend proved to have been based on historical events, and the excavations turned out to be breathtaking.

There was a huge palace with a large central courtyard, a throne room, long corridors, many of which led to store-chambers containing enormous jars (*pithoi*) for oil and other agricultural produce, official quarters, private quarters for the family of the king, bathrooms, lively frescoes in blue and red showing young princes, beautiful women, dolphins, birds, priests, bulls, double axes and seals, and most important of all, clay tablets bearing hieroglyphics that Evans hoped to decipher.

Who were these people that left behind this amazing art and architecture? What was their cilivization? When did they live? Slowly, the mystery unfolded, but it still keeps many archaeologists busy.

The Minoan Period

The story of Crete begins shortly after 3000 BC, with the slow replacement of stone by copper, although earlier Neolithic settlements have also been discovered at many sites, most notably Knossos, Festos and Agia Triada, places that were important palace sites in the period that followed. These first settlers, who arrived in Crete between 6000 and 5000 BC, introduced agriculture on the island basing it on the cultivation of cereals, olives, grape vines and the herding of animals. They also imported the cult of the fertility goddess, with her big buttocks and heavy thighs, a "steatopygous" figure of the African type. The Neolithic culture of Crete is like the Neolithic culture of mainland Greece and has left us some decorated pottery and clay figurines of animals, but it is the next period that was most important.

Around 2600 BC, new people arrived on Crete. These new settlers, who also penetrated mainland Greece, came from western Anatolia. They worked with copper and later with bronze. They did not destroy the culture already existing on the island. Rather they embraced and absorbed it and created the famous Minoan civilization, so called by its discoverer Sir Arthur Evans after the legendary ruler of Crete, King Minos. Evans, basing his chronology on pottery styles, came up with three distinct periods: Early Minoan

Right: Ivory carving depicting a bull jumper (Archaeological Museum of Iraklio).

(2500-2100 BC); Middle Minoan (1950-1750 BC); and Late Minoan (1550-1400 BC). Each of these periods he further divided into three sub-periods. In the meantime, academicians have come up with a more extensive system for the period between 2600 and 1150 BC, dividing it into four periods, the Pre-, Old, New and Post Palace Era (that is, Pre-, Proto, Neo- and Postpalaticum). It concludes with the Sub-Minoan Era, 1150-1100 BC.

For over 1000 years the Minoans lived peacefully – weapons were scarce and no city fortifications have been found. A seafaring economy developed based mainly on the trade with metalware and agricultural products. Traveling to western Anatolia, the Aegean and the West, the Cretans carried their pottery with its spiral designs, their carved seal stones and their perfumes and wines, which they exchanged for the goods of their neighbors – leather from Cyprus, gold and silver from the Cyclades, stone from Milos. Its ports – Zakros and Palekastro in the east, the little islands of Mohlos and Psira in the north – were its centers of commerce with Asia Minor. Increasingly, Crete welcomed and assimilated the influences of Anatolia and its art, starting in the Early Minoan Period (2100 BC). spreading from the eastern part of the island to the central area of Knossos and Festos and to Keratos in the west through a new route that ran from east to west.

In approximately 2000 BC, Crete experienced a profound change, a fact that can be deduced from the sudden change in the style of pottery. The famous Kamares vases with their eggshell surface and polychromy were introduced, as was the establishment of direct commercial relations with Egypt. This is the Middle Minoan period when the complex palaces of central Crete were built: Knossos, Malia, Festos and Agia Triada, together with other royal residences and large towns. Many of the palaces were de-

stroyed during the Middle Minoan Period (1850 - 1750 BC), probably by an earthquake, but were rebuilt around 1700 BC. Life in the palaces seems to have been pleasant and carefree, the nobles affluent, the institution of kingship secure – a centralized government with a large civil service and a highly organized society. Religion played an important role and was practiced within the palaces as well as on mountain peaks and in caves.

After 1700 BC, grander palaces were built on the ruins of the old with architectural innovations such as columns made of cypress trees, and sky-lights over patios. Toward the end of this era, around 1600 BC, Crete experienced a veritable renaissance. Its art shed its oriental influences. Politically the island was also at a climax: The Cretan navy ruled the Aegean and the Mediterranean – making

Above: An Etruscan plate tells of the encounter between Pasiphaä and the Minotaur. Right: Gold coin left over from the days when the ancient Greeks lived in Knossos.

Crete a real thalassocracy. Relations with the neighboring peoples increased while the "oriental trade" experienced a recession due to the invasions of the Hyksos in Egypt, the expansion of the Hittites in Asia Minor and the arrival of new waves of people in Greece proper.

Minos (which should be understood as a title like Pharaoh) ruled unchallenged. "Minos," wrote the historian Thucydides in the fifth century BC, "is the first sovereign, as we hear, that possessed a navy and the control of the sea we now call Hellenic; his power spread to the Cyclades and other islands of the area which he held for a long time and where he appointed his sons as leaders. He purged the seas from the pirates as much as he could, obviously in order to better assure the safety of the revenues from these islands."

We find the name Minoa given to towns and whole areas in Laconia, Sicily, Syria, Arabia, the Cyclades. A colony was established in Corcyra, commercial relations were strong with the XVIIIth dynasty of Egypt, everywhere we see signs of the spreading of the Cretan civilization.

But around 1450 BC the palaces of Festos, Agia Triada and Tilissos were destroyed by fire. Who set it? Rivals of Minos or enemies from abroad? And why is it that Knossos flourished for the next 50 years? Had the Mycenaeans, called by Homer "Achaeans," taken Knossos and were they the ones who introduced new forms of architecture, new weapons, a new pantheon of gods, a new social and political organization, a new calendar, adapting the Cretan writing to their own language and needs? It seems likely.

But in 1400 BC, Knossos too was destroyed through pillage and fire. Was this a result of earthquake, war or internal revolt? Scholars differ in their conclusions. What is certain is that this brought to an end the great era of Minoan history, while the ascendancy of the Mycenaeans continued on the mainland until the invasion of the Dorians, "the people from the North."

The Classical Period

Minoan culture did not disappear completely, however. A part of the population took refuge in the inaccessible east, later becoming known as the Eteocretans, or "real" Cretans. The rest of the people were enslaved by the Dorians who began their invasion of the island around 1200 BC. The new conquerors were able to assimilate the native population, so that by the opening of the classical period Crete had become fully Greek. During its long history, Crete has kept this Greek character despite repeated wars and foreign occupations and despite its occasional forced isolation from the Greek mainland.

In Crete, the retention of place-names throughout long periods of historical change is remarkable and by comparison with other areas, quite unusual. Prehellenic and ancient Greek place-names, even in altered form, are quite common all over the island. Some of these names were artifically "historicized" and re-in-

27

troduced after Crete's return to the folds of Mother Greece.

The era of classical Crete eventually succumbed to the overwhelming power of the Greek mainstream, but not without passing on its deities and customs, legislation and institutions. The Cretan Zeus, the Gortina legislative tablets and the Cretan Assembly are indications of this process.

Pax Romana

During Roman times Crete participated in eastern Mediterranean affairs, in its capacity as a perfect stopover on the way to the Roman Eastern Empire. It was well-off financially but politically without any importance. Crete was the last Greek region to be conquered by Rome after considerable resistance.

Above: Church of the Archangel Michael in Rotunde, a relic of the great Byzantine Empire. Right:The division of Crete into four districts under the Venetians.

The Roman period was more than merely peaceful: It brought to an end the internecine wars between Cretan cities. Christianity was introduced early in the island and triumphed over paganism. Tradition has it that the island was visited by St. Paul in AD 59. Paul stopped at Kali Limenes, met with Titus, and appointed him Bishop of Gortina, asking him to continue his missionary work in Crete. Besides the remains of his church in Gortina, many other churches in Crete are dedicated to Titus.

Crete and Byzantium

As part of the Eastern Roman Empire, the island was just another "eparchy" (administrative district) of the Byzantine Empire which had become a Euro-Asian world power after the division of Rome in AD 395. Crete emerged from this mysterious period in the year 824, when Arabian pirates with a flotilla of 40 ships conquered the town of Gortina. They subsequently established a fortified spot where Iraklio stands today, calling it Rabd-el-Khandak.

Nikiforos Fokas, the Byzantine commander and later Emperor Nikiforos II, succeeded in liberating Crete in 963. It seems strange, but although the Arabs remained on the island for 137 years, they left no noteworthy relics. Perhaps the Byzantine invasion was a little too thorough. One thing is sure, the population of the island had been decimated and the new rulers felt it necessary to settle people there from all corners of their vast empire. Village names such as Sklaverohori recall Slav settlers, Armeni must have been founded by Armenians, and there were many Greeks, notably twelve noble families from Constantinople, who were supposed to guarantee the rule of law. These twelve *arhontopoula* (noble children) live on in numerous folk songs.

Crete and Venice

In 1204, a new calamity befell the Byzantine Empire: The Fourth Crusade, on its way to the Holy Land, veered towards the rich city of Constantinople to loot and conquer. Among the booty was the island of Crete "a diamond in the midst of the Mediterranean," the link between the Middle East and Western commerce. The island was eventually purchased by the Venetians, who considered it indispensable to their lucrative eastern trade. Thus, starting in 1211 and for the next 450 years, Crete became part of the Venetian Republic. It is interesting to note that a modern traveler to Crete, especially if he arrives by sea at the port of Iraklio, will be faced with the double lions of Venice, set on the walls of the fortress. The image of peaceful transfer of power, prosperity and satisfaction belies the reality.

The Cretans fought continuously and courageously against this new conqueror, and for the first three centuries rose in a series of bloody but unsuccessful revolts and revolutions in order to keep their Greco-Christian identity intact against the assaults of the Roman Catholic enemy. It is actually said that during this unbroken series of unsuccessful revolts, each generation of Cretan men married, sired a son to ensure a new generation of fighters, and then returned to the mountains to fight the invaders.

With the fall of Constantinople into the hands of the Ottoman Turks in 1453, the hopes for liberation died and, by necessity, the two elements, the Orthodox Cretans and the Catholic Venetians, began a slow but steady rapprochement which became especially pronounced among the middle classes of the larger cities. By the middle of the 16th century, Crete's cultural life had been more or less homogenized. The net result was a renascence of artistic and literary life combining Greco-Byzantine and western European elements. For a brief and golden period in the 15th and 16th centuries, Crete was the first place in the general Greek area that was able to latch on to

Above: The Venetian Loggia in Iraklio.
Right: It was the Turks who introduced coffee drinking.

some of the intellectual developments in western Europe after a long period of silence. The Greek mainland itself was at that point under the Turkish yoke.

It was during this period that significant people were born and raised in Crete: Domenikos Theotokopoulos, for example, named El Greco (the Greek) in Spain, Georgios Hortatsis, a superb writer of popular plays, a literary genre hitherto unknown in the Greek-speaking area; and Vitsentzos Kornaros who wrote the masterpiece of the Cretan renaissance, the *Erotocritos*, the most popular work of Greek literature for 200 years, a stereotypical Italian romance transformed into an original epic in Cretan dialect and still recited by Cretan shepherds from memory. In architecture and in art, the Venetian influence is strong in such masterpieces as the church of Agios Markos in Iraklio, the famous Loggia – the club of the Venetians – across from the Morosini fountain, and the lovely Agios Titos church with its stone façade. The fortresses around the city of Iraklio – built by the famous Venetian architect Michel Sanmicheli –and its port are awesome with their thick battlements and recurring theme of lion reliefs.

Although the Venetian rule in Crete had been a colonial rule of systematic economic exploitation, of intolerance towards the Greek Orthodox ecclesiastical hierarchy, demanding in the tone of its communications and cruel in the collection of taxes, it also proved intellectually stimulating in the fields of poetry and the other arts.

Crete and the Turks

This brilliant period ended with the coming of the Ottoman Turks in 1641. In a sudden change of course, they set foot on the outskirts of Hania as their fleet was ostensibly headed for Malta. The Venetians were taken by surprise. By then, the Ottomans had conquered most of the Greek mainland, and after a twenty-one-year campaign against the main cities of Crete, they were able to take the last big bastion of Crete – Candia – by 1669.

The 21-year siege of Candia, one of the longest such military operations in history, was not only recounted in various ways by later popular and folkloric literature, but has also been the subject of extensive examination by historians. All Mediterranean powers at the time had vested interests in the outcome. Besides Venice and the Ottoman Empire, there was also Genoa, the Holy See under Clement IX and King Louis XIV of France. Diplomatic efforts failed in the face of brute force, especially on the part of the French, who entertained a convenient double standard when it came to the Turks (they were interested in keeping the Habsburg Empire in check).

A recent account of the siege of Candia, of the "Cretan War" in general and its parallels with the siege of Vienna by the Turks is given by E. and R. Eickoff in *Venedig, Wien und die Osmanen.* The siege was recorded by a Cretan poet – Marinos Zane Bounialis – in his moving epic *The Cretan War.* Bounialis implicates – apparently not without reason – a Venetian traitor, the engineer Andrea Barozzi as having supplied details about the fortifications and their weak points to Köprülü, the Turkish general. The Turkish leaders met with Barozzi just outside the fort.

"They descended there, were they were instructed by him, and they saw and measured and he said to the vizir that this is the easy way: From here they could pierce the fort and get inside."

Indeed, during the last months of the siege, the Turks abruptly changed objectives: The fort was stormed from Sabionera (Sandy Place), the side near the port, and St. Andrea where the fort abutted on the sea. A truce was signed and soon the island was abandoned for ever by its Venetian conquerors and most of its native population. The Cretan refugees filled the main economic centers of

31

Western Europe and western Greece and bringing with them their knowledge of ancient Greek culture. For Crete, though, this was the beginning of a steady and dramatic decline, a dark period of sacrifice and struggle.

The peasants in the countryside, too poor and illiterate to leave their island, were ultimately to suffer most. They began a long resistance against this new and cruel conqueror, a conqueror of different culture, religion and habits.

This was a period of violent change in the political, social and economic life of the island and dramatic events in religious affairs, since the earlier sporadic conversions to Catholicism were followed by an extensive Islamization of the Cretans, sometimes through the soft path of economic incentives and at other times through forced conversion. These Islamized Cretans, who, by the mid-18th

Above: Even priests did their duty as freedom fighters in those days. Right: The erstwhile mosque of Pasha Hassan.

century numbered nearly 200,000 out of an entire population of 250,000, were not only lost to the Orthodox church but to Hellenism as well. The so-called Turco-Cretans emigrated to Asia Minor and still speak Greek.

Once being under Ottoman domination, Crete became an *eyalet* (or *vilayet*), a province governed by a *vali* as governor general, and a large staff which included the *mufti* (the chief justice), the *reis effendi* (the recording secretary), the *defterdar* (the treasurer), and a considerable number of clerks. The *eyalet* of Crete was divided into three smaller units, the *sanjaks* of Hania, Rethimno, and Candia. Within the social and economic structure of Crete under the Turks, the non-Muslim population represented the class most liable to suffer from taxes, duties, impositions, and general insults. Since the *pashas* were rarely stationed in their post for a long time, they showed little interest in reforms and a just administration; an effective *vali* could not survive the pressures exerted on him from below by the *janissaries*, the *beys*, and the *aghas*. It was the latter who really set the tone, and any administrative higher official could easily lose his post by being deposed by the independent janissaries, the elite troup of the sultan's army. As for the remaining Christians, they had little in the way of rights. Their high taxes gave them practically nothing in the way of roads, public services or improvements in communications. All fertile land was in the hands of the Turks. The only consolation for having not succumbed to Islam was that the Turkish system allowed them to practice their religion, conduct their own affairs, and educate their children in the Greek language.

Cretan Revolts

No wonder, then, that the history of Crete in the period of the *toukokratia* (Turkish occupation) is a story of maladministration, cruel oppression, continuous terrorism and frequent massacres. It is also a story of successive revolts by the Christian population against the Muslim overlord. The Cretan revolts have been chronicled by folk poets, narrated by novelists, and sung in the *rizitika* songs by the inhabitants of the highland villages of the White Mountains who expressed their desire for rebellion against the Turks and for their freedom, through these allegorical and symbolic songs. Among these folk songs, the most important recounts in over 1000 lines the revolt of Dhaskaloyiannis in 1770. It was lead by a teacher named John, who fought against immense odds, relying on promised help from Orthodox Russia. This support did not materialize and the revolt collapsed. John was finally caught and flayed alive by the Turks. The best known song about him is the version dictated by Barba-Pantzelio, an illiterate cheese-maker, to an amanuensis in 1786.

"They handed him over to the torturers; afterwards they flayed him, right up to his eyes and his nose: Bitterly he screamed at the tortures they inflicted. When they had done the worst with him, the mercy of death came on him."

Other superb accounts of the Cretan rebellions have been given in the fictitious histories of Nikos Kazantzakis and Pandelis Prevelakis, who have described so well the physical, racial, and social make-up of these revolts. *Capetan Mihalis* by Kazantzakis (translated as *Freedom or Death* in English) is the story of the author's father who fought in the 1889 revolt, while the trilogy of Prevelakis, *The Cretan*, describes the uprisings from 1866 to 1906, and has as a sequel *The Tale of a Town*, the town being the birthplace of the author, Rethimno, the quiet, magical town in the middle of northern Crete, which witnessed the expulsion of many Creto-Turks in 1923 with the exchange of populations.

Until the end of the 19th century all the Cretan revolts failed, but they do compose a unique story of blood and heroism, legend and romance. From 1770 to 1898,

Crete was continuously in revolt. Each revolt had its own evolution, its colorful personalities, its heroic battles, perhaps some elements of cold-blooded manipulation by the Great Powers.

The Christians, chafing at the discriminatory rules of law and the unequal conditions of life under Ottoman rule, petitioned the Porte, and often the Great Powers, for reforms. They usually sought relief from the egregious tax burden, and more civil rights. Often one Great Power or another supported the rebels for its own higher strategy, but usually only verbally. As it became clear that upheaval was imminent, the Muslim inhabitants of the countryside, being at the mercy of the Christians, flocked to the walled towns of Iraklio, Rethimno and Hania; Christian inhabitants of the towns, being at the mercy of the Muslims, attempted to flee to the mountains but were often trapped inside the towns and massacred.

Over the centuries, the Cretans holed up in their mountain retreats began to form representative committees. Councils from these villages (*dimogerontes*) and select warriors (*oplarhigi*) spearheaded the effort for the cause of a free and Greek Crete. The struggle intensified after the formation of a Greek state in 1830. Volunteers frequently arrived on the island, and the mother country also provided weapons in large quantities.

Of course, the main aim of the Cretans was not to defeat the sultan's army militarily, which was not possible, but rather to draw the attention of the Great Powers to the fate of Crete and maybe in that way get some concessions out of the Porte. The ultimate goal, however, was unification with Greece.

Probably the most bloody rebellion took place in 1866, after the local pashas decided to put up resistance against some

new administrational directive sent down by the central government. The beacon signalling to all of Europe was a mass suicide at the Arkadi Monastery, which was being attacked by 15,000 Turks. Kostis Giamboudakos, seeing that the situation was hopeless, set fire to the remaining munitions, killing almost all 967, women, children and fighters, who had found refuge in the monastery. Quite a number of Turks died there too. This event is alive in Cretan consciousness, and is recalled annually in a ceremony. At the time, well-known revolutionaries, novelists, and poets such as Garibaldi, Victor Hugo and Swinburne spoke with admiration about it and wrote fiery poems to commemorate the event. In his *Ode to the Insurrection in Candia* of January 1867, Swinburne notes that:

"...In the hundred cities of Crete... Such glory was not of old... Though her name was great upon earth... And her face was fair on the sea... So fair, who is fairer now... With her children dead at her side... Unsceptred, unconsecrated... Unapparelled, unhelped, unpitied... With blood for gold on her brow..."

Greek interference and growing escalation of the fighting led to the Great Powers' intervention, resulting finally in the acceptance of the Organic Statute of 1868, which offered Crete the chance of self-administration. If the statue had been complied with, the conditions of the Christians in Crete would have improved. However, nothing happened until 1878, when the Pact of Halepa inaugurated a more satisfactory regime for the Christians and gave them virtual self-government. The pact became the Magna Carta of the Christians from that day on. If it had been executed in good faith, the results would have been satisfactory, despite the fact that it was full of ambiguities that could alter its meaning.

Under the first Governor General of Crete it was interpreted in a broad spirit and worked well but under his successors

Right: Ships from the international defense forces in Hania harbor.

Chania. Ships of the International Forces in the medieval harbour.

the imperfections of the pact became apparent. With the Ottoman Empire falling apart at the seams, no straight message was received from Turkey. The directives of the governors were vague, the agreement between the Cretan Assembly and the government ceased to be clear, and the authority of the General assembly was undermined by the veto powers of the Sultan which turned the Assembly into a consultative rather than a legislative body. The result was agitation, new petitions and endless friction, ending with the revolutionary movement of 1896-98, when the Great Powers intervened in a direct and decisive way.

Crete and the Great Powers

The island of Crete had posed difficult political problems for the Great Powers since the 17th century. In the center of the eastern Mediterranean, halfway from Europe to Africa and halfway from Malta to Syria, Crete commanded then as it still does today the strategic sea lanes from north to south and from west to east. Its large population of Muslims at the end of the 18th century and the emotional meaning this had for Greeks only heightened the sensitivity of its foreign relations. Greece, Turkey, England and Russia had direct interests in Crete. Greece, committed to the "Great Idea," the vision of incorporating the unredeemed Greeks of the Ottoman Empire into a single Greek state, was looking forward to the redemption of the Greek majority of the historically Greek island of Crete. As a consequence, Greece unconditionally supported *Enosis* (union to the mother country).

Turkey, unwilling to relinquish those territories which formed a connecting link between the European portions of the empire and Egypt, but also acting as the defender of the large Muslim population in Crete, wished to retain Crete as a province. England was the least favorable to Cretan aspirations. For England, Crete, along with Gibraltar, Malta, Cyprus and the Suez Canal, controlled the

35

sea lanes that led to the riches of India; it was essential to the "internal communications" of the British Empire. Russia's attitude fluctuated. For Russia, Crete was a strategic outpost needed to protect her access to the eastern Mediterranean. All the powers, but especially the Ottoman Empire, were concerned that concessions to Greece on Crete could lead to demands for similar concessions in other parts of the Balkan peninsula and possibly widespread war. The other European states formulated their politics following the demands of treaty obligations, sentiment, and power politics.

France, her idealistic philhellenic notions influenced by her revolutionary and Napoleonic ideology, supported Greece in her Cretan policy. Italy was ambivalent. Crete was of no immediate interest to her but the Venetian occupation of Crete and of other Aegean islands in the past

Above: Commander of the international forces on Crete. Right: Cretan delegates in 1911.

made her speak of certain "historic rights" in the area. The European powers had played an important role during the Turko-Venetian war and especially during the siege of Candia. Prodded by the Holy Sea and ambiguous in their policies the French had led in numbers but other nations sent their armies against the "infidel Turk" too. Armies from the Papal, Italian and German states took part in the 21-year siege.

The British did not, but followed events closely because of their economic interests in the area. They had already opened the first foreign consulate in Hania in 1520. Ten years after the fall of Candia, in 1679, the French opened a consulate too and French commerce flourished all through the 18th century. Russia's development lagged behind the Western Powers. But it consolidated its position in European affairs after the accession to the throne of Peter the Great. Then, under the wily Catherine the Great (1763-1796), Russia's expansion got up a head of steam, especially in the Balkans and the Mediterranean,

The orthodox unity provided a motive for this expansionist movement. It culminated in the Orloff revolt, in which Russia instigated a Greek upheaval against the Turks on the island. The Russo-Turkish war of 1770-74 ended with the Treaty of Kutchuk-Kainardji, which imposed on the Porte "the protection of the Christian religion and its churches" and defined Russia's role as the protecting power of the Balkan peoples who looked towards her for guidance from then on.

This was not the first time, however, that the weaknesses of the overextended and somewhat exhausted Ottoman Empire had become obvious for anyone to see. For the Great Powers of the day, it was time to negotiate secretly and openly for the bits and pieces that were being left behind by the retreating giant. In the Treaty of Tilsit (1807), Crete was officially left to the French. Two years later,

Οἱ ἐγκαθειρχθέντες εἰς τὰ Εὑρωπαϊκὰ πολεμικὰ Κρῆτες Βουλευταὶ κατὰ τὸ ἔτος *1911*.

Les Deputés Crétois gardés sur les vapeurs de guerre Européens en 1911.

at the Treaty of Vienna, England expressed its desire for the island -and for Cyprus as well, by the way, which it received in 1878.

The expansionism of these powers was somewhat dampened by Greece's rebellion against the Ottoman Empire. Still, their influence could be felt, especially when it came to determining the borders of this new power.

During the Greek Revolution of 1821, the Cretans fought long and hard. However, the Great Powers decided to exclude Crete from the new kingdom of Greece and their approaches to the Cretan problem took different paths. France, although interested in ultimate unification, was unwilling to take any initiatives on her own. England, on the other hand, opposed unification, first because of fears that Greece would act as an extension of Russian influence and second because of her own ambitions in Crete. Russia was willing to preserve the status quo as long as she was allowed to pursue her interests elsewhere.

Thus came about a series of bloody revolutions culminating in the 1866-68 Great Revolution, followed by the revolts of 1878 and 1889, when the Cretans were, obviously, the great losers since they had no policy or central leadership, and thus always resorted to action which was effective only in dramatizing their plight, not in changing it. Change was impossible without a combination of revolutionary (destructive) forces with conciliatory (constructive) forces. These isolated and ineffective actions only became productive when Eleftherios Venizelos, a young Cretan leader, relying on the developing political maturity of the Cretans – nurtured by increasing participation in their own government – realigned their policies towards a pragmatic combination of "guns and negotiations" *(toufeki ke pazari)*.

Venizelos and Crete

The entrance of Eleftherios Venizelos in active politics of his island came at a

A. B. Y. Πρίγκηψ Γεώργιος
S. H. R. Le Prince Georges

difficult time. This was the post-Halepa period which saw the gradual solution of the Cretan Question after a great deal of negotiation and infighting. Four main factors dominated the period 1878-1898: 1. Turkey showed a reluctance to implement the Pact. 2. The Cretan parties were involved in intense infighting. 3. The Greek government and the Greek powers played an increasingly important role in directing Cretan affairs and policy. 4. The Great Powers' position vis-à-vis Crete was hesitant, to say the best.

Venizelos was born in 1864 in Hania on the northwest coast of Crete. He was educated at the University in Athens and then returned to Crete where he opened a law firm, coedited an influential local newspaper, and at the age of 24 won a seat as a liberal in the Cretan Assembly. He was superbly trained as a lawyer, well-read in European literature and political thought, and was a born leader.

Above: Prince George of Greece. Right: The spirit of Venizelos is alive and well.

He played a vital, important role in the series of intricate and interlocking steps by which Crete passed from Ottoman domination to autonomy and then to union with Greece, and went on to become the most important statesman of modern Greece, becoming prime minister several times between 1910 and 1933. He died in exile in Paris in 1936.

The inevitable failure of the reforms of the sultan led to increasing insecurity and sectarian violence on the island and culminated in the great fire of the Christian sector of Hania in January 1897 which started a new revolt on the island – the famous Akrotiri revolt. It was followed by a new demand by the Christians for union with Greece.

The Greeks landed a force on the island, but the admirals of the European powers, who were stationed in Souda Bay, also sent an international landing party and put an end to the fighting by occupying Hania and bombarding the positions of the insurgents.

Finally, through a series of intricate negotiations – during which Venizelos played an important role – the powers imposed a settlement, with all four holding Hania: The British held the Iraklio area, the Russians the area of Rethimno, the French the Sitia area in the east, and the Italians the southeastern area of Ierapetra.

These foreign powers also tried to introduce long overdue reforms. Their intent was to negotiate autonomy under Ottoman suzerainty but a tragic incident changed the situation. In August 1898, 14 British soldiers and the British vice-consul were murdered by the Turks in Iraklio. In the wake of the Iraklio "massacres" the powers decided that all Turkish influence had to cease. On November 3rd, 1898, the troops of the sultan started withdrawing from the island, ending 257 years of Ottoman rule.

A new arrangement was agreed on. Crete would become independent under

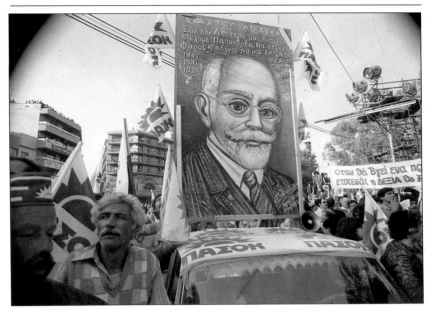

the nominal suzerainty of the sultan and the protection of the four powers and would be governed by Prince George of Greece as High Commissioner of Crete. With the new autonomy, a legal structure had to be drawn up for the island, so a committee of 16 was chosen.

Venizelos was made chairman of the committee and was involved in the drafting of the legislation. On January 24, 1899, in the new elections, Venizelos became the representative of Hania in the Cretan Assembly, which accepted the constitution of the Cretan State *(Kritiki Politia)*. In April, he was appointed Councillor for Justice in the primary Greek cabinet of Prince George.

It did not take long for differences to appear between the liberal, republican Venizelos and the authoritarian prince. As an impassioned supporter of ultimate unification with the Greek motherland, Venizelos could not, would not agree to the kind of wish-washy politicizing of the prince from the Danish-German House of Schleswig-Sonderburg-Glücksburg.

After a short but acrimonious clash with Venizelos, Prince George dismissed him from the government on March 18, 1901.

In protest against Prince George's despotic rule in Crete, on March 10, 1905, Venizelos and a group of his friends established a new revolutionary camp at Therissos, a virtually inaccessible village south of Hania. Amazingly enough, he was able to persuade the representatives of the Great Powers to meet with him and discuss Crete's political future, and even more amazingly, he was able to persuade them to withdraw their support from the Prince. The revolutionary camp was disbanded in November.

During 1906, Great Powers gradually took over the responsibilites of the Prince. The Constituent Assembly also grew in importance as a governing body. The Prince left Crete in September.

The revolution by the Young Turks against the sultanate, and renewed Ottoman retreats in the Balkans gave Venizelos and his supporters renewed impetus

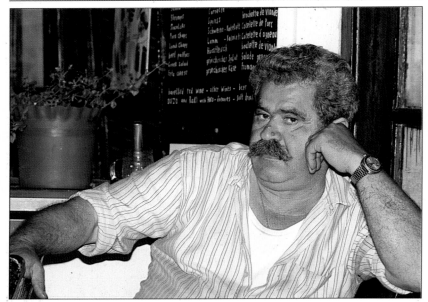

to demand unification with Greece in 1908. But the Great Powers were still hesitant and imposed their veto.

In March of 1910, after renewed elections, Venizelos became President and Prime Minister of Crete, but not for long. He was called to Athens by the leaders of the Military League in Greece, a group of reformists, who had taken power in a coup in August 1909. On September 12, Venizelos resigned his Cretan positions and on October 5 he became Prime Minister of Greece.

On October 14, 1913, Crete finally achieved union with Greece. At the fort of Firka in Hania, on December 6, Venizelos, together with King Constantine of Greece, ceremonially raised the Greek flag over Crete. Venizelos' Cretan period had ended and his position as head of the Greek government propelled him to the rank of international statesman.

Above: Invaders come, invaders go, but here it's business as usual. Right: Nazi medallion depicting their landing on Crete.

Crete and Greece

The unification process with Greece was the final stage in a long Cretan dream that had often looked like a nightmare.

As one of the Greek provinces, Crete had its own Governor General to coordinate its diverse services – agriculture, education, public works, justice. The island was divided into four *nomi* (districts) Iraklio, Hania, Rethimno and Lassithi, governed by a prefect nominated from Athens, with a mayor for each commune.

Greece ultimately sided with the Allies during World War One, a politically logical decision, as the arch-enemy Turkey had become a German ally. It turned out to be quite profitable in terms of territory. But the new Turkish Republic was neither as weak as one might have thought, nor was it about to accept the Treaty of Sèvres lying down. Another war broke out between the two countries, in which Turkey ultimately gained the upper hand. In 1922, an exchange of

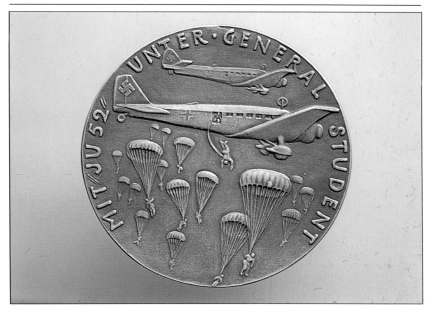

population took place and Crete received 13,000 Greek refugees from Asia Minor while approximately 11,000 Turco-Cretans (Cretans who had been Islamized) left Crete and were resettled in the area of Smyrna where one can find them today dressed in Cretan fashion, using the Cretan dialect, and mourning their lost life on their beloved island. The feeling of "lost paradise" created by the expulsion and exile of these islanders is beautifully and movingly portrayed in the masterpiece of the Cretan novelist Pandelis Prevelakis, *Tale of a City*. Another portrayal of this period is the recent film *Rembetiko*, which describes the harsh life of the Greeks expulsed from Turkey who were also considered *rembetiki* (outcasts) in their new-old homeland.

The Battle of Crete

With the coming of the Second World War and the occupation of Greece by the Germans, the Cretans again rose to the occasion and started the famous Battle of Crete, a fight against another brutal conqueror that cost them many lives and long guerilla warfare against the German forces immobilized in the Cretan mountains. For a moment it seemed that Crete was going to be spared the occupation. British, Australian and New Zealand forces descended on Crete, driven from the Greek mainland by the invading Germans. The Greeks were jubilant. The king and the government were in the hands of their allies and the brave Cretans!

Winston Churchill stated, "We intend to defend to the death, without thought of retirement, both Crete and Tobruk... Let there be no thought of cutting our losses." Yet in spite of defiant words and postures, Crete was attacked and taken by the Germans after twelve days fighting only. According to C. M. Woodhouse, General Bernard Freyberg, who took over command of the Allied forces in Crete, had received important information regarding the German plans to occupy Crete. He was ordered, however, to ignore the information relating to movements of German forces so as not to betray its source. For this reason the Maleme airport west of Hania was inadequately defended. The decision was fatal.

On May 20, 1941, the Germans attacked, with 7,000 parachutists and glider troops of the Seventh Airborne Division landing around the Maleme airfield. It was an impressive sight as the northern skies blackened with a multitude of airplanes dragging gliders, and the small space below filled with descending parachutes. For the local population it evoked biblical comparisons with the plague of locusts in Egypt. Next day more troops landed along the north coast. Iraklio was attacked from both the east where paratroopers landed amidst the vineyards, making their way towards the fortress, and the west near the airport. The British troops, including the Australians and

Above: The German military cemetery in Maleme near Hania. Right: Peace finally, after years of war and occupation.

New Zealanders, helped by Cretan citizens, put up a magnificent resistance, using at times knives, clubs, and their bare hands and causing heavy casualties among the enemy. But the Germans continued to pour forces onto the island. Soon, 20,000 troops had arrived. By May 31, it was all over. Almost half of the force of British, Australian and New Zealand troops was left behind, either killed or captured on the island. The loss for the Allies approximated 15,000 men while the count for the Germans varies from 6,000 to 15,000. Some of the Allied soldiers and officers who were left behind, and were not captured, were able to reach the south coast of Crete and, eventually, Egypt. Others were sheltered by the Cretan fighters in the White Mountains and the Psiloritis for the duration of the war.

The battle of Crete has been the subject of considerable criticism on the part of British and allied commentators. Although the major reason for the defeat was without any doubt the lack of enough air power on the side of the British and a commitment of 1,200 planes by the Germans, other questions remain. Why, for example, had the defences of Crete not been improved? Why were the forces so badly armed while the Cretans had not been armed at all? Unforgivable mistakes? Simple miscalculation? We will never know. We know, though, that the strong resistance of the island disrupted Hitler's plans for the invasion of Russia, which thus started later than anticipated. This delay had serious consequences for the outcome of the Russian campaign and the war in general. Moreover, according to Churchill, this was a Pyrrhic victory for Goering "for the forces he expended there might easily have given him Cyprus, Iraq, Syria and perhaps Persia."

Soon the Germans brought the necessary military material (tanks, trucks, artillery) to organize the occupation and the defense of the island. A guerilla campaign started in Crete from the first day of occupation. The Cretan fighters were supplied by the British from Egypt, who also provided officers and agents. The

situation was dismal in the occupied island, with insufficient food, forced labor, raids and executions by the German and Italian troops. But acts of heroism and bravado by both Cretans and Allies are also recorded. The most famous of these incidents was the kidnapping of the German Commandant Karl Kreipe, who was taken from his headquarters (the famous Villa Ariadne, from which Evans worked on the excavations of Knossos) to the mountains of Crete, shipped to Egypt by the British agents on the island and later flown to London by the Allies. The Allies' agents were often helped in their communications by Cretan messengers. One of these messengers was George Psychoundakis who later wrote his memoirs in a book called *The Cretan Runner*. The book has been translated by another famous fighter of the island, the Englishman Patrick Leigh Fermor, who, as the peasants recall, "was a giant who could reach a mountain peak with only one big jump!" The guerilla warfare immobilized a large number of German troops in the mountains and so slowed down other attacks by the Germans. Crete was finally liberated on May 23, 1945, almost exactly four years after its fall. The count was chilling: One out of every six villages was destroyed, her large cities had lost 35 percent of their populace, the economy of the island was in ruins.

Crete Today

After all these bitter experiences, how can Cretans today go to Germany as workers, own VWs, speak German, serve German tourists, even erect a German memorial outside Hania and take care of the German cemetery at Maleme?

What a strange people the Cretans are, and what a strange place is modern Crete! Old men sip their coffee at a mosque turned into a cafe, unaware of the history

Above: Looking into the future between progress and tradition. Right: Campaign poster rhetoric, growing more heated from right to left.

of the place, or probably pretending to be. Strong odors emanate from a raisin-processing plant next to a garden with the heavy smell of jasmine. Young Cretan girls in mini-skirts stroll past an ogling old Cretan in baggy pants and knee-boots. Markets are full of fresh fruit, vegetables and mounds of herbs from the Psiloritis – some you buy for their medicinal properties, some to flavor food, and others to use as aphrodisiacs – aromatic thyme, oregano, basil and camomile fill the air with their heady scent. This is the atmosphere of Crete, whether approaching the port of Iraklio, looking at the White Mountains that rise all around Hania or making one's way along the winding roads of gentle Rethimno. At the end of a long day of exploration, which has included an exhilarating excursion in the Malaxa Mountains for an aerial view of Souda Bay, sip *tsikoudia*, the pure Cretan raki, at the Venetian port of Hania, and eat sea urchin salad or the remarkable *staka*, a distillation of pure butter. It is an unforgettable experience.

And when night comes and the noises of the city subside the lines of Prevelakis come to mind:

"... let me simply pray that you may one day drop anchor off Rethimno some summer evening at the hour when the sea is sweet-scented as a water melon and the women are anointing their hair with oil of jasmine and coming down for a stroll along the quay. Then rest your elbows on the gunwale and gaze form afar at the magical city, which will itself be looking at you through thousands of eyes and will make its waters a mirror to the lights streaming from your boat and will wink back at you from its own innumerable little lamps ..."

But these hours of peace and romantic introspection are rather rare in the island these days. Tourism has arrived in Crete – somewhat late, but in full force – in the last 15 years. Roads have been built, innumerable hotels and pensions have sprung up in every corner of the island, package tours have been promoted, and hordes of Germans, Swedes, Italians und

British have descended on the island. The Venetian Morosini Fountain, in the center of Iraklio, is surrounded by hundreds of mopeds whose owners drink espresso while asking for the traditional *bouyatsa* at Kir Kor's "modernized" cafe. Music pours out of tavernas but it is seldom the traditional *mandinada* anymore. To see the wild *pentozali* dance one has to be invited to a Cretan wedding since it is seldom performed in public places anymore. Cretan baggy pants and knee-high boots have been exchanged for "Athenian finery." *Tsikoudia* is being offered to the tourists while the local population prefers its whisky straight.

Behind this façade, a brisk export trade of tomatoes, grapes, raisins (the major crop of the island), olive oil and flowers keeps the economy of the island strong. The ferry-boats that continuously work the lanes between the ports of Crete and mainland Greece (and Italy on occasion), carry not only full loads of passenger cars but heavy multiwheeled intercontinental trucks – many refrigerated – that reach all the major cities of Europe. There is an infrastructure that supports all this agricultural production and trade; machine shops, repair shops for cars, trucks, buses, tractors and ploughs, plastic pipe factories, the ubiquitous noisy and sputtering motorcycles; and there is a work force with greasy clothes, hands and faces, that struggle for their daily bread. The demand for scarce agricultural labor remains high and during the olive gathering or grape picking seasons many travelers and foreigners come here to seek employment.

The resulting traffic congestion, pollution and population pressure in the cities makes life difficult. The resources of the island (fresh water, game, beaches, forests) are under extreme pressure by the increased industrial, tourist, recreation, and agricultural demands. The ecology of the island is seriously threatened by overhunting, pesticides, fertilizers, herbicides (especially those used to combat cane brush), disposal of factory wastes from olive presses into scarce and valuable streams, and lowering of the water table by irrigation. The introduction of mechanical rotary cultivators and small diesel driven water pumps has permitted the cultivation of otherwise useless land on hills. Sadly, the construction work involved in building the new roads to reach remote villages and fresh pastureland has left ugly scars on the virgin landscape. This development has enormously increased the cultivated acreage of grapes, adding to the problems created by monoculture and the subsidies required to support it. It is said that the population of noisy cicadas has increased because of the overhunting of birds.

But the pressure to survive on the local farmers is so intense that these problems seem non-threatening for the moment and the state is powerless to enforce

Right: This Cretan villager surely has a great deal to tell.

badly needed environmental measures. But, high up on the rugged mountains, in remote beaches and villages off the beaten path, there is still magic. Whether one sits on a deserted beach as the fishermen bring in their catch of the day or, in a quiet corner of a monastery listening to the evening chants of the *esperinos*, heavy scents come to you of orange, almond and lemon, mixed with the odors of olive oil and garlic, the cicadas sing on into the dusk – wild and uncontrollable like the Curetes' cymbals in the cave of Zeus – not to hide the cries of a baby god, but to signal the presence of an island that has produced and nourished rough mountaineers, gentle poets and shrewd merchants – brave people who fought and suffered to keep their freedom, individuality and love of life.

5000 years ago, Crete created the first maritime empire of the world. Today, it is only a province of a developing country, with all its problems. However, due to its place in the Mediterranean world, its people and its history, it has not ceased playing an important role in the world. As the main US military base in the eastern Mediterranean Crete has found a strange destiny, which it shares with the other large islands of the Mediterranean – Cyprus, Rhodes, Sicily.

"A precarious, a restricted, a menaced life, such is the common fate of these islands. Their private life, if you will. But their outside life, the role that they played in the foreground of the stage of history is of an importance which one would not have expected from such miserable worlds. History in the large – the so-called *grande histoire* – washes the shores of these islands. You could say that it abuses them... Those islands on the path of powerful maritime routes are inevitably linked to the history of the Great Powers. Thus, an aspect of the grande histoire will always superimpose itself on their daily existence." (Fernand Braudel, *The Mediterranean*).

HANIA

**HANIA CITY
AKROTIRI PENINSULA
OMALOS PLATEAU
SAMARIA GORGE
SFAKIA / GAVDOS
WEST AND SOUTH OF HANIA
GRAMVOUSA
WEST COAST**

The westernmost part of Crete is dramatically isolated from the central and eastern part of the island by the massive ridge of the **Lefka Ori** or **White Mountains** which, for most of the winter months, are covered with snow and all but inaccessible. On the southern side of the island this ridge drops precipitously into the sea making a great barrier with few, if any harbors. One part of this ridge runs to the nothern sea coast at **Kalami** where the modern national highway cuts slightly inland. The older highway can still be followed, and affords the opportunity to visit many small and interesting villages.

The northern coast is marked by three great promontories jutting out into the sea. One of them, **Akrotiri**, forms the northern side of the great **Bay of Souda,** the largest natural harbor in the Mediterranean. The other two, uninhabited and desolate, form the **Gulf of Kissamou** and **Hania Bay**. Between the northern and southern shores run a number of virtually impenetrable valleys and ravines that link the two coasts. It is not surprising that the *kri-kri*, or Cretan ibex, the animal symbol of the independent and stubborn character of the Cretan people, has taken its last refuge in these isolated regions of the island.

Despite all the formidable mountains Hania is comparatively rich agriculturally. Apart from winter rains there is an abundance of springs that irrigate the ground. The valleys are carpeted with great groves of orange, lemon and grapefruit and in the more mountainous areas these groves give way to walnut trees. Olive groves are found everywhere and many different varieties are grown. Hania's vineyards are excellent, and the cheeses of this region are duly famous.

To a certain degree, the Prefecture of Hania is less well known to tourists as there are comparably few Minoan ruins and even fewer well-excavated sites. Some sites have been identified with famous ancient cities of considerable reknown such as **Aptera**, **Pergamon** (Platanias), the city mentioned in the Aeniad as having been founded by the Trojans after the fall of Troy, or **Diktyna** on the **Rodopou Peninsula**.

Many of the ruins are spread out over fields and valleys and afford good opportunities for hikes into the countryside and surrounding mountains. There is a reliable public transportation system that makes most of the sites accessible but by far the best manner of travel is by renting a car or motorbike.

Preceding pages: Goats. A dialogue. Venetian port in Hania. Left: In a cafenion.

HANIA

0   100 m

← to Kastélli Kissámou

HANIA CITY

There is something magical about **Hania** quite apart from its minarets, Venetian palazzi, and the narrow streets of the old town. Its dramatic backdrop of mountains face out towards the vast Cretan Sea. Its climate is determined by hot winds rising from Africa that are confronted by less temperate winds from the north. These extremes have had an effect on the volatile character of Haniotes. In the winter Hania is decidedly Gothic, an ambience that gives way to a sensually sun-drenched atmosphere in the summer. In antiquity Hania was known as Kydonia and extensive Minoan remains have been found on **Kastelli**, which was then,

and was to remain until well into the Middle Ages, the acropolis. During the Roman period Kydonia was, along with Knossos and Gortys, a major administrative city. It remained so until the Arab conquest of the island in 828, when it was sacked, reconstructed and renamed *al-Hannim*, from which Hania was derived after the Byzantines retook the city. Little if anything remains from these centuries to indicate the importance of Hania.

In the late 13th century the Venetians took Hania and under them it became the administrative center for the west of the island. The acropolis, now known as the Kastelli, was heavily fortified and a working harbor was constructed with arsenals and administrative offices. After absorption by Greece in 1913. Since then, further dramatic changes have affected Hania. The great Venetian walls that circumscribed the old town were, for the most part, torn down and Hania began to expand in every direction so that today it is a sprawling urban complex and the center of economic life for the western part of Crete. In World War II it suffered severe bombing and the old town was heavily straffed for several days prior to the Nazi occupation. The Kastelli, with its pallazzi and the memories of centuries, if not millenia, has remained almost a ruin since then. Despite this, old Hania still evokes the past and its twisting lanes and winding backstreets, dominated by Ottoman lattices and Venetian frontages, have seduced more than one visitor with their magical aura.

Getting Around

Quite apart from its many neighborhoods Hania is really two towns: The old and the new. The old town also has two parts, one older and one comparatively newer, and is built around and behind two harbors, the inner and the outer harbor. Since visitors coming to Hania inevitably reach the new town first it is probably best to orient oneself from there. New Hania has as its center an enormous cruciform **market** that was erected after the union of Crete with Greece in 1913. In the early hours of the morning, huge quantities of meat, poultry, fish, vegetables, fruit and cheeses are piled up ready for sale. It is the perfect place to get a sense of the busy and volatile Haniote and its little shops are stocked with spices, herbs, jars of honey and pickled vegetables.

Until late in the 19th century, to the east of the market there was a permanent encampment of Bengazi Arabs who, for some obscure reason, had been exiled to Crete. Old prints of this encampment show its palm trees and tents in between

the daring sea attacks of the Ottoman corsair Barbarossa in the 16th century Hania was completely rebuilt and expanded. A new, or outer harbor was built and great walls marked the new limits of the town which held out until its final conquest by the Ottomans in the early 17th century. The Turks loved Hania and quickly transformed what must have been lively noisy quarters into quiet lanes dotted with fountains and centered on neighborhood mosques. The old Venetian palazzi were soon renovated to provide the quiet solitude of the harems and gardens for which Hania was so well known.

The Cretan revolts against Ottoman rule in the 19th century culminated first in the autonomy of Crete and then in its which are tethered camels and goats. The old market (this was a commercial center even before the present building was put up) also had large numbers of Abyssinian *hamals* or porters, and the minaret of their mosque can still be seen slightly east and to the south of the present market. Off the square in front of the market runs **Tsanakaki Street** on which the post office and telephone service are located, and slightly farther on are the gardens and zoo. There is an old-style coffee shop here as well as an open air cinema: A favourite spot for families until late in the evenings during the summer and fall.

To reach the old town, the most convenient approach is to walk down **Halidon Street** where the **Metropolitan Church** of Hania is located. It was built in the late-19th century by a Muslim as a votive offering to the Virgin Mary after she interceded to cure his son of a fatal

Above: Folkloric wares and chess games.
Right: Restaurants and cafés in the Venetian port.

illness. Behind the cathedral and to the right sprawls a section of Hania that was put up shortly after World War II, after the old houses that crowded against the city wall that cut across Halidon Street were razed through the ill-directed energies of a local mayor. To get an idea of the old character of the town in this area one should wander through the narrow streets to the left of the **cathedral** and behind Halidon Street to the east. Elegant Venetian façades still stand as well as the defaced stone surfaces marking wall fountains that almost inevitably indicate the proximity of a neighborhood mosque.

Directly across from the cathedral and down a small alleyway is the **Catholic Church** of the Capuchins, and not far from it, also on Halidon Street, stands the **Archaeological Museum** of Hania, which is housed in what was formerly the **Mosque of Yusuf Pasha** and prior to that the Venetian church of **St. Francis**. The museum is small but well worth a visit as it contains sarcophagi, pottery and other artifacts dating from Minoan down to Late Roman times, all from the Prefecture of Hania. The building itself is exquisite and adjacent to it is a small garden filled with interesting fragments as well as an old fountain dating from the Ottoman period. Almost directly across from the Museum is a small **Turkish bath** that is now being used as a foundry.

Halidon Street opens out into the harbor area. To the right rises the **Kastelli**, the oldest part of the old town, and to the left is the newer part, mostly built up in the 16th century. The Kastelli can be reached by walking up **Kanevarou Street** to the right of the square. Another approach is from **Karoli-Dimitriou Street** – also to the right. The latter approach skirts some of the oldest walls of the citadel, with columns and rubble of 3000 years embedded in their fabric. Once on the Kastelli there is little to see today other than the ravages of the last world war but some of the cleared areas

58

contain the foundations of Minoan houses and pavings that reveal Hania's most ancient past.

Continuing along this street will lead into a quite different quarter known as the **Splantzia** or **Hiones**, also known as *Koum Kapi*. Rising above it is the single minaret of the old **Mosque of Ibrahim Sultan** which is now once again (as it had been before the Ottoman period) the church of **St. Nicholas** (Gr. Agios Nikolaos). At the entrance to its square is the small, elegant, and derelict 15th-century church of **San Rocco**. The Splantzia is a fascinating place to wander through, with many tiny streets and cul de sacs. From here almost any street to the north will take you down to the inner Venetian **harbor**. Along it are the **arsenals** and worksheds built by the Venetians, and central to them is the majestic façade of the **rector's palace**. At its western end the harbor opens up into the outer harbor and the newer part of the old town.

The **outer harbor** has a wonderful frontage of Veneto-Ottoman houses and shops marking its entire course. It is a beehive of activity in the evenings and certainly the touristic nerve center of Hania. In some ways this is unfortunate as it means that it has lost its natural life. Houses have been converted into pensions, hotels, bars and discos that make it noisy and quite unlike the quarter that had a unique life of its own until very recent times. This part of Hania, behind the harbor front, is still known to many as the **Colombo** and there are still a few Haniotes who speak a dialect that was peculiar to this part of the city. It has two landmarks: The old **Mosque of Hassan Pasha** with its great onion dome, and the **Pharos**, or lighthouse. The mosque was built on the substructure of the old Venetian "dogana" or customs house and until very recent times a small cemetery linked it to the adjacent building. This now houses a hotel as well as some restaurants, but was once a local *medresse*, or school where Muslim children studied the Quran. It functioned as late as 1900. The other landmark, the Pharos, marks the end of the protective mole. Renovated by Ali Pasha in the mid-19th century, it is built on old Venetian foundations. A walk out to the Pharos early in the morning provides one with a spectacular view of the old town bathed in limpid colors, backed by the majesty of the White Mountains.

The Colombo was once divided into two main quarters: The **Ovraiki** and the **Top Hana** – two names dating back to the Venetian and Ottoman times. The Ovraiki is the first of these quarters and its limits are marked by **Halidon, Zabeliou** and **Kondylakis Streets**. This was the old Jewish quarter of Hania in medieval times and the old synagogue of Etz Hayyim, formerly the Venetian fifteenth century Church of **St. Catherine**, can be seen on Parodos Kondilaki.

Past the Ovraiki is the **Top Hana** which was the principal Muslim quarter

Above: The Turkish lighthouse on the Hania pier. Right: The Katholiko Monastery near Gouverneto.

until the 19th century, and before that an elegant Venetian neighborhood as can still be seen from the fronts and high structures that mark the narrow streets. On Zambeliou Street an old *hamam*, or **Turkish bath** marks one corner and a short distance from it, to the east, is a corner house with a base for a minaret and nearby fountain that indicates its former life as a neighborhood mosque. As in the case of many places of worship in Crete it was, prior to its conversion to Islam, a Venetian chapel.

At the end of the outer harbor, facing the lighthouse, is the **Firka**, an old Ottoman fortress that was built into the ruins of the Venetian bastion. It is now the **Naval Museum** and in the spring and summer months concerts of Cretan music, dancing and theatrical performances are held in an outdoor theater.

If one continues along the sea front, the Venetian bastion to the left marks the end of the sea wall. Rising above the sea is the **Xenia Hotel**, built on the uppermost part of the fortification. The street that cuts between these two sections of the old fortifications is known as Theotoko-poulou (El Greco) and just to the left of the entrance it is the old Venetian church of **St. Salvadore**.

It is in the process of being restored and has a fine Venetian interior with delicately groined arches as well as a small arched recess that, according to its Latin inscription, is dedicated to an image of the Virgin Mary. The floor is set with stone slabs that covered the burial places of Venetian notables. During Ottoman times the building was converted into a mosque and its *mihrab*, pointing to Mecca, has amazingly survived re-conversion to Christianity. In the course of the restoration an earlier, and most likely Byzantine apse was found imbedded in the later Venetian additions.

A walk up Theotokopoulou street leads into an old **Veneto-Turkish quarter**. One of the more interesting houses is the wooden structure just to the left on entering the street. Though not very old (mid-19th century) it is a very good example of the type of Ottoman house that characterized certain parts of the old town of Hania but has been, for the most part, either razed or destroyed by fire.

The road that continues past the front of the bastion supporting the Xenia Hotel continues along the sea front to **Nea Hora**. Here are some of Hania's finest fish restaurants as well as a small beach that attracts locals and tourists in the summer months. Directly across from the beach is the island of **Agii Theodori**, today a nature reserve on which the Cretan ibex is allowed to live.

AKROTIRI PENINSULA

(Unless otherwise stated all distances are calculated from Hania.)

The promontory of **Akrotiri** can be seen from Hania and is easily reached by following the road marked for the airport or the village of **Kounoupidiana** (6 km).

At the left turn into Akrotiri a signpost marks the way to the **tomb of Eleftherios Venizelos**, the great statesman of modern Crete and Greece. From here there is a magnificent view west over Hania and along the entire coast.

Akrotiri is currently being developed and there are fine tourist facilities and a very good beach at **Kalathas** and farther on at **Stavros** both of which are on the western side of the peninsula. If you continue straight on at the Venizelos turn-off, the road leads directly to the airport, skirting **Souda Bay**. An interesting diversion can be taken to **Sternes** which is a very old village. Just after entering, to the right, is a large Venetian country house, now in ruins, and adjacent to it the substructure of a Byzantine church dating from the sixth century.

The airport turning, just before Sternes to the left, passes an abandoned Venetian monastery of the 15th century and then continues on to the Greek Orthodox monastery of **Agia Triada** (16.5 km) which has a very fine church of the 17th cen-

Vardiés
Akrotíri
Mavromoúri
Stavrós
Cave of Lera
Moní Katholikó
(Monastery)
Moní Gouvernéto
(Monastery)
Akrotíri Maleka
Órmos
Kalathás
Akrotíri-
Koumarés
Moní Agía Triáda
(Monastery)
Horafákia
Kalathás
Hordáki
Kalórrouma
Skloha
528m
Kólpos Hanion
Kambáni
Mouzourás
Kounoupidiana
Káthiané
Peninsula
Kydonia
(Castle)
Profítis
Ilías
122m
Argoulidés
Paxinós
HANIÁ
Korakiés
19
Anemómili
Korakiés
214m
Pithári
Arónio
Stérnes
Vigles
195m
Darátsos
Maráthi
Galatás
Vamvakópoulo
Soúda
Órmos
Souda (Castle)
to Pireás
Óasis
Perivólia
New Road
to Réthimno
Ligidés
Marmarás
Nerokoúros
Tsikalariá
Soúdas
Mourniés
Kalámi
Varípetro
Kopránà
Maláxa
Zoúrva
610m
Metóhi
AKROTIRI PENINSULA
Megála Horáfia
Aptera
0 2 4 6km
444m
Mongila
Kalíves
Pláka
Kókkino
Horió

tury. Beyond it, to the north, the road leads to the **Gouverneto Monastery**, whose church is small and has an elegant Venetian renaissance façade (20.5 km).

After Gouverneto, a short walk leads to the **Katholiko Monastery** and the cave of **Panagia Arkouditissa**, or the Bear Virgin which, while dedicated under this name to the Virgin Mary, has revealed artifacts indicating that it was once dedicated to the bear goddess Artemis. Not far from this cave is another cave that was used by a famous Cretan saint, St. John the Hermit.

THE OMALOS PLATEAU

The **Omalos Pateau** in the White Mountains is best reached by car. If a hike through the Gorge of Samaria is planned as well, a hike that necessarily begins at the plateau, then it would be advisable to book an organized tour with a

Right: A monk sounding the vespers at Agia Triada Monastery.

bus or even a taxi in order to get to Omalos. After passage through the gorge, namely, the itinerary can be arranged either to end in Hora Sfakion or Paleohora on the south coast after a boat ride, or to go back north via the road.

The road to Omalos (39 km) leaves Hania to the west and ascends through fertile countryside. A stop should be made at **Alikianos** to visit the 14th-century Church-of-St-George (Agios Georgios), which is known for its fine frescos. The village also boasts the remains of an old Venetian country manor that belonged to the Damolino family.

Not far from here is **Fournes**, where a left turn will take you on a short trip to **Meskla**, on a road that winds through orange groves. In this village there are two small 14th-century churches that are among the most important in Crete – the **Transfiguration** and the **Church of the Savior**. Both have wall paintings of the same period. Returning to Fournes, continue on to **Lakki** which is worth a stop if only to take in the breathtaking views of the White Mountains. It is also the last place for tanking up on fuel. After leaving Lakki the ascent leads through increasingly wild, stark, and barren mountain country until the Plateau of Omalos is reached. For centuries this plain's produce fed the lower villages, and the surrounding mountains provided rough grazing for herds of goats. In the last century it was here that the initial stages of the Cretan rebellion against the Ottomans began and one of the great leaders, Hatzi-Mihalis Giannaris, rests in a small tomb on the hill of **Agios Panteleimon**. (To reach the entrance to the Gorge of Samarias one continues on the Omalos road marked for **Xyloskala**.)

The Omalos Plateau has an eerily deserted atmosphere; for most of the year it has few inhabitants. When the tourist throng heads towards the Samaria Gorge in the summer, shepherds and the few farmers move to the overhead plateau.

At an altitude of 1080 m, Omalos is surrounded by a formidable granite mountainwall. It is snow-covered in the winter, marshy in the spring melt and refreshingly cool on summer evenings.

The tiny hamlet of **Omalos**, the only settlement on the plateau, has a restaurant and a few rooms to rent. It could serve as a base for travelers who want to take their time exploring the gorge, as camping inside the park is now forbidden, or for those who want to walk the plateau. It has a wide variety of wild flowers, many rare, endangered species of birds of prey and *kri-kri* on neighboring slopes.

This wild area in the heart of the White Mountains is a paradise for hikers and nature lovers. Serious hikers should get information from the Greek Mountain Club (EOS). It operates the **Kallergi Hut**, a one-and-a-half hour walk from Omalos at the base of the peaks. A caretaker rents beds and serves meals, as well as giving information about climbing the peaks in winter and finding slopes suitable for advanced skiers.

Pahnes, at 2453 m just shorter than Mount Psiloritis, is a two-day hike from the Kallergi Hut. **Mount Gingilos**, beginning at the top of Samaria Gorge, is lower than Pahnes but its near vertical slope makes it more formidable. Its path is marked sporadically with orange paint and it is best to stick to it, for peculiar rock formations and powerful winds make it hazardous. The payoff for those who do conquer it is a splendid panoramic view, perfect for observing larger birds of prey or *kri-kri* who have taken refuge on upper levels to escape the crowds walking the Samaria Gorge.

SAMARIA GORGE

Hikers should probably receive badges at the end of their trek through the Samaria Gorge which say "I can't believe I walked the whole thing!" Every evening in the tavernas and bars of Hania, conversation between people of all ages and countries, most rubbing their shins and thighs, consists of anecdotes about their

different experiences along the 18-km route of the longest gorge in Europe.

The walk through the Samaria Gorge can be one of life's more awesome experiences, a journey to what looks and feels like the veritable navel of the huge island of Crete. To enjoy it fully, wear sturdy, waterproof walking boots and carry only light provisions, binoculars and water. Allow at least six hours to walk and explore the gorge and its environs. Severe leg strain and accidents occur most often when people are rushing down the steep path at the beginning of the walk from Omalos.

Take the early morning bus from Hania or wherever one has stayed overnight so that the walk from Omalos is begun by at least eight o'clock. This allows enough time to have a refreshing swim, take photographs or sunbathe on a rock and still get back in plenty of time to be sure of catching the last boat from Agia Roumeli at the end of the day's hike. It is a tiring day, but the spectacular scenery makes it all worth while. The gorge is a huge ravine caused by the erosion by surface water. A light jacket or pullover will protect against the morning chill, although you will probably be carrying it by the time you reach the bottom in the hotter months.

The descent begins on the *xiloskalo*, wooden steps once made of logs, a dizzying walk that carries you down a 1000-m plunge in the first couple of kilometers. Nevertheless, it is a safe walk on a wide path that has a hand railing. During the summer, several thousand people a day cross the gorge. The hectic stampede down this first section may not seem conducive to a spiritual atmosphere but the hordes will spread out over the length of the track.

Agios Nikolaos *(St. Nicholas)* is a whitewashed chapel which sits in a clear-

Left: The Samaria stream pushing its way through the "Iron Gates" of the gorge.

ing between massive cypress trees. It is located about 2 km after the beginning of the trail. In this area, there is a terrace of coniferous trees. Herbs such as sage, thyme and Cretan dittany as well as wild orchids, irises and peonies are found here but some of these are rare species, so look but don't pick. Lizards and occasional snakes glide in the undergrowth. The Cretan ibex or *kri-kri* is too elusive to be seen – sometimes the bearded vulture can be seen soaring overhead.

Shortly before the 7-km marker stands the deserted village of **Samaria**, reached via a bridge crossing a stream. You should note that each marker gives the distance between it and the next marker. When one reaches the 0 marker, there are still a couple of kilometers before the end of the trail.

The village of Samaria, slowly eroding with time, was inhabited by the Viglis family, descendants of one of the 12 aristocratic Byzantine clans. The residents were all relocated in 1962 when the area was offically made a park. The church of

Ossia Maria, named for a converted Egyptian courtesan, was founded in the late 12th century. The Venetians called this church the "San Maria," which was corrupted to become "Samaria," also the name of the gorge.

The most interesting artifact in the chapel, now on Mount Athos, was an icon showing Ossia Maria brandishing a claw-hammer in order to slay a terrifying beast in the Samaria Gorge. The dragon's lair was probably on Mount Gingilos, the other imposing peak north of **Mount Volakias**. The mountain has a sinister reputation in local folklore, and is said to be the abode of Satan, and of various demons, including vampires.

After this point, the cliff faces become higher and the rocks crossing the stream closer together. Just before the *sideroportes*, the famed "Iron Gates," sits the

Above: View of the so-called Xiloskalo, the steps leading down the gorge of Samaria. Right: Shrine in the White Mountains above the Gorge of Samaria.

little church of **Aphendis Christos**, built as a shrine by Sfakiote mountaineers. The Sfakians proudly state that in two and a half centuries of Turkish rule in Crete, they never got past the Iron Gates into the gorge. One such attempt by the Ottomans was crushed by 200 Sfakian soldiers under the leadership of Yannis Bonatos during the 1770 rebellion led by Daskalogiannis.

The highlight for many walkers is the passage through the **Iron Gates**, where the sheer rock walls rise on either side to just less than 300 m. The path has disappeared under the swirling water of the stream and the two walls are only 2.5 m apart at the narrowest point. Looking up, the feeling is of being in an abyss, with only the far-off rays of the sun faintly glinting far, far above.

After the narrowest of the Iron Gates, the path emerges into a broader valley and gentler landscape covered with olive trees, pines, oaks and platenos. Past this is the now-deserted old village of **Agia Roumeli**, whose residents were also displaced when the park was opened in 1962. Near this site is a ruined Turkish fortress and a Venetian church. The church is reported to have been built on an ancient temple to Apollo belonging to the city of Tarrha. Excavations show that it was inhabited from the fifth century BC until about the fifth century AD. During the Hellenistic period, it banded together with half a dozen cities on the southern shore to form the Confederation of Oreioi. The temple of Apollo must have been one of the most important shrines of the ancient Cydonians, the predecessors of the modern Sfakians.

After this point, it is a short walk to today's **Agia Roumeli**, with some accommodation, tavernas and facilities for swimming in the Libyan Sea. From here, a return to Hania can be made by small motorboats that ply between Agia Roumeli and Paleohora via Sougia to the west, or Sfakia to the east. From both these ports one can return to Hania by regular bus. Itineraries vary during the year and can be checked in Hania.

SFAKIA

Hora Sfakion and its forbidding mountainous terrain have an almost mythical quality about them. It has been claimed that no one has ever conquered this region of Crete nor its fierce inhabitants. This may be questionable but is quite believable as one enters the passes that climb up to Askifou. The port was quite important until the last century, as ships docked there from North Africa and Egypt, bringing goods that were carried by donkey and camel caravans up to the markets of Hania and Rethimno. If you have reached Hora Sfakion by boat after passing through the gorge you have no alternative but to take a coach back to Hania. This obviates the possibility of exploring the countryside and villages at leisure, and on foot. By far the best way to see Sfakia and the Askifou Plain is to rent a car or motorbike from Hania.

Take the road from Hania marked for either Souda or Rethimno to the east. Just before reaching Souda (6.5 km) you can

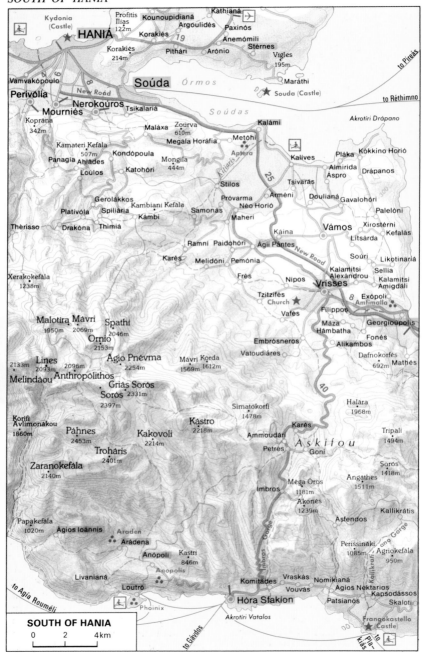

Kydonia (Castle)
Profitis Ilias 122m
Kounoupidianá
Kathianá
Argoulidés
Paxinós
HANIÁ
Korakiés
Anemómili
Stérnes
Korakiés 214m
Pithári
Arónio
19
Vígles 195m
Vamvakópoulo
Soúda
Órmos
Maráthi
to Pireás
Perivólia
New Road
Souda (Castle)
to Réthimno
Mourniés
Nerokoúros
Tsikalariá
Soúdas
Akrotíri Drápano
Kopraná 342m
Maláxa
Zoúrva 610m
Kalámi
Kalíves
Pláka
Kókkino Horió
Kamateri Kefála 507m
Megála Horáfia
Metóhi
Panagía
Kondópoula
Aptera
Almirída
Áspro
Drápanos
Ahládes
Katohóri
Mongilá 444m
Tsivarás
Loúlos
Stílos
Douliané
Gavalohóri
Gerolákkos
Próvarma
Arméni
Paleloni
Plativóla
Kambianí Kefála
Spiliária
Néo Horió
Xirostérni
Kefalás
Thérisso
Drakóna
Kámbi
Samonás
Maheri
Vámos
Thimiá
Ramní
Paidohóri
Kaina
Soúri
Litsárda
Karés
Melidóni
Pemónia
Ágii Pántes
New Road
Likotiniariá
Sellia
Kalamitsi Amigdáli
Xerakokefála 1238m
Frés
Nípos
Kalamitsi Alexándrou
Vrisses
Exópoli
Amfímalla
Tzitzifés Church
Vafés
Filippos
Georgioúpolis
Malotíra Mávri 1950m 2069m
Spathi 2046m
Máza
Hámbatha
Fonés
Ornió 2153m
Embrósneros
Alikambos
Dafnokorfés 692m
Mathés
Lines 2093m 2096m
Agio Pnévma 2254m
Vatoudiáres
Anthropólithos
Mávri Kórda 1569m 1612m
Melindáou
Griás Sorós 2331m
Halára 1968m
Sorós 2397m
Simatokorfí 1478m
Korifí Avlimonákou 1860m
Kástro 2218m
Karés
Tripali 1494m
Páhnes 2453m
Kakovolí 2214m
Ammoudári
Petrés
Askifou
Goní
Sorós 1418m
Troháris 2401m
Angathes 1511m
Zaranokefála 2140m
Mega Óros 1181m
Ímbros
Akónes 1239m
Astendos
Kallikrátis
Papakefála 1020m
Ágios Ioánnis
Araden
Anópoli
Kastrí 846m
Perissináki 1085m
Agriokefála 950m
Aradéna
Anopolis
Livanianá
Loutró
Komitádes
Vraskás
Vouvás
Nomikianá
Ágios Néktarios
Patsianós
Kapsodássos
Skaloti
Phoinix
Hóra Sfakíon
Akrotíri Vátalos
to Agía Rouméli
to Gávdos
Frangokastello (Castle)
to Pla-kiás

SOUTH OF HANIA

0   2   4km

choose to take either the old highway that goes through Souda or go on the new national highway which bypasses it.

The Venetian fortress on the **Islet of Souda** in the Bay of Souda was built in the late 1500s but didn't fall to the Turks until 1715. It played an important role during World War II, first in the evacuation of the Allied Forces in 1941 and later in supplying the troops during preparations for the Battle of Crete. The village of **Souda** and its harbor area is the main port of Hania as well as an important naval base; and photography is forbidden for security reasons. The village is of little, if any, interest and can easily be skipped.

Shortly after passing Souda the road begins to skirt the flank of a large promontory. In order to ascend the promontory for a breathtaking view out over the Bay of Souda and Akrotiri take the right turning marked for **Aptera**. The site of ancient Aptera is sometimes called Paleokastro after the huge Venetian fortress which dominates it today. Scattered in every direction around it are the ruins of the city which was founded in the fifth century BC. Dominating as it did the entrance to the Bay of Souda it was important during Roman and Byzantine times until its destruction during the Arab conquest of Crete in AD 828. From Aptera, access to the old highway can be gained by taking the route marked for **Stilos** or **Agii Pantes** and then on to Vrisses.

Alternatively, you can take the route down to the national highway on the coast. Shortly after getting onto this road two other routes to Vrisses (and on to Sfakia) are feasible. The old road with access to fine beaches and tourist facilities is that marked for **Kalami/Kalives** to the left. Otherwise, the main national highway can be followed and at the sign for Vrisses a right turn should be taken. The drive along the new highway from Kalami to Vrisses passes the **Drapano** promontory which has several interesting villages and at **Georgioupolis** (38 km) follows the coast to Rethimno. There are tourist facilities as well as access to a fine beach. Should you be interested in fresh water swimming, shortly after passing Georgioupolis there is a sign marked for Kournas to the right.

Lake Kournas is reached after a short drive (4 km). This is the largest freshwater lake in Crete and the water is quite refreshingly cool even in the summer months. There are restaurants and a great deal of opportunities for quiet walks in the vicinity of the lake. After this diversion return to the Vrisses turn-off and drive on to the village of that name. In the summer, **Vrisses** is a refreshing place to stop and rest, as it is surrounded by great plane trees and watered by many springs. There are some good cafes and tavernas, selling local specialities, one of which is yoghurt and honey.

Out of Vrisses continue on the main road. Shortly after leaving the village the road divides. The one to the right is marked **Embroseneros**. The one straight on leads to Sfakia. This village is in itself of little interest other than for the castle of Ibrahim Alidakis, a local Muslim who was active in the defence of the area against Christians during one of the rebellions in the 19th century. The drive to it, however, is very beautiful and if continued to its terminus provides many opportunities for hikes into the foothills of the mountains of Sfakia.

The Askifou Plain

Having taken this diversion, return to the road marked for Sfakia. From this point, the terrain begins to change quite dramatically as one ascends up to the **Askifou Plain** through the Katre Ravine to Kares. Side roads, marked for **Maza** and **Alikambos**, lead to small villages with Byzantine churches, both painted in the interior by the 14th-century Cretan painter Ioannis Pagomenos. The church in Alikambos dates to 1323, that in Maza was painted two years later. Pagomenos is somewhat of a rarity in Byzantine art as he signed his paintings and consequently it is possible to follow not only his development as a painter, but also his travels, as several churches in the region of Kandanos are signed by him. He had a highly personal style and, as he was a native Cretan, it is through him that we obtain an insight into a still relatively unknown school of painting that developed on the island under strong influences from Asia Minor and the monastic traditions in painting, rooted in Cappadocia.

Returning to the main Sfakia road, the route ascends sharply through rugged mountain country to the **Askifou Plain** and the towns of **Kares** and **Goni**. If there is time to stop, these villages are worth visiting, as they have good examples of local architecture and there

Above: The coast at Hora Sfakion. Right: The old donkey path from Anopoli to Aradena.

are also some good tavernas. From the Askifou Plain it is also possible to climb up to **Mount Kastro**.

In the winter months, the green lush valley gives way to snow and this is a favorite outing for Haniotes. On leaving **Goni** the road begins a sharp and tortuous descent along the **Imbros gorge**, one of the most dramatic drives in Crete, cutting through the heart of the Sfakia region. The road terminates at **Hora Sfakion** on the Libyan Sea. The village is usually bustling with arrivals from the Samaria Gorge waiting to take buses back to Hania. There is some accommodation of a modest nature and several good tavernas. Out of Hora Sfakion to the west there is a small road that leads to the ancient sites of **Phoinix** and **Loutro**, its port. According to tradition it was here that St. Paul was shipwrecked. Further inland and accessible by tracks are sites of other ancient cities that were destroyed in the 19th century and in many of the villages there are quite fine Byzantine churches.

A good road leads from Hora Sfakion to **Anopoli**, where there is the Church of the Transfiguration. From here a rough road leads to **Aradena**, with the church of St. Michael, dated to the early Byzantine period. Farther on from Aradena is the village of **Agios Ioannis**, built high above the Libyan Sea and backed dramatically by the Sfakiote Mountains. In the vicinity of the village are several important caves, one of which, called Drakolaki or the Dragon, is said to be inhabited by Neraidis even to this day.

To the east of Hora Sfakion the road leads to **Komitades**, a village known for being the meeting place of Sfakiote revolutionaries in the 19th century. Beyond Komitades the road leads into the Prefecture of Rethimno. The return to the nothern coast can be made from this direction via Plakias and Rethimno. The shorter route by far is simply to return to Hania by retracing the route from Hora Sfakion through the Imbros gorge and Askifou Plain.

GAVDOS

Out of Hora Sfakion there is a boat service to the island of Gavdos and its sister island, Gavdopoula, some 40 km off the Cretan coast. Gavdopoula is uninhabited, save for a few shepherds. **Gavdos**, the larger of the two, has a good number of villages and was known in antiquity as Clavda. It was here, according to some, that Calypso seduced Odysseus and held him prisoner in her "vaulted cave" for seven years. This island was a Saracen pirates' nest long into the Middle Ages after Crete had been returned to Byzantine hands.

Gavdos, little more than a barren rock except in its interior which is covered in dwarf pines and herbal brush, is the home of about 35 year-round residents, most of them fishermen or shepherds. A few families spend the summer in Gavdos but return to Crete in the fall because employment is scarce. Emigrants have formed the community Gavdiotika in Paleohora.

Daytrips are possible on the boat from Paleohora or Hora Sfakion during the tourist season. The boat trip takes about two hours. Those who want to stay overnight on the islet can book a room through Brown's Travel in Paleohora or can look for one in the port of arrival, **Kalergiana** or in the main village of **Kastri,** reached on foot in about an hour from Kalergiana, or in other small settlements. 90 percent of the overnight guests are Greek.

Gavdos was probably inhabited as early as Neolithic times, though the first permanent settlement dates from the post-Mycenaean era. *Kaudos* was the name the Romans gave to Gavdos and this is the name of the islet which St. Paul blew past during a storm which eventually shipwrecked him in Malta. During Byzantine times, Gavdos had a population of almost 8000, and was the seat of a bishopric, which probably included the

GAVDOS

0   2 km

village of Sfakia. It was abandoned during the later Byzantine era when pirates used the eastern side of the islet as one of their lairs.

It's hard to imagine that Gavdos was once a thriving island when **Kastri**, its most important agglomeration, is almost a ghost town with six families remaining. Camping is possible almost everywhere but bring bottled water and basic provisions because these supplies come from the mainland and there are shortages of both.

Activity in Gavdos centers around the beaches during the day and the few tavernas or a campfire at night. The north and east of the island have a low coastline with good beaches at **Potamos** and **Sarakiniko** in the north and **Korfos** in the east. The south and west coasts are high and rocky.

Gavdos is a good place for lovers of solitude and a simple life style. Tempera-

tures can be oppressively hot during July and August but a gentle evening breeze usually makes the evenings pleasant. The Libyan Sea is warm enough to swim in most of the year and is very clean. Snorkeling and spear fishing are fairly good here because the inhabitants have not dynamited all the fish away, as has happened off much of the coast of Crete.

Talk has been bandied about for some time about building a hotel and paved roads, but no definite plans have been made for either. The natives of this southernmost part of Europe have felt overlooked in the general improvement plan for Crete. Requests have been made for upgrading of the sanitary facilities, electrical hookups (there is neither a central electrical plant, nor proper medical care – a doctor is on the island only in the summer months).

If Gavdos is still too "civilized" for your taste, an excursion can be made to the tinier islet of **Gavdopoula**, uninhabited except for a few shepherds and their flocks.

Right: Fishing with tried and true means on the south coast.

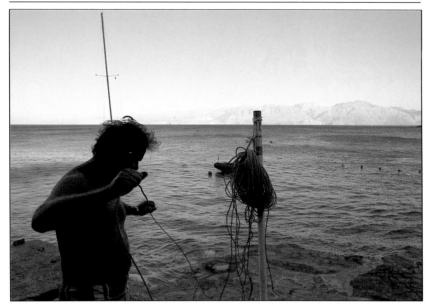

WEST AND SOUTH OF HANIA

If possible, try trips to Omalos, Sougia and Therisso (Gr. Therissos). All provide magnificent views of the mountains and begin by taking the turn-off marked for Omalos/Therrisso just west from Hania.

If there is time, it is worth while to take a left turn marked for **Meskla**, where there is a fine church from the fourteenth century. If you continue on, the road leads up into the mountain foothills through orange groves to **Therisso** and its gorge. By far the best way of making this day trip is to hike, as the countryside and gorge are breathtaking.

West of Hania, the Libyan Sea and southern coast can be reached by three main routes: 1. via Alikianos to Sougia (70 km), 2. via Tavronitis to Paleohora (74 km) and 3. directly west through Kastelli Kissamou (42 km) and then down the western coast of the prefecture to Elafonissi (57 km). All three trips are well worth the time and effort as the countryside and terrain of each are quite different

and striking. They also offer opportunities for some energetic hiking on the surrounding mountainside, swimming, and visits to several ancient sites of importance. Most of the latter have been only partially excavated, if at all, and the remains of theaters and other buildings protrude out of fields and hillsides. There are, as well, a great number of medieval Byzantine churches that are especially prevalent in the region around **Kandanos** (57 km).

From Hania to Sougia

Of the three trips to the south this is certainly the most arduous but also very beautiful. It passes the western flank of the White Mountains and twists and winds down to the sea past several ancient sites that are seldom visited. Take the southwestern road from Hania, marked for **Agia** or **Alikianos**. Just before Alikianos there is a small church off a left turn, called St. George (Agios Georgios), that was decorated and signed in the early 15th century by Pavlos Provatos whose work is quite different from that of the earlier painter Pagomenos who also worked in this area.

After leaving Alikianos the road begins to ascend the White Mountains and continues on, passing many small villages until, at **Apopigadi** (1331 m high), it resumes its long descent to the sea. At **Rodovani** the road cuts to the east and arrives at the ruins of **Elyros** which during Roman and Byzantine times was one of the most important cities in southwestern Crete. It was an important bishopric and there are remains of what must have been a fine fifth-century early Christian church with a floor mosaic. Elyros was destroyed during the Arab conquest of Crete in the early ninth century and never recovered its fortunes, and today it is possible to make out only the remains of its aqueduct, a few remnants from the walls, and a theater. In the village are the remains of a basilica of the 6th century with a fine floor mosaic.

From Elyros the road passes **Moni** in which there is a church dedicated to St. Nicholas with frescoes from the 14th century. At Moni the road takes a sharp bend and then descends south to **Sougia** which was the port of Elyros.

There are only few remains from before the period of its destruction in the ninth century. There are also some tavernas, and reasonable places to stay though with limited facilities.

Should you wish to take a short hike, it is possible to walk west along the coastal road to another ancient sea port at **Agios Kirkos**. In antiquity it was known as Lissos, which was the port for Hyrtakina, a city located slightly to the north. While not as famous as Elyros, Lissos was well known for its temple to Asklepios, the famous god of healing. Some of the remains of which have been identified and can be seen today. Of special interest is a section of floor mosaic from the temple itself.

A further hike northwards will take you to **Prodromi**, which is built on the site of the ancient Hyrtakina. If you are driving, it is possible to return to Rodovani and from there continue on westward to **Maza** and **Temenia**. At the junction take the road south to Paleohora.

From Hania to Paleohora

The road leading directly west out of Hania skirts the sea as far as the Rodopou Peninsula. The entire coast is in the process of being heavily developed touristically. Many of the accessible beaches are now lined with pensions, hotels and tavernas, though there are still several open and relatively undeveloped beaches near **Kato Stalos** and just after leaving Platanias. One should be wary of strong undertows in the sea. Just beyond Agia Marina on the coast west of Hania, one can see the islet of **Agii Theodori**, which

Above: A Shrine by the wayside. Right: A friendly encounter.

was known in ancient times as Akytos. Legend holds that its craggy form is the distorted head of a prehistoric monster petrified by the gods when it tried to eat the islet.

A cave on the island, dated to the 3rd century BC, was thought to have been used as a sanctuary, along with one of a slightly later date at Agia Marina, one of the few Minoan sites unexcavated on the main land. Excursion boats from Agia Marina sail around Agii Theodori, now used as a preserve for the ibex, so that one has a chance to see them.

At **Tavronitis**, just before reaching the **Rodopou Peninsula**, there is a major turn-off to the left marked for Paleohora. This road leads through the region of Selinos down to the Libyan Sea. The main road out of Tavronitis goes on to Kastelli Kissamou and out of there farther west to unite with a road that follows the western coastline, also down to the Libyan Sea.

This itinerary to the south and Paleohora runs through the eparchy of **Kidonia** and then into that of **Selinos**, the principal village of which is **Kandanos**. It provides many opportunities for side trips, hiking and visits to some of the many small but important churches that are occasionally not too easy to find – but well worth the effort by the adventurous.

Initially, the road out of Tavronitis passes through rich and verdant agricultural land. **Voukolies** is an interesting place to stop and investigate. After the Ottoman conquest of Crete many of the Cretan (and Venetian) families in this region and that of Selinos converted to Islam and the village became an important center for marketing local produce. There are two churches of some interest: St. Constantine (1452, Agios Konstantinos) and that of the Archangel Michael dating from 1392. There are also some Venetian remains including a tower with a spring credited with having curative powers.

After Voukolies, a steep ascent begins through the harsh mountains of the region. A worthwhile side trip out of Voukolies leads off toward **Kato Kefala** after which it passes between two ridges. At **Ano Kefala** (just before Platanes) there is a side road to the left that leads to **Sembronas** through terrain being quite magnificent and deserted. Through this region it is possible to feel some of the grandeur and solitude that pockets of Crete still retain. This road, at Sembronas, joins the major road that goes to Sougia from Alikianos.

Should you wish to visit the more isolated and typical villages of this region, the road to **Platanes** (which has a small church dedicated to St. Demetrios, with wall paintings from 1372) can be taken at Ano Kefala. At **Palea Roumata** you can continue on – in circular route – around the valley and, returning to Palea Roumata, take the road marked for Kakopetros, which will get you back on the main route to Kandanos and Paleohora. The road to Kandanos from **Kakopetros**

passes through typical, but less harsh landscape than that met with in the diversion to Platanes, and begins a sharp ascent at **Floria**, where there are two churches, located in the upper and lower parts of the village. One, that of St. George (Agios Georgios), in the lower village dates from 1497 with frescoes painted by Georgios Provatopoulos.

The other church, Agion Pateron (in the upper village) has unfortunately lost its paintings. The mountain ridge that this road passes over marks a sharp north-south division after which one is in the region of Selinos. After passing the peak, the road begins its descent to the Libyan Sea. This is a comparatively rich countryside, marked with many small villages out of which one can take fine walks into the hills. Many of these villages give access to more or less isolated churches of great importance, interest, diversions and stops throughout this region are well worthwhile.

Kandanos is surrounded by magnificent olive trees with low, writing, age-blackened trunks. Although accommodation is limited and sparse, this is a good place to stay if you wish to hike in the surrounding hills, explore the many small churches dating from the 14th to the 16th centuries or even to visit the ancient site of Kandanos which is located in the hills above the present village (to the south). Around Kandanos, as far as **Kakodiki** and **Kaniskades**, the villages are more in the nature of compounds and the churches are small and intimate and have not been systematically studied. In Kandanos there are Agios Ioannis and Archangelos Michael – the oldest, and both dated to the early 14th century. **Skoudiana** has an especially interesting church, the Panagia, which is one of the few extant churches in Crete dating to before the Arab Emirate (sixth century).

Left: This village priest has found a quiet spot. Right: Plain and simply beautiful.

Kakodiki has several dependent villages in all of which are small churches. **Veidikali** has a church painted in the early 14th century by Ioannis Pagomenos (the Panagia) and in **Tzinaliana** is Agios Isidoros which has a magnificent Jesus as the *Pantokrator* and decorations reminiscent of Monreale in Sicily, dated to the 15th century. The road south from Kandanos descends through olive groves and the Libyan Sea can be seen stretching toward Africa.

Paleohora is located on a small isthmus – the promontory of which is dominated by one of the very earliest Venetian monuments on the island. This fortress, known as **Selino Castle**, has only in recent times been abandoned. Paleohora itself is a pleasant enough village with a good beach and reasonable facilities that are being developed for tourists.

West of Paleohora there are two possible itineraries that lead back into the mountains and valleys of **Selinos** and to some of its most isolated villages. However, it is not advisable to attempt to

From Hania to Kastelli Kissamou

reach the most western part of the island from this direction.

Leaving Paleohora to the west there is a turn-off marked for **Agia Triada**, and at **Kondokinigi** the road forks again. The most interesting villages are reached by taking the route to **Agios Pavlos** and from there to **Sklavopoula** where several Byzantine churches appear to have been erected not long after Crete was re-taken by the Byzantines in the tenth century. Most of this region of Selinos was settled by Bulgarians, Slavs and Armenians who were brought in to re-populate isolated pockets of the island. Agios Giorgios in Sklavopoula is one of the very early churches with remnants of frescoes dating from the late 13th century. At **Voutas** there is another church with 14th century frescoes, Agia Paraskevi. Returning to the northern coast from Paleohora it will be necessary to retrace the route north through Kandanos on to Tavronitis.

Above: Everyday life in a Cretan village.
Right: The south coast and the Libyan sea.

As the most western part of Crete cannot be reached from the south coast, it is necessary to go west and then south along the western coast. This region of Crete is known as **Kissamou** and was named after its principal city. It lies on the coast between two great promontories that jut out into the Cretan Sea to form the Gulf of Kissamou.

The first of these, **Rodopou**, is a mountain ridge that is for the most part uninhabited, except for the village of **Afrata**, near which recent evidence was found of human remains dating back 20,000 years. It is possible, though not recommended, to hike to the tip, where only a few remains of the ancient city of **Diktyna** can be seen. The road is quite pitted and the some 12 km distance that it covers is barren and of geological interest, but, after the first kilometer or so, quite repetitious and marked by nothing extraordinary. It is perhaps best, should one wish to visit the tip of the promontory, to take a local boat. The **monastery of Gonia**, located not far past **Kolimvari** on the east side of the promontory, is relatively late and most of what remains is from the late 17th century. There are a few fine icons in the monastic church, also of this period.

Out of Kolimvari, an interesting diversion can be made by taking the road south out of the village leading to **Spilia**. There are several fine churches here. Especially noteworthy is the church of Archangelos Michael which has an ornate carved wooden ikonostasis dating from the 16th or 17th century.

At **Drakona**, not far from Spilia, there is an ancient church with decorations from before the Arab Emirate in the ninth century. The nearby village of **Episkopi** got its name as a result of being the residence of the Bishop of Kissamou. The cathedral church of Archangelos Michael is especially interesting as it has a rotunda built over the nave in the style that was typical of churches in Crete prior to the ninth century.

The area around Episkopi has several villages and sites that have been identified with ancient cities – though remains are scanty and of little interest.

To return to the main highway and Kissamou, the road north can be taken from **Vassilopoulo** to **Nohia**, which was apparently a Minoan site. Some scholars have even identified it with Pergamon, the city founded by Aeneas after he fled the burning city of Troy.

Once past the isthmus of Rodopou, the road descends to Kastelli Kissamou and in the distance the second promontory, Gramvousa, can be made out. The town of **Kissamou** was originally the port of an ancient city to the south called Polyrinia. During the 16th century, Kissamou was reconstructed by the Venetians and given a large fortress from which it got the name **Kastelli**.

The countryside around it is very rich and some of Crete's finest wines come from its vineyards. Out of the town, **Polyrinia** can be reached by taking the route marked for Paleokastro on an as-

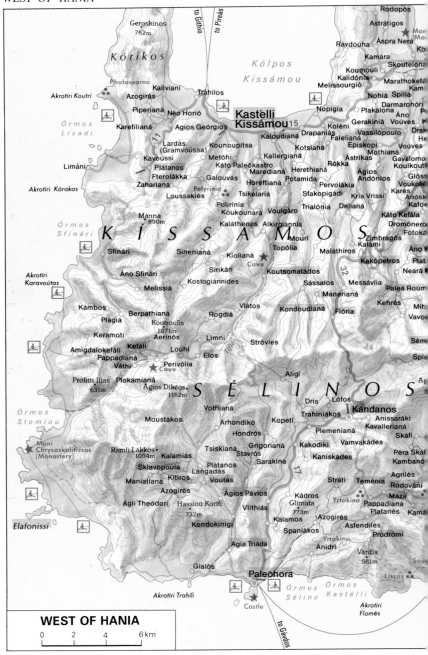

Rodopós
Astrátigos
Ravdoúha Áspra Nerá
Geroskinos
762m
Kamára
Skoutelóna
Kórikos
Koumoúli
Kólpos
Kalidónia
Melissourgió Marathokefá
Kissámou
Kam
Phalassarna
Nohiá Spiliá
Kalivianí Tráhilos
Akrotíri Koutrí
Azogirás
Nopigia
Darmarohóri
Piperianá Néo Horió
Plakálona Áno
Plakálona P
Órmos
Karefiliana
Agios Geórgios
Gerakiniá Voúves K
Koléni
Livadi
Kaloudiana Drapaniás
Vassilópoulo Drak
Faleliana
Kounoupitsa Kotsiana Episkopí Vouves H
Lardás
(Gramvoússa)
Kayoússi Metóhi Kallergianá Mothiana
Vouves
Limáni
Plátanos Káto Paleókastro Rókka Ágios Gavalomo
Maredianá Herethianá Andónios Koulkoutl
Akrotíri Kórakas
Fterolákka Galouvás Potamida Glóss
Zaharianá
Horeftianá Pervolákia Voukolié
Polyrinia Karés
Loussakiés Tsikalariá Sfakopigádi Kria Vríssi Anósk
Polirinia Trialónia Deliana Kafo
Mánna Koukounará Voulgáro
Káto Kefála
890m
Kaláthenes Aïkirgiánnis
Dromónero
KISSAMOS
Zimbrágos Fotoka
Sfinári
Mouri Kalámi Áno
Topólia Maláthiros
Sinenianá Kioliána
Kaköpetros Plat
Áno Sfinári Cave
Koutsomatádos Neará
Akrotíri
Sirikári
Karavoútas
Kostogiánnides
Sássalos Messávlia Paleá Roúm
Melissiá
Maneríana
Kámbos Vlátos Kehrés Mir.
Berpathianá
Rogdiá Kondoudianá Flória Vavo
Plagiá
Koutroúlis
Keramoti
1071m
Aerinós Limní Sém
Amigdalokefáli Kefali Loúhi Strovles
Pappadianá Spir
Váthi Perivólia
Profitis Ilias Plokamianá Cave Aligí
631m
Ágios Díkeos *SÉLINOS*
1182m
Dris Lófos
Vothianá Kándanos
Trahiniakos
Órmos
Moustákos Kopetí Anissaráki
Arhondikó Kavalleriana
Stomíou
Hondrós Plemenianá Skáfi
Moni
Ramli Lákkos Tsiskianá Grigorianá Kakodiki Vamvakádes
Chrysoskalítissas
1004m Kalamiás Stavrós Pèra Skáf
(Monastery)
Sarakina Kaniskádes Kambanó
Sklavopoúla Plátanos
Langadás Agrilès
Maniatianá Kitiros Voutás Stráti Temenia Rodováni
Azogirés
Máza
Elafonissi Ági Theódori Ágios Pávlos Kádros Yrtakina Pappadianá
Hassiou Korifi Vlithiás Glimata Platanés Kama
732m 773m Azogirés
Kálamos
Kondokinigi Spaniákos Asfendilès Prodrómi
Yrtakina
Agia Triáda Ánidri
Várdia Sou
581m
Gialós
Paleóhora Lissos
Órmos *Órmos*
Akrotíri Trahíli *Sélino* *Kastélli*
Castle Akrotíri
Flomés

WEST OF HANIA
0   2   4   6 km

to Githio
to Pireás
to Gávdos

Kastélli
Kissámou 15

80

cending road. Polyrinia itself is a jumble of ruins that range from Ottoman to Venetian and far back into Roman and Dorian times. The site is very beautiful and well worth a trip.

Directly to the west of Kastelli Kissamou, and reached by a somewhat circuitous route, is the ancient site of **Phalassarna** (59 km). This city was a serious rival to Polyrinia in antiquity, and while little remains of it today the site dominates a magnificent beach and views of the sea as well as the western coast of the Gramvousa Peninsula.

The ruins of the city are situated inland today, as this end of Crete was thrust upwards by about 9 m during the sixth century AD as a result of an earthquake. It was this, rather than rivalry, that caused the decline of the city.

An interesting sea trip can be made by hiring a boat at **Trahilos**, not far to the west of Kastelli Kissamou, and going round the northern tip of the coast at Gramvousa. Here you can see the massive fortifications of the erstwhile Venetian castro. There are some beautiful and almost completely isolated beaches along the coastline.

GRAMVOUSA

Gramvousa, a triangular islet north of Phalassarna Beach in the northwest corner of Crete, is attached to the mainland by a series of shoals and reefs. To visit uninhabited Gramvousa and its wilder and larger northern neighbor, **Agria Gramvousa**, hire a caique in Kastelli.

Flat-topped Gramvousa is historically important because the Venetians built an impressive **fortress** on the rocky northwest tip in 1579, after they had conquered Crete. They refused to relinquish it or their other strongholds at Souda and Spinalonga.

Gramvousa fell in 1692, 23 years after the surrender of Iraklio to the Ottoman troops, when two Neapolitan commanders sold Gramvousa to a pasha and absconded with the money. After some years, when the islet was deserted, 900 Cretan veterans captured the fortress during the Greek war of independence. They installed refugees there, mainly women and children, who were joined by islanders from Psara and Kasos, driven off by the Turks. Without any source of income, they were forced to turn to piracy.

Eventually, Capodistria was compelled to intervene and the matter was turned over to the European powers. They restored the islet and the rest of Crete to the Turks who used it to blockade boats of Cretan rebels fleeing to the independent island of Antikythera. The high walls of the ruined fortress have a romantic profile, especially when seen in moonlight. The slope up to the fortress is pitted by bullets and shells from the many conflicts, and the characteristic escutcheons

Above: Cloister steps. Right: The cloister of Chrisoskalitissa in the southwest of the island.

of the lion of St. Mark were removed from the walls by the Turks. Families from the nearby mainland often make excursions to the cove on **Cape Tigani**, south of the islet and cross to Gramvousa to fish, for its waters are known for abundant fish and seafood, such as crab.

THE WEST COAST

It is feasible, though the road is less interesting and more difficult, to reach the southwest coast of Crete by taking the road south from **Platanos**. This inland route affords access to the west coast at several points but follows a mountainous ridge. By far the more interesting route is that which runs south out of **Kaloudiana** to the east of Kastelli-Kissamou.

This road follows the bed of the Tiphlos river and passes two villages of note: **Voulgaro** and **Topolia** (46 km); in and near both of which are fine churches still decorated with frescoes. At **Latziana** the church of St. Barbara (Agia Varvara) was constructed almost entirely

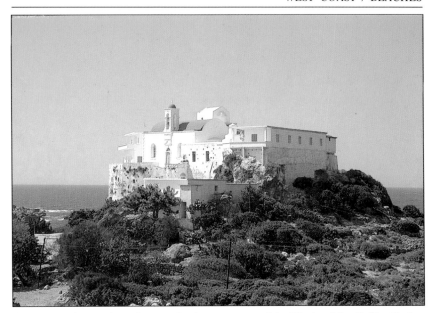

from the antique ruins of a temple that once stood there.

Not far from Topolia the road enters the **Koutsomatados Ravine**. Not long after entering it care should be taken to watch for the signs for the **cave of Agia Sofia** which is one of the largest caves on the island. Out of the ravine the road runs on to **Elos**.

This village may well have been part of the ancient *Inakorion* and today is included in what are called the Nine Villages or *Enneahoria* – though there are, in fact, more than nine. The countryside is magnificent and great forests of chestnut trees thrive here.

At **Kefali**, one of the nine villages, the road flanks the eastern side of Mount Elias. After reaching **Vathi** it begins to degenerate rapidly and the last few kilometers to the coast are difficult. Both Kefali and Vathi have fine churches and afford rich opportunities for hikes in the nearby hills.

The road reaches the sea at **Ormos Stomiou** and continues south to the Monastery of the Virgin of the Golden Stair – or **Chrisoskalitissa** (57 km). There is a legend that of the 90 steps that lead up to it, one is made of gold, but it has never been discovered as only a person who has never sinned will be able to recognize it.

Past the monastery, the road leads down to the coast at **Elafonissi**, an island located just offshore that can be reached by wading and swimming from what is certainly one of the most beautiful beaches in Crete, washed by the Libyan Sea and warmed by the winds of Africa.

Offbeat Beaches

Crete is 260 km long; so if you are willing to wander off the beaten track, secluded beaches can be found at any time of the year. Those craving isolation might prefer to visit in the spring or fall. The seas surrounding this southernmost of the Greek islands are warm enough to swim in from April to October.

Nudism is prohibited on the beaches of Crete except in the specifically desig-

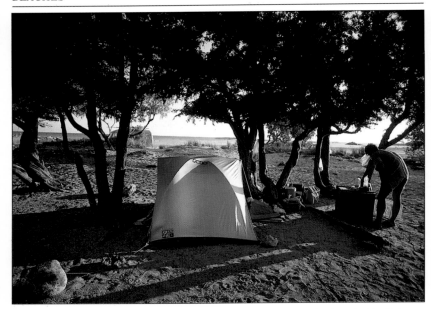

nated areas but some of the remote beaches are unofficially allocated for skinny dippers. If bathers are discreet and do not offend other families or conservative islanders, chances are they will not run into trouble.

The **town beach of Hania** is a ten-minute walk west of town and other, better beaches lie in the same direction. A bus goes as far as the sandy beach of **Kalamaki** but it is better to get off before this and go to one of the less populated sandy stretches. Better yet, head to **Akrotiri Peninsula** in the east, dotted with isolated beaches, many within walking distance of ancient monasteries for those who get bored with lying in the sun. In between Kounoupidiana and Stavros, especially in the **Bay of Kalathas**, are sandy coves that attract more locals than tourists.

Stavros, at the end of the Akrotiri Peninsula, is the locale used in the last scene

Above: A camper's paradise on the beach of Elafonissi.

of *Zorba the Greek* when the Englishman dances with Zorba. The beach is lovely, in a circular bay with a shelving bottom that makes it safe for children. A mountainous mass dominates the far side of the bay. Behind the beach is the **Cave of Lera**, known for its interesting stalactites and said to have been used as a sanctuary as early as 1200 BC until the Hellenistic period.

East of Souda there are fine beaches at **Kalyves** and some kilometers farther on in the idyllic village of **Plaka** which has not yet been inundated with tourists.

One of the thrills of swimming at **Georgioupolis's** gently curving beach, is to wade through the ley streams of bubbling fresh water that flow into the sea.

Phalassarna beach near Kastelli Kissamou stretches for many kilometers and is used mainly by campers. It is undeveloped, has some ancient ruins and nice sand, unfortunately marred by an oil slick.

If you opt for complete isolation, hike for three hours from the village of **Kali-**

viani to the lovely white sand beach opposite the islet of Gramvousa. It's a pity it is also plagued with patches of tar and torn plastic.

Tempting beaches lie below the spectacular cliff off the winding coastal road leading to Paleohora. The road drops at **Kambos**, making it easier to reach the small beach there, as well as the one at **Sfinari**.

The small islet of **Elafonissi** can be reached by wading from the coast. An idyllic retreat, mellow pink in tone due to coral fragments in the sand and good for snorkeling, the atmosphere can be marred by garbage left by picnickers.

Compared to the northern coast of Crete, the southern coast is still less accessible. With the exception of the area around Ierapetra, you will not find the kind of big hotels here that are typical of the northern coast. Your compensation for that, however, will be remote and tranquil inlets.

Paleohora, flanked by Venetian ramparts, has been discovered by younger travelers but the place is still lowkey. The beaches to the east tend to be nicer than the western ones, which are spoiled by plastic greenhouses. To the east, the beaches are often pebbly but more isolated and favored by nudists.

There is also a popular beach at **Sougia** with rooms for rent, some tavernas and even a discotheque.

The beach near (now deserted) **Agia Roumeli** is usually frequented only by hikers trekking through the Samaria Gorge, because otherwise this village is only accessible by boat.

The scenic fishing village of **Loutro** is also only accessible by boat. From here a 20-minute walk takes you to the beach of **Phoinix**. Near **Hora Sfakion** the sea offers crystalline water but is more rewarding to make a side trip to **Frangokastello** with its beach of fine sand, hospitable tavernas and moderately-priced accommodations.

CRETAN WEDDING

Although weddings in Crete in recent years have become less elaborate than they once were, much of the tradition is still maintained. "Thus, for the families involved, the marriage negotiations have the quality of participation in a kind of ritualized contest" (E. Friedl, *Vassiliska).* When boy meets girl, intermediaries get involved, marriage contracts are drawn, courtship and engagement follow, and, finally, the wedding ceremony takes place.

In Crete, in earlier generations, it was possible for a woman and a man never to have seen each other until the first formal occasion for meeting. Most of the times today, though, a young man may have met a girl in a feast *(paniyiri)*, and may have asked his father to look into the financial and social status of her family. In turn, a young girl may have seen a young man at a local festival and may have asked her family to investigate the situation. But neither of the two young people is supposed to know anything about the negotiations between their families. Secrecy is important since the families do not believe they can get accurate information if the villagers know they have an interest in the matter.

Once information is on hand, the father of the would-be groom or bride sends three to four well-respected members of the community as intermediaries, to start the negotiations *(proxenia)*. Sometimes, these intermediaries *(proxenitades)* use socks of different colors as a sort of sign for their intentions without openly declaring them from the outset. At times, they also wear their cloths backwards for good luck! After the first pleasantries, the aim of the visit is stated and the group gets down to serious business, exploring the amount of dowry the family is willing to give. When later transmitting the information to the interested parties, both the size of the dowry and the qualities of the young people are exaggerated by each group. The game, then, is to find out the actual truth.

Once the main parts of the marriage contract are agreed upon, the two young people meet formally and, if they feel that "the chemistry is right" the formal engagement takes place at the home of the bride, usually on a Saturday night, while during the previous day gifts are sent by the groom to the bride in big baskets full of dried fruit, liquor, food, dresses, and cosmetics.

Saturday afternoon the friends of the groom pick up the groom and march in procession to the bride's house to "give her the groom" *(tis pigenoun ton gambro)*. A priest is always present to give his blessing. The party lasts from Saturday night through Sunday, sometimes. Next day, the bride sends sweets to the groom and his family *(ta boxalikia)*

Above: Even modern couples maintain traditional marriage customs. Right: Again and again typical specialities are served up.

wrapped in special clothing, the so-called *boxades*.

When the house of the groom is ready and the bride has finished preparing her dowry, the formal date of wedding is announced and the whole village is invited, together with the relatives of the young people. The week preceding the wedding, family and friends help with the preparations. The dowry is exhibited – sheets, pillow cases, blankets, curtains, towels, carpets, tablecloths and napkins, embroideries and, most importantly, a mattress filled by a happily married couple. Friends throw walnuts, sugared almonds *(koufeta)* and coins on the mattress and place a little boy on it, so that the first child will be a male.

The mother-in-law prepares ring-shaped biscuits with special care for the bride's cake *(kouloura)* which she decorates with sculptured birds, animals, fruit and abstract disigns. The dowry is complete when items of furniture are purchased consisting of a bed, a table, some chairs, a wooden wardrobe, and cooking

86

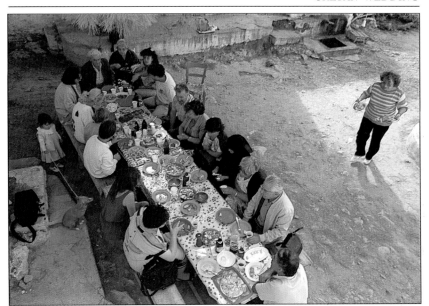

and serving utensils. On Friday, before the wedding, the dowry is collected in a small pickup truck and taken to the couple's house accompanied by young men singing and laughing. While on Saturday, the house of the bride is decorated and dinner preparations are made.

On the afternoon of the wedding day the young men prepare the groom while young women help the bride dress in her white wedding gown, a gift of the groom. Both the groom and the bride have to wear one used old item to avoid "the evil eye." The groom is supposed to place a coin in his right shoe so that he may become wealthy while the girlfriends of the bride write their names on the bridal shoes to secure a good groom too.

By late afternoon all is ready. The bells start ringing, the priest with the marriage sponsor arrive at the groom's house and the procession starts towards the bride's house to pick her up for the church ceremony. As the procession marches towards the church, friends and relativves sing Cretan songs written for the occa-

sion *(mandinades* and *rizitika)*. During the ceremony, the marriage sponsor *(kumbaros)* holds the limelight together with the couple. He is responsible for the decoration of the church, provides the white candles which are held at the ceremony, the wedding crowns and the *koufeta,* the sugar covered almonds arranged in small packages of white netting, which are distributed to each of the guests after the ceremony.

Immediately after the church ceremony a pomgranate, the symbol of fertility, is thrown down and as it breaks up in pieces family and friends wish the couple a large and happy family. Then, the whole procession forms again and moves towards the bride's home, with the bride and groom often on horseback with family and friends following on foot, amid songs and music played by musicians, hired for the occasion, in their *laouta* (lute) and *lira* (Cretan lyre). At this point, the young men start shooting blanks to express their happiness and virility. Their *baloties* are heard all over the

87

TASSOULA MAMALAKIS' LYRA

Dressed in a long black dress, Tassoula Mamalakis has a delicate Victorian air, emphasized by the serious expression on her pale face. This image is dispelled when she picks up her lyra and begins to sing classical Cretan songs with great conviction. Her eyes glint and the power of her voice and instrument increases as she continues, giving a glimpse of the determination that propelled her to achieve her dream of becoming a professional lyra-player, the only woman performing today.

Tassoula began studying the violin but switched over a decade ago to the lyra because she feels it gives a more authentic expression of the spirit of Crete. This is not unusual because many young Cretan women study the lyra. But she surprised everyone by beginning to play in *kentra* (clubs with music).

Her parents had supported her in playing the lyra as a hobby but did not approve of their only child playing in nightclubs. Their attitude changed when she married Stratis Mamalakis, a *laouta* player. She admits, "If I hadn't married Stratis and started to play with him, my family never would have accepted my profession."

Tassoula is from Amari near Rethimno, once the stronghold of lyra music in Crete. She spends her summers in Crete, playing together with her husband at weddings, *panigyria* (festivals), and at *kentra*, including Zamania, Lefka Ori and Kondaros in Hania. In the winter she stays in Athens because "the music scene in Athens is more lively than in Crete during the cooler months. Most Cretan clubs are closed."

Tassoula encountered prejudice from both men and women who felt only a true *pallikari* (brave man) could play the lyra. Those that spend an evening listening to her spirited playing, usually overcome their prejudice.

area and signal the beginning of the *glendi* (feast). The wedding feast goes on for hours and sometimes days with a lot of singing *(ta tragoudia tis tavlas)* dancing (the famous complicated dances of *sousta* and *pentozali*) and eating young roast lamb *(rifaki),* entrails *(gardouba),* stuffed cheeses, sweets, and to top it off, the wedding cake.

Eventually, the wedding feast ends and the bride ist accompanied to the groom's home by her brothers. All cry as they leave the girl with her new husband.

Although some of these customs have slightly changed over the years, one has the feeling that there is a continuity in Crete that ties the joyful Minoan frescoes with their scenes of games and feasts to the medieval poems of courtly love, like the national poem, *Erotokritos,* to the wild and rowdy songs of courtship and marriage of modern Crete.

Above: Souvenirs of Crete. Right: Tassoula Mamalakis with her lyre.

HANIA

Access / Local Transport

AIR: **Olympic Airways** has several flights to and from Hania and Athens each day. Schedules vary according to season and should be checked with Olympic Airways, Tel: (0824) 27701.

BUS: From Hania to Rethimno (58 km) and Iraklio (137 km) there is a public coach service several times a day. There are also services to Omalos (39 km), Paleohora (75 km), Hora Sfakion (72 km) and Kastelli Kissamou (42 km).

From Hora Sfakion to Rodakino, Plakias and Agia Galini there are daily coach services. The central bus station in Hania (KTEL) is located on Kydonias St., Tel: (0821) 23052.

FERRIES: There are several daily ferry boat services connecting Hania (Souda) with Piraeus (Athens). These normally leave in the evenings and arrive in the mornings. Exact times and companies vary and should be checked.

There is a ferry boat service out of Kastelli Kissamou once a week that connects with Antikythera, Kythera, Neapoli Voion, Monemvasia and Gythion. There is also a weekly service to Elaeraka and Kyparissi, Tel: (0822) 22024.

From Paleohora, there are three sailings a week to the island of Gavdos. There are also boats out of Hora Sfakion for Gavdos. Information: Paleohora, Tel: (0823) 41214, Hora Sfakion, Tel: (0825) 91292.

Accommodation

LUXURY: **Amphora**, Tel: 42998. **Casa Delphino**, 19 Theophanous St., Tel: 42613. **Kontessa**, 15 Theophanus St., Tel: 23966. **Porto Del Colombo**, Tel: 50975. **Kydon**, Tel: 26190.

MODERATE: **Doma**, El. Venizelou 124, Tel: 21772/3. **Enetiko Limani**, Tel: 29311. Domeniko, Zambeliou 71, Tel: 55019. **Xenia**, Theotokopoulou St., Tel: 24561. **Domenio**, Tel: 53262. **El Greco**, Tel: 22411. **Lissos**, Tel: 24671. **Porto Veneziano**, Tel: 29311. **Samaria**, Tel: 51551.

BUDGET: **Meltemi**, 2 Angelou, Tel: 40192. **Stella's**, 10 Angelou, Tel: 43756. **Loukia**, Akti Kountourioti, Tel: 21821. **Manos**, Akti Kountourioti, Tel: 29493. **Peraieus**, Zambeliou 14, Tel: 54154. **Amphitriti**, Tel: 22980. **Aptera Beach**, Tel: 22636. **Diktynna**, Tel: 21101. **Hellenis**, Tel: 28070. **Kriti**, Tel: 21881. **Kypros**, Tel: 22761. **Canea**, Tel: 24673. **Avra**, Tel: 23654. **Nea Ionia**, Tel: 22706. **Averof**, Tel: 23090. **Phidias**, Tel: 52494.

Restaurants

The **Karnagio** in the old Venetian Harbor (next to the Rector's Palace), **Akrogiallia** in Nea Chora. There are also a number of good and reliable restaurants in the backstreets of the harbor areas. **Kytarro** (chinese and vegetarian), **Oleander** (international cuisine), **Tamam** (local specialties), **Zorbas Café Ouzeria** (appetizers), **Jimmis** and **Faka's** (simple tavernas).

Museums

Archaeological Museum, Halidon St., open daily from 8.45 am to 3 pm, closed on Tuesdays. **Naval Museum**, at the Old Harbor, open Tuesdays-Sundays, 10 am-2 pm, Saturdays also 7-9 pm. **Historical Museum**, 20 Tzanakaki St., open Mondays-Saturdays, 9 am-1 pm.

Churches

Metropolitan Church, Venetian Church of St. Francis, Church of San Rocco, Church of St. Nicolaos, Church of St. Catherine, Venetian Church of St. Salvadore.

Banks

National Bank, Hatzimichali St. **Bank of Greece**, Venizelos St. **Commercial Bank**, Hatzimichali St. **Ioninan and Popular Bank**, Tzanakaki St. 4. **Credit Bank**, Chalidon St. 106. **Bank of Crete**, Pl. 1866.

Beaches

WEST OF HANIA: Agioi Apostoloi (4.5 km), **Galatas** (5.5 km), **Agia Marina** (8 km), **Platanias** (11 km). **AKROTIRI PENINSULA: Stavros** (14 km). **EAST OF HANIA: Kalami** (16.5 km), **Kalyves** (20.5 km), **Almirida** and **Plaka** (25 km).

Car Rentals

Avis, Karaiskaki St. 26, Tel: 21196. **Blazakis**, Fotiadou Pascha St. 6, Tel: 24618. **Zouridakis**, Hatzimichali Giannari St. 12, Tel: 24403. **Canea Travel**, Karaiskaki St. 46, Tel: 24780. **Manolikakis**, Fotiadou Pascha St. 10, Tel: 21837. **Spanoudakis**, Ver Pascha St. 52, Tel: 23427. **Hertz**, Tzanakaki St. 21, Tel: 20366. **Kontadakis**, Konstantinou St. 31, Tel: 25583.

Cinemas

Apollo, Botsari Street. **Asteri**, Skalidi Street. **Olympia**, Konstantinou Street. **Pantheon**, Place 1866. **Rex**, Skalidi Street.

Greek Mountain Association

EOS Hania, Akti Tombazi 6, Tel: 24647. Refuges in the White Mountains at Kalergi and Volika.

Post / Telegraph / Telephone

Hania: The area code is 0821.

General Post Office: Tzanakaki St. 3, open 7.30 am-6.00 pm.

The **Central Telephone/Telegraph Office** (OTE)is located at Tzanakaki St. 5.

Shopping

The **Covered Market**, Halidon Street, is lined with many shops selling a variety of Cretan handicrafts. **Top Hanas**, Angelous Street, offers old Cretan embroideries and carpets. **Carmela's**, Angelous Street, sells modern ceramics and silver work.

Taxis

Place Dikastirion, Place 1866, Central Market, Sintrivaniou Place, Place Kotzambassi, Venizelou St., 1897 St., Iraklio St., Souda St., Markopoulou St., Zymbrakakidon St.

Tourist Information

The **Greek Office of Tourism (EOT)**, is in the Pantheon Building on Kriari St. 40, Tel: 26424.

Travel Agencies

Canea Travel, Karaiskaki St. 46, Tel: 24780. **Akrotiri**, Ver Pascha St. 8, Tel: 26610. **Kriti**, Fotiadov Pascha 10, Tel: 23212. **Patris** 1866 Place, Tel: 23751.

OUT OF HANIA

Provinces

Kydonia (capital: Hania), **Kissamou** (capital: Kastelli), **Selinon** (capital: Kandanos), **Apokoronas** (capital: Vamos), **Sfakia** (capital: Hora Sfakion).

Accommodation

MALEME: **Crete Chandris**, Tel: (0821) 62221/5.
GALATAS: **Panorama**, Tel: (0821) 31700. **Creta Maria**, Tel: (0821) 51335.
AGIA MARINA: **Santa Marina**, Tel: (0821) 68570/1. **Amalthia**, (Tel: (0821) 68542.
KASTELLI KISSAMOU: **Oscar**, Tel: (0821) 68773. **Helena Beach**, Tel: (0822) 23300/4. **Castle**, Tel: (0822) 22140/1. **Kissamou**, Tel: (0822) 22086. **Peli**, Tel: (0822) 22343.
PALEOHORA: **Elyros**, Tel: (0823) 41348. **Elman**, Tel: (0823) 41412/4. **Lissos**, Tel: (0823) 41266.
STALOS KATO: **Dolfin**, Tel: (0821) 68507. **Pavlakis Beach**, Tel: (0821) 68309.
HORA SFAKION: **Xenia**, Tel: (0825) 91206.
SOUGIA: **Pikilassos**, Tel: (0823) 51242.
GEORGIOUPOLIS: **Gorgona**, Tel: (0825) 61341.
KOLYMVARI: **Rose Marie**, Tel: (0824) 22220. **Dimitra**, Tel: (0824) 22244.
OMALOS: **Xenia**, Tel: (0821) 93237.
PLATANIAS: **Villa Platanias**, Tel: (0821) 48333.
RAPANIANA: **Olympic**, Tel: (0824) 22483.
SOUDA: **Knossos**, Tel: (0821)89282. **Parthenon**, Tel: (0821) 89245.

Camping

HANIA: Tel: (0821) 51090, 100 persons, 33 tents.
AGIA MARINA / HANIA: Tel: (0821) 685545, 68565, 240 persons, 80 tents.
PALEOHORA: **Loupassis Camping**, Tel: (0823) 41225), 41130, 120 persons, 40 tents.
KISSAMAS: Mythimna, Tel: (0822) 31444-5, 54 tents.

Festivals

Contact the Tourist Association for exact dates as they vary. All church festivities *(panigiria)* feature Cretan music and dances.
HANIA: During August there are theater performances, concerts, exhibitions.
AGIA MARINA: Church festival 17.7.
AKROTIRI: Horafakia 15.8.
VAMOS: Summer music festival with famous artists from Greece and Crete.
VOUKOLIES: Commercial festival on Good Friday.
GEORGIOUPOLIS: Church festival Tou Sotira 6.8; church festival in Kournas 29.8.
ELOS: Chestnut festival 20.10.
THERISSOS: Festival of Holy Mary 15.8.
KALIVES: Church festival Agia Paraskevi 26.7.
KANDANOS: Memory day for the battle of Crete 20.5.
KASTELLI KISSAMOU: Wine festival at the beginning of August.
KOLIMVARI: Church festival 15.8., in Tavroniti church festival 14.9.
OMALOS: Church festival of Agios Pantelimonas in Fourni.
PALEOHORA: Music festival 1.-10.8.
PERIVOLIA: Church festival *tou sotira* 6.8.
PLATANOS: Festival of Agios Akinitos 12.8.
PHALASSARNA: Festival of Agia Paraskevi 26.7.
POLYRINIA: Festival of Agion Pateron 7.10.
SOUDA: Navy week in June.
FRANGOKASTELLO: Festival of Agios Nikitas 15.9.

Beaches

WEST OF HANIA: Kato Stalos, Platanias, Maleme, Phalassarna, Elaphonissi. **EAST OF HANIA**: Kalyves, Plaka, Georgioupolis. Akrotiri: Kalathas Bay, Stavros. **SOUTH COAST**: Paleohora, Sougia, Loutro, Frangokastello.

Caves

Lera (Stavros), **Agia Sophia** (Topoliana gorge), **Spilia Panagias** (Gouverneto), **Drakolakkos** (near Anopolis), **Chonos** (Omalos).

Gorges

Samaria gorge, Eligias gorge, Aradena gorge, Imbros gorge (all South coast), Topoliano gorge (Kastelli Kissamou), Therissos gorge (near Hania), Agia Irini gorge (near Hania).

Monasteries

Gouverneto, Agia Triada, Korakies, Gonia, Kolimvari, Chrisoskalitissas.

Small Islands

NORTH COAST: Agii Theodori, Agria Gramvousa, Imeri Gramvousa. **WEST COAST**: Elaphonissi. **SOUTH COAST**: Gavdos, Gavdopoula.

RETHIMNO

RETHIMNO CITY
ARKADI MONASTERY
PREVELI
PLAKIAS
FRANGOKASTELLO
AMARI VALLEY

RETHIMNO CITY

The prefecture of Rethimno lies just to the west of the center of Crete, occupying a broad swathe of territory on a north-south axis between Mount Psiloritis to the east and the foothills of the White Mountains in the west, its northern and southern coasts, on the Aegean and Libyan seas respectively, fringed with expanses of fine sandy beaches.

On the north coast, the capital city of **Rethimno** is conveniently situated midway between Crete's major sea- and airports of Iraklio in the west and Hania in the east. Lacking a natural harbor and being traditionally a center for artistic and intellectual activities rather than commercial ones, Rethimno has escaped much of the development that marks both Iraklio and Hania. Its old city is still the main part of town, and the charm of its post-Byzantine past, principally that of the medieval Venetian occupation, is very much alive.

Rethimno rests on a wide isthmus of land, joined to the mainland by a rocky hillock, on whose crest stands a 16th-century **Venetian fortress**. Ever since Late Minoan settlers began to arrive in the

Preceding pages: A view of Rethimno. Left: An idyllic spot for an antique.

area in the 13th century BC, the promontory seems to have had something of importance built upon it. In the fourth century BC, temples to Artemis, Apollo and Athena were raised there and after that, sometime during the Byzantine, Saracen, and Genoan possessions of Crete, a fort of some sort was erected, as is indicated by the traditional name for the hill, **Paleokastro**.

When the Venetians took control of Rethimno in 1210, they occupied this old castle and immediately began building a line of walls, towers and gates across the entrance to the isthmus in order to protect the city on its landward side. These fortifications and the old castle also were eventually reduced to rubble by a series of mid-16th-century pirate and Ottoman raids, some led by the notorious Turkish privateer, Barbarossa, scouring the Aegean in the pay of the Turks. In 1573, the Venetians began constructing the present fortress, which was completed in 1583. In 1645, after a 23-day siege, it was overrun by the Ottomans, who occupied it until forced out by the allied powers of Britain, France and Russia in 1898.

While virtually no trace of the Venetian walls remains today, their invisible presence nevertheless continues to define the "real" city of Rethimno as distinct from its somewhat colorless modern ex-

St. Spiridon Church

Venetian Fortress

Chapel

Gateway

Archaeological Museum

O. Argyropoulou

O. Liggou

O. Makedonias

O. Cheimaras

O. Damvergi

Platia Karamanli K.

Customs House

Hotel Ideon

O. Plastira

Venet. Harbour

Kathehaki G.

O. Melisinou I.

O. Salaminas

O. Melisinou I.

O. Minoos

Rimondi Fountain

O. M. Renieri

O. Klidi St.

O. Radamanthous

O. Thessalonikis

O. I. Petihaki

O. Korai

O. Portou

Odeon

O. Paleologou

Internat. Press

Prefecture

Platia Georgiou "B"

Riga Fereou

O. Dikastiriou

O. Veraron

O. Petihaki

Soutiou

Loggia

Paraliaki Leoforos

O. Mavili

O. Nikiforou - Foka

O. Patelarou

Minaret

Nerantzes Mosque, Minaret

Sant. / Gravel. Bea

Prok.mea Eleftheriou

Tourist Police

Theod. Arambatzoglou St.

San Francésco Church

Ethnikis Antistáseos

O. Tsoudèrou

Public Library

Arkadiou

Stadium

Court of Justice

O. Sifi Vlastou

O. Dimakapoulou

Library

Ag. Varvaras

Cathedral

O. Manioudaki

O. Tompazi

Youth Hostel

Mosque

Park

Goora Gate

O. Tzanempou- niali

Validés Minaret Mosque

O. Gerakiri

L.P. Koundouriótou

Pl. 4 Martiron

Tessaron Martyron Church

Telephone & Telegraph Office

Varda Kaller

L. Igoumenou Gavrill

Public

Daskaláki

L.P. Koundouriótou

Internat. Press

To Ha

St K

O. Timeleonda Vasou

O. Iliakaki

Dimitrakaki St.

Garden Hotel Jo-An

Hotel Brascos

O. Hatzidaki

O. Siganou

Preveláki

O. Dimokratias

Tick Offic

St. Konstantine Church

O. Kriari

House of Birds

O. Koumoundourou

O. Them. Moatsou

Hospital

O. Trantallidou

Bank

to Agia Galini

Hotel Olympic

RETHIMNO

0 — 100 m

to Hania

---

tension rising along the east-west highway between Iraklio and Hania. The only extant part of the original fortifications is still considered to be Rethimno's main entrance. This is the best place to begin a tour of the city.

Getting Around

The Goora Gate is located just off the Iraklio-Hania Highway as it passes Rethimno's **Church** and **Square of the Four Martyrs** and its **Public Gardens**. Here the traveler can find agencies selling tickets for ships embarking from the ports of Hania and Iraklio. The square marks the spot where, in 1824, four Rethimniots were beheaded and hung on

plane trees for refusing to convert to Islam, while the gardens, built on the ground of the old Turkish cemetery, are a wonderfully verdant refuge from the heat and dust of the summer as well as being, in July, the nigh-time site of the city's annual **Wine Festival**. The **Goora Gate** is still known as the "Big Gate" (Megali Porta) even though it is now not a gate at all, but a street barely wide enough for a modern truck to go through. Spanning the entrance from above is a portion of an arch that is now the only existing trace of the Venetian walls.

As in the old days, the gate leads immediately into the **market area**, a small but bustling cornucopia of fish, meat, cheese, bread and fruit and vegetable

to Hania
to Pireás
to Iráklio

Dolphin
Sculpture ★

EOT
acilities

élou
Mussa
que
1. Agnostou
Comm. Bank
tion NTOG
st Office

L. Sot. Venizélou
Hotel
Xenia

O. Psarou N.

O. Giamboudaki

O. Hortátzi

O. Papandreou G.

Maroúli
Z.
Kastrináki
N. & M.
Olympic
Airways

O. Maroúli

O. Papadáki K.

O. Portalíou

to Iráklio

cling private houses and impossible to get to. Further down the main market street and just to the west of tree-lined Platanos Square, is the very accessible **Nerantzes Mosque and minaret**.

The finest of its kind in the city, the Nerantzes Mosque is believed to have originally been built as a church during the Byzantine era and subsequently converted by the Ottomans. Today, it serves as both a tourist attraction and a concert hall and offers an excellent 360-degree view of Rethimno from the top of its minaret's 120 stairs.

Platanos Square is lined with plane trees, restaurants, cafés, diving, antique and leather goods stores. At its far end (to the north) is the **Rimondi Fountain**. Named after the Venetian rector, Antonio Rimondi, who had it built in about 1629, it is architecturally a virtual time capsule of the city's history in the last 2000 years, the pillars being Corinthian, the lion heads Venetian, and the back wall a Turkish restoration. In 1930, its overhead vault was torn down to allow motorized vehicles to penetrate more deeply into the residential area around the fortress, the most beautiful part of old Rethimno.

When the Venetians built the present fortress to withstand continuing Ottoman assaults, the Cretans thought it beneath their dignity to enter and rebuild their houses outside the fortress walls. They in fact refused to seek protection inside until the final Ottoman attack made death the only other alternative.

These houses are, for the most part, those that visitors see today lining the defensive warren of streets that make up the old quarter. Built in Venetian times, some have wonderfully sculpted marble portals and superb interior courtyards and fountains. Quite a few also display the subsequent addition (by Turkish overlords) of overhanging projections of second-storey living rooms, built to allow the ladies of the house to observe, from behind latticed screens, the goings-

stores as well as tourist shops, leather goods, clothing, hardware, photography, music and book stores, a library (with books in English), antique shops, saddle makers and metal working establishments. There are very good workers' cafes and tavernas in the area, and also, just outside the Goora gate and on the street to its left before entering, a musical instrument maker's shop specializing in Cretan *liras*, the long-necked, three-stringed type of violin that is the principal sound and instrument in Cretan music.

To the east of the gate is the **Valides Mosque**, the spire of its minaret tantalizingly visible from both the Square of the Four Martyrs and the market street, but its entranceway closed off by encir-

97

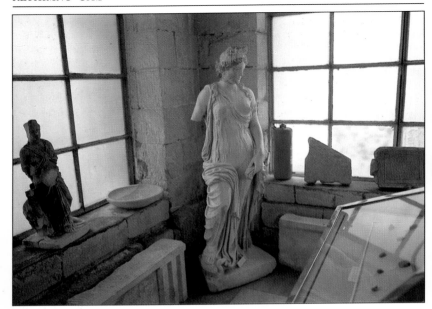

on in the streets below without themselves being seen.

The **fortress**, built by the Venetians with forced labor and unconditionally surrendered by them to the Turks, has long been a blot on the communal memory of Rethimno, a symbol of anguish and enslavement as well as, in August 1944, martyrdom as Rethimniot women leapt to their death over its walls rather than be taken as hostages during the German withdrawal. Hence, until recently, the fortress was allowed to fall into ruin, with the devastation wreaked upon it by the retreating German army in 1944 left virtually untouched. It is now in the process of being extensively restored and is very much worth a visit if only for its view of the city and the sea. In summer, concerts by popular Greek singers are often given in its lovely amphitheater.

Opposite the fortress entrance is the new **Archaeological Museum**. Original-

Above: Aphrodite in marble in the Archaeological Museum of Rethimno.

ally the site of a Venetian prison and maintained as such by the Turks, it fell into disuse after the latter's departure. Recently restored, it replaced the Loggia (see below) as the city's new museum in 1986. Although there has been little systematic archaeological digging in the Rethimno area, the museum has a representative collection of items from all periods since human habitation began in Neolithic times. There are tools, jewelry, pottery and votive idols from the Neolithic period, pottery from Minoan times, vases, figurines, statuettes, seals, jewelry, weapons, tools, coins, sarcophagi, gravestones and architectural fragments from the Classical period of Roman and Byzantine rule on the island. Also included are certain pieces from Egypt.

The fact that only little exists from the days of the Turkish occupation is yet another indication of how thoroughly the Rethimniots went about obliterating that part of their past which is most recent and, in some ways, the most difficult and painful.

The lovely **Venetian harbor** is but a five-minute walk away from the fortress east along the northern sea wall. Colorful and intimate, ringed with caiques and cafés and restaurants specializing in grilled meats and seafood, it is a world unto itself and a perfect place to retreat from the bustle of the city in day or night.

Begun by the Venetians in 1300 (the lighthouse was restored in the mid-1980s), it has yet to be completed to the satisfaction of seafarers save the owners of the smallest types of fishing and pleasure craft. The problem is one of continually accumulating sand and silt that requires constant dredging to keep the channel to the interior of the port open, a truly Sisyphean endeavor. At approximately the center of the curve of the harbor, there is a narrow street lined with Cretan handicraft and jewelry shops. It leads back into the city towards one of Rethimno's most cherished landmarks – the **Loggia**. The Loggia, recently the city's Archaeological Museum until that was moved to the old prison outside the entrance to the fortress (see above), was built in the 16th century as a clubhouse for Venetian gentlemen.

Opposite it to the north was a large clock tower, built, the locals say today, so that the gentlemen would know when to stop their gaming in order to arrive home at a decent hour, presumably for lunch, since the clock was a solar one. At night, apparently, time didn't matter. This tower formed the last substantial part of the original city walls to remain standing into the present century. Unfortunately, in 1945, the day after the German occupation of Crete ended, it was razed to the ground in the middle of the night by a property owner wanting to gain access to Arkadiou Street, then as now the main shopping street running behind the beach front and past the Loggia.

The wide expanse of Rethimno's **public beach** is a comparatively recent but welcomed addition to the attractions of the city, having achieved its present excellent state only after the construction of a second jetty to the south of the city center in the 1960s. Before that, as old photographs testify, the sea came virtually up to the windows of the beachfront houses.

In the center of the curve of the beach is a relatively new single-storey structure containing a snack bar, showers and bath houses as well as the city's **tourist office** or **"EOT"** (eh-ot) as it is known to the Greeks. This is an invaluable source of information on all aspects of both the city and prefecture of Rethimno, including the availability of rooms in hotels, pensions, and private houses.

At night the road along the beach is closed to traffic, a practice formerly reserved for Sundays. Indeed, the Rethimniots still observe the age-old Mediterranean custom of displaying marriageable daughters and sons on an evening stroll *(volta)* along the seafront.

Another stroll that is especially recommended, particularly in the evenings, is on the road around the western edge of fortress promontory. There you can sit and watch the sun sink into the Aegean Sea from an *ouzeri* just below the fortress, and examine the curious **church of St. Spyridon** (Agios Spiridon). The façade of this church is flush with the rock face of the promontory, its interior built into a blast hole dynamited by beseiging Turks in an unsuccessful attempt to tunnel under the fortress walls during their assault on the Venetians and Rethimniots in 1645.

Within the city, there are many other sights to see and opportunities for rewarding walks, particularly through the old quarter. The city has a lively and congenial warmth that is best absorbed by encountering the Rethimniots themselves, young and old, as they go about their daily lives in a manner that must be as little changed over the centuries as the streets themselves.

Outside the city, with Rethimno as a base, there are numerous extremely rewarding excursions to be made.

ARKADI MONASTERY

Nearest to Rethimno is the **Monastery of Arkadi**. This is the most renowed monastery in Crete, particularly as the site of the 1866 martyrdom of hundreds of Cretan rebels and their women and children, who blew themselves up in the monastery's gunpowder room rather than be captured by the besieging Turks. You can see a drawing of the monastery on the 100 drachma note.

Located on a plateau in the foothills of Mount Psiloritis, the monastery is only 22 km to the southeast of Rethimno, but takes some 50 minutes to reach, the road is narrow and winding and, in its final as-

Above: The weather-beaten Renaissance monastery of Arkadi. Right: The monks appear to have gotten used to the hordes of visitors.

cent, skirts the edge of a ravine so that it must be traveled with care.

The present-day monastery is principally a memorial to the 1866 martyrdom and is made up of four separate clusters of buildings. Sitting among a grove of trees to the left (or west) of the parking area is a **pavilion**, dedicated to the fallen heroes of the rebellion. Within is an ossuary, containing the skulls of several of the martyrs. The building at the far, (i.e. northern) end of the parking area is a **tourist rest center** with a souvenir area and a dining room, from the balcony of which there is a fine view of the valley leading north down to the Aegean.

The huge entrance gate and front wall of the monastery itself, destroyed by cannon fire in 1866, were rebuilt in 1870. Inside the gate are arcades leading to the monks' cells, although most of them now are no longer in use. Opposite the entrance is the magnificent façade of the monastery's main church of **St. Helen and Constantine**, built in about 1587 during the Venetian occupation of Crete.

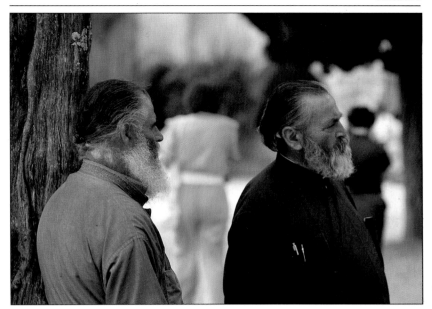

For one thing, it has two naves. The beautiful façade of yellow stone combines freely Renaissance and Baroque elements. Over time the Mediterranean winds have added their own special design to the stone. The belfry with its three arches, crouched atop the two naves is one of the main eye-catchers, however.

To the left of the church, and behind the present-day refectory, is the famous **Gunpowder Room**. It was here that nearly a 1000 men, women and children took refuge on November 9, 1866, and, when the Turks broke through the stiff resistance at the front gate, died in the explosion which ensued when Kostis Giambudakos, the renowned hero of the event, fired his pistol into a barrel of gunpowder. It was truly a shot heard round the world, and the international furore it aroused over the continuing colonialization of the Cretans contributed significantly to the eventual liberation of the island ten years later. The monastery's **Historical Museum**, to the right of the main church, contains mementoes of this martyrdom, including a three-dimensional reconstruction of the surrounding topography, showing how the Ottomans approached and encircled Arkadi.

Hike from Arkadi to Thronos

If you don't have an automobile, you can reach the monastery of Arkadi from Rethimno using public transportation. The way there is lined with beautiful old olive trees, their trunks twisted into gnarled and imaginative knots. The olive harvest takes place between the beginning of December and the end of January. Usually a net is stretched under the tree and the fruit allowed merely to fall into it. Sometimes the tree is also hit with a stick, a tedious job. More recently they have started using compressed air to blow the olives off the tree. Anyone needing a job to survive in Crete over the winter will have no difficulty in finding work hitting trees. The pay is about US$ 20 a day.

The final section of the road goes along a deep gully and then up to an elev-

101

Palelóni
Kefalás
Soúri Likotinariá
Sellía
Alexándrou
Kalamítsi Amigdáli
Exópoli

Ormós
Almiroú

to Soúda
to Pireás

Venetian
Fortress

RÉTHIMNO

Amfímalla
Georgioúpolis

Geráni Atsipópoulo
Cave Prínes Gállos Anógia
Aspropouliáni Vedéri Agia Irini
692m Drámia Frandzeskianá Mili
Mathés Mouri Metóhia Somatás Roussosp
Dafnokorfés Episkopi Karoti Gonia Hron
Kato Kastéllos Kapediar
Lake Fílaki Koufi Valsamónero Ágios Andréas Kastéllos Pras
Koúrna Arhondíki (Castle) Kastéllos Vríssinas
Kournás Kastéllos Kaloniktis Áno Valsamónero Arméni 858m
Cave Pátima Ágios Monopári Mirt
Tripáli Zourídi Konstantínos Ágios Geórgios Óros S
1494m Káto Póros Palélimnos Karé
Monastery Káto Maláki Gouledi
Sorós Agioúpoli Roústika Saitoúres Áno Maláki Ambeláki Falanna
1418m Asigoniá Lappa Moúndros Koúmi Fotinós
Maroulloú Assóna Ambelos Viglotópt
560m 570m 596m
Velonádo **NOMÓS**
Arolíthi **RETHÍMNOU**
Kallikrátis Miriokéfala Vilandrédo Ágios Vassílios
Roumbádo Armós
Allónes 706m
Kali Sikiá
Vour- Angouselianá Lofiá
douvas Krioneritis Katsogrída 673m Lam
Agriokefála Kakáves 1312m Tsilivdíkas Koxaré
950m 1258m 1228m 928m Ágios Ioánnis Atsipádes Mixórrouma Da
Kirimianoú Kouroúpa Agía M
Kapsodássos 815m 984m Pélagia
Skalotí Sellía Mírthios Frati
Argoulés Áno Rodákino Marioú Xirón Óros
Káto Rodákino Plakiás 904m Akto
Frangokástello Kastri Castle Assomatós Lefkógia V
(Castle) Paralía 402m Korifí Damnóni Káto Moní Préveli
Kóraka 207m Tímios (Monastery) Ke
Akrotíri Ormós Stavrós Korifí
Akrotíri Kalógeros Stavrós Pláka Ammoúndi 433m Gianniou 378m Ag
Kakómouros Piso Moní Préveli
(Monastery)

LIVIKÓ   PÉLAGOS

SOUTH OF RETHIMNO

0   2   4   6   8km

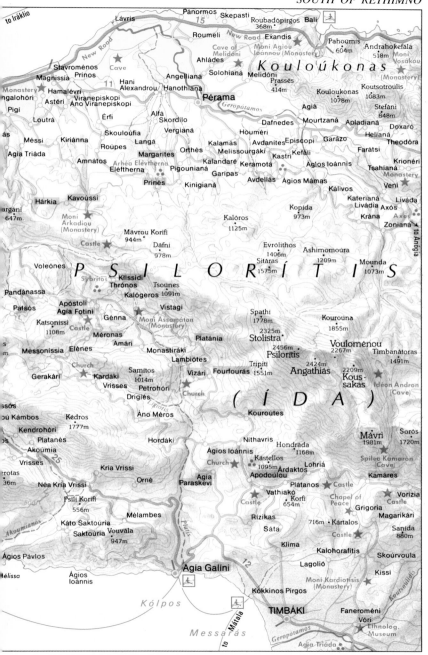

to Iráklio

Pánormos Skepasti
Lávris
Roubadópirgos Bali
368m
15
Roúmeli
New Road Exandis
Pahoúmis
604m
Andrahokefála
518m
Moni
Vosáko
Cave of
Melidóni
Moni Agiou
Ioánnou (Monastery)
Ahládes
Kouloúkonas
(Monastery)
Stavroménos
Cave
Angelianá
Solohianá
Melidóni
Prassés
414m
Koutsotroúlis
Magnissia
Prinos
Hani
Alexandrou
Hanothianá
Koutsotroúlis
Hamalévri
Monastery
ngalohóri
Viranepiskopi
Ano Viranepiskopi
Pérama
Koulonkonas
1078m
1083m
Astéri
Geropótamos
Agiá
Stefani
848m
Pigi
Loutrá
Érfi
Alfá
Skordilo
Dafnedes
Mourtzaná
Apladianá
Doxaró
ás
Messi
Kiriánna
Skouloúfia
Vergianá
Houméri
Episcopi
Garázo
Heliáná
Theodóra
Agia Triáda
Roúpes
Langá
Kalamás
Avdanites
Kefáli
Faráfsi
Krionéri
Amnátos
Margarites
Orthés
Melissourgáki
Kastri
Agios Ioánnis
Tsahianá
Arhéa Eléftherna
Kalandaré
Keramotá
Eléftherna
Pigounianá
Garipas
Monastery
Prinés
Kinigianá
Avdellás
Agios Mámas
Veni
Kálivos
Katerianá
Liváda
Hárkia
Kavoússi
Kopída
973m
Livádia
Axós
Axe
arganí
647m
Moni
Arkadiou
(Monastery)
Kalóros
1125m
Krána
Zonianá
to Anogia
Castle
Mávrou Korifi
944m
Dáfni
978m
Evrólithos
1406m
Ashimomoura
1209m
Sitáras
1575m
Mounda
1073m
Voleónes
P S I L O R Í T I S
Sybritos
Klissidi
Thrónos
Tsounes
Pandánassa
Kalógeros 1091m
Patsós
Apóstoli
Agia Fotini
Vistagí
Spathi
1778m
Kouroúna
1855m
Katsonissi
1108m
Génna
Moni Assomáton
(Monastery)
Méronas
Amári
Platánia
2325m
Stolistra
Vouloménou
2267m
Messonissia
Elénes
Monastiráki
2456m
Psiloritis
Timbanátoras
1491m
Lambiótes
Tripiti
1551m
2424m
Angathiás
2209m
Gerakári
Kardáki
Samitos
1014m
Vizári
Fourfourás
Kous-
sakas
Idéon Andron
(Cave)
Vrisses
Petrohóri
Drigiés
Church
ssós
Áno Méros
Kouroútes
(Í D A)
ù Kámbos
Kédros
1777m
Kendrohóri
Platanés
Hordáki
Nithavris
1168m
Hondráda
Mávri
1981m
Sorós
1720m
Akoúmia
Ágios Ioánnis
Kástellos
1095m
Ardaktos
Lohriá
Spileo Kamarón
(Cave)
Vrisses
Kria Vrissi
Orné
Agia
Paraskevi
Apodoúlou
Platanos
Castle
Kamáres
rotas
36m
Néa Kria Vrissi
Vathiakó
Korfi
654m
Chapel of
Peace
Vorizia
Castle
Psilí Korifi
556m
Grigoria
Magarikári
Akoumianos
Mélambes
Káto Saktoúria
Saktoúria
Vouvála
947m
Rizikas
Sáta
716m
Kártalos
Castle
Sanida
880m
Klima
Kalohorafitis
Skoúrvoula
Ágios Pávlos
Lagolió
Kissi
Mélissa
Ágios
Ioánnis
Moni Kardiotissis
(Monastery)
Kólpos
Agia Galini
Kókkinos Pirgos
Faneroméni
Vóri
Ethnolog.
Museum
Messarás
TIMBÁKI
Geropótamos
to Mátala
Agia Triáda

ation of just over 500 meters where you'll find the monastery.

The visit to the monastery can be followed up by a pleasant hike on a gravel road to Kavoussi/Harkia. The monastery still owns some property in the area. After a couple of hundred meters you come to a pretty pinery, and about a quarter of an hour later to a cement bridge where you turn left. The road straight ahead leads to Kavoussi. 20 m later a wide road turns off to the right. However, follow the small gravel road that runs along a stream lined with oaks. This road is seldom used. It climbs gently through pastures dotted with rocks and bushes. Stay on the main road, disregarding any forks to the left or right. After about an hour's walk, just before reaching the top of the plateau, turn for a last look at the monastery. The road forks, but head right. The gravel road twists and turns

Above: Winds of hurricane strength often pound the island. Right: A donkey waits patiently while the vines are pruned.

down the mountain until you can spot the terraced hillside that gave **Thronos** its name (it has a broadcasting antenna on it). After about a quarter hour you once again encounter the wide road that you left behind at the cement bridge after the monastery of Arkadi. It girds the mountain with the width of a highway. The huge aisle that was cut to build the road is one of the great eyesores in the landscape. The piles of rubble that were pushed to the side of the road have been deeply furrowed by rain and wind. Follow the new road for a bit, and after a long right-hand curve you come to the spring **Petra sto Nero**. Its water is supposed to heal kidney and gallbladder complaints, and on weekends people often come to take some water home in large canisters. Stay on the road until, after another long curve, a mule path forks off to the right. A few minutes later you arrive in the borough of **Klissidi**. Turn right at the next intersection (a covered bus stop) and walk for ten minutes into town. Here you have a view

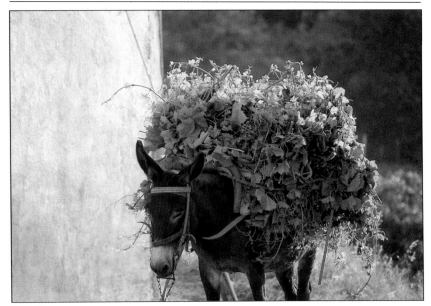

of the **Amari basin**, while to the left the houses of **Kalogeros** village sprawl on the mountain slope with the Psiloritis range in the background.

The modern village of **Thronos** was founded on the remains of a Graeco-Roman city named Sybritos. The **church of the Panagia** in the center of town merits a visit, for it is built on the ruins of a much larger early Christian basilica, and floor mosaics can still be partly seen on the square on front of the church. The view from here or from the neighboring *kafenion* (café) is of the village's luxuriant gardens and the peaks of the Psiloritis that remain snow-covered until spring. The bus from Thronos to Rethimno runs only once a day (mornings) and returns in the evening, so you must go back the same way on foot.

West of Rethimno

There are two fine swimming areas bordering the New Road to Hania just west of Rethimno: The beaches of Gerani and Petres River. **Gerani Beach** is seven kilometers to the west just below a small bridge over the Gerani River. Here, next to a tiny chapel nestling in a grove of tamarisk trees, is a small camping area and a taverna. There is also a **cave**, discovered during the construction of the New Road and immediately locked up to protect its Neolithic finds. Permission to visit can be obtained from the proper authorities. Ask at the Rethimno Tourist Bureau (EOT) on the beachfront.

The **Petres River Beach**, 16 km to the west of Rethimno, with the often snow-covered white mountains (Levka Ori) in the background, is a 7-km stretch of almost undeveloped seafront, covered by fine sand interspersed with clusters of shady trees. One of the reasons, perhaps, for its lack of development is the strong offshore currents, which are dangerous for even the best of swimmers. They are present no matter how placid the sea might seem. There are two tavernas as well as camping facilities located just off the main road at the beach's center.

Turn south at this point, off the New Road to the village of **Episkopi**, from which side trips can be made to the rarely visited areas around the village of Argiroupoli or to Lake Kournas, the only fresh water lake on Crete.

Argiroupoli and its environs formed a retreat for Cretan aristocracy during the Venetian occupation from the 13th to 17th centuries, a fact evident in some of the local architecture, while in the nearby village of **Miriokefala**, the church of the monastery of the Panagia offers some of the earliest Byzantine frescoes on Crete, from the 11th and 12th centuries.

Further into the mountains is the village of **Assi Gonia**, birthplace of George Psychoundakis, author of *The Cretan Runner*, and the site on St. George's Day (April 23) of a highly recommended village festival during which the sheep are blessed.

West of Episkopi is **Lake Kournas**. Said to be bottomless, it covers approximately 65 hectares of the relatively arid Cretan landscape with pure, fresh water. There is a taverna just up from the water's edge serving fish from the lake, but swimming in its waters is strongly discouraged. Sudden whirlpools have claimed the lives of several people foolish enough to ignore the warnings, one of them having been a professional scuba diver attempting to reach the bottom of this dangerous water hole.

The site has also given rise to various legends. Bullets fired from one side are said to be swallowed up by some mysterious force before they can reach the opposite shore. In addition, the lake is believed to be haunted by the ghost of a young girl who was raped and killed by her father somewhere in the vicinity.

From Kournas, a reasonably good road, paralleling the north coast New Road, eventually crosses this road and

leads further east to the lovely tree-shaded fishing village of **Georgioupolis**, nestling at the mouth of a river at the far western end of the above-mentioned Petres River Beach. From here, the traveler can proceed further west on the New Road to Hania or south along the road through the enchanting riverside village of **Vrisses** to Sfakia and the fortress of Frangokastello.

South of Rethimno

The main road to the south begins at the Square of the Four Martyrs in the center of Rethimno. Signposts direct the traveler along the side of the Public Gardens and, at the southern edge of the city, into the foothills which span the area between the western range of the White Mountains and the eastern massif of Mount Psiloritis (Ida).

The village of **Armeni** lies only ten minutes' drive into the hills outside Rethimno and offers a pleasant and easy-to-reach respite from the summer crowds of the city. There are several tavernas and cafés along its shady main street, and some interesting old houses off the eastern side of the road. About 2 km before reaching the village from Rethimno there is, on the right, about 100 meter after the turn-off for Somata, a **Minoan necropolis**. Uncovered in 1969, it has yielded many artifacts including several painted sarcophagi now on display in the Archaeological Museum at Hania. About 4 km south of Armeni, the traveler can turn eastwards towards the village of **Kare** and cut over to the beautiful valley of **Amari** (see below) or continue on to the southwest or southeast of the prefecture of Rethimno.

PREVELI

Another 12 km further along the main road to the south from Armeni is the turn-off to the west leading to the monastery

Right: The idyllic Preveli monastery overlooking the sea.

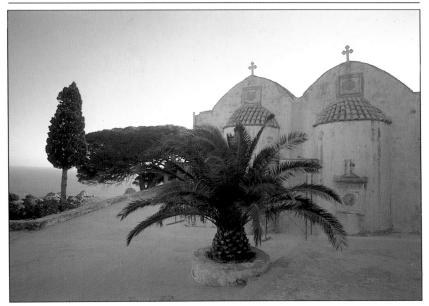

of Preveli and the beaches of Plakias and Frangokastello, plus the fortress.

The monastery of Preveli is about a 15-minute drive directly south of a turn-off to the left, as the main road passes through the village of **Asomatos**. On the way, along the side of the winding, tree-lined **Megalopotamos river**, one comes to the ruins of a 16th-century monastery, now abandoned but still impressive.

Taking the bridge across the river to the left and following the road south (over another tiny bridge) will lead you to the sea, where a small taverna has recently been opened. From here, it is a 10-minute clamber over the seaside rocks to **Preveli Beach**, isolated and idyllically fringed with palm trees, but suited only to those truly willing to rough it.

Continuing past the ancient monastery but staying on the right side of the river leads one to the present-day **Preveli Monastery** (Moni Preveli). It was rebuilt after the Turks burnt it to the ground in 1866 for supporting resistance movements. It sits on a bluff on the southern side of the mountain and has a magnificent view of the Libyan Sea.

It was from here that hundreds of British, Australian and New Zealand soldiers were evacuated following the 1941 German invasion of the island, and transported to safety in Egypt by Allied submarines. A marble plaque on the wall outside the main church recalls this event as do a pair of silver candlesticks donated to the monastery after the war by the grateful survivors of the Allied troops.

Preveli Beach may be reached from a curve in the road about 200-300 m before you come to the monastery and from here there is a 20-minute downhill trek over rocky fields and walls, the return being much more difficult than it would be from the mouth of the Megalopotamos River.

Hike to the Palm Beach of Preveli

The point of departure for this five-hour round trip is the village of **Asomatos**. Leave the village on the asphalt

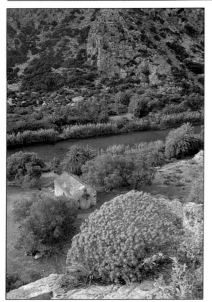

road leading to Rethimno. 800 m from the village limits a dirt road leads to the right toward the **Kourtaliotiko Gorge**. At a sharp turn is a cement-paved road leading downward that soon becomes a gravel road. Go straight along the right bank of the Megalopotamos that flows from the Kourtaliotiko gorge. The hitherto trafficable road ends in about one km in front of a small chapel. A little further on you will find a path leading down to the river. The village of Asomatos is now behind you.

A five minute hike leads to an abandoned olive mill with an inscription indicating the year 1890. A young Greek couple have turned the inside into a little campsite, with sleeping mats, covers, sleeping bags and various cooking utensils. At the old mill take the dirt road to the right. After about 300 m you will come to a wide asphalt road leading right

Above: Wilderness near the palm beach of Preveli. Right: Crystalline waters off the coast near Preveli.

along the Megalopotamos to Preveli monastery. The narrow strip of land between the road and the river is covered with olive and citrus trees. After about five minutes you can leave the road and rejoin the footpath on the river bank, which reveals a luxuriant vegetation of planes, reeds, high myrtle bushes and ivy.

About a quarter hour after having left the mill, you come to an arched Venetian bridge gracefully nestling against the backdrop of the massive cliffs of the Kourtaliotiko Gorge. To the south lie the ruins of the old Preveli cloisters also known as *moni mega potamou,* the cloisters of the great river. Cross the river and take the gravel road that stretches along its left bank. The ruins are now on the other side of the river.

A quarter of an hour after leaving the first bridge you arrive at a second arched bridge, which takes you across the stream. Disregard the fork off to the left and follow the gravel road on the left bank of the Megalopotamos. You soon arrive at the dilapidated buildings of cloisters with an intact chapel. The road forks 25 m after the chapel. The right-hand path takes you in five minutes to an olive grove. Go to the left, up the slope on the left bank of the river. The river itself carves its way deeper and deeper into the rock. The path you follow, on the other hand, continues, gently rising and falling, above the gorge amidst low scrub growth.

About an hour after having crossed to the left bank over the Venetian bridge, you pass under some telegraph lines. An exclave on the cliff about 200 m further offers the first superb view of the palm-covered estuary of the Megalopotamos. A little further, miles and miles of the coastline come into view before the path loses itself between jagged rocks on its way down to the estuary. After a solid two-hour walk from Asomatos you have reached the palm beach of Preveli. The trees are protected.

At the foot of the cliff a local has built a small hut where he sells drinks and sandwiches during the summer months. The sign "Mini Market" suggests that the place is jumping in summer and certainly without much concern for nature conservation. Even in winter one group of Greek "beach bums" never leaves the beach. These fellows, all with dreadlocks, spend their days on the beach, drawing Socratic circles in the sand with their toes and defining their philosophical horizon by staring out to sea. Here, they surely find all the peace and quiet needed for meditation during the winter months. According to reports from other travelers, the beach tends to look like a garbage dump in summer and the police have raided the place on occasion.

You can wade across the estuary to the other side using a small sand strip between the river and the sea. The road leads upward here. After about a 20-minute climb, a path branches into a gully leading right into the wall of the gorge. If you go straight ahead, the path leads to an asphalt road and from there to the upper Preveli cloister which is worth a visit. On the left of the gorge, when looking towards its opening, is a path leading – after approximately a quarter hour – to a small cleft with a few scattered palms. Shortly thereafter you come across the telegraph wires you already passed under on the other side of the gorge. The path then remains about halfway between the edge of the gorge and the road further up (that passes under the third and fourth telegraph poles counting from the gorge). It is in good repair. After bypassing a few great rocks it leads down an incline into the river valley. On the way down, after crossing a stone wall, you suddenly come across the **Agia Fotini** chapel hidden amongst olive trees. The interior of this inconspicuous little church is decorated with frescos from the 14th century. The road continues through an olive grove, down to the river, and upstream to the ruins of the Kato Preveli cloister and the Ventetian bridge. After the bridge you can walk along the path between the road and the river, then on the road itself for a while and finally rightward on the gravel road leading to the olive mill. When you have reached the building there is a mule path that climbs leftward up to the little chapel from which you can now return to Asomatos as you came.

PLAKIAS AND FRANGOKASTELLO

Accessible swimming can be enjoyed at the seaside village of **Plakias**, some 10 km further along the main southwest route from the turn-off for Preveli at Asomatos. The road leads through the small but spectacular **Kotsifou gorge** and the hillside village of **Mirthios**, which has good tavernas and an excellent view of Plakias below.

Above: The fine sands of Frangokastello beach, once a Venetian stronghold. Right: Fortress walls in the scorching sun of the southern coast.

Long a favorite of the people of Rethimno, Plakias is now experiencing a considerable boom as a tourist center, with new hotels and rooming houses springing up every year. The best bathing area is on the left (or eastern) side of its lengthy beach, while the majority of tavernas and cafés are on the western side in the tiny tree-shaded fishing hamlet that is Plakias itself. In addition, there are many small and secluded beaches and coves over the rises to the east and west of the central area. It is also possible to walk from here eastwards to the monastery of Preveli, which was described earlier in the chapter. It takes about two hours, but the wonderful scenery en route makes it well worth the effort you have made.

To the west of Plakias, another 24 km over a rather rough road along the coast, is the famous fortress and beach of **Frangokastello**. The fortress was built by the Venetians in the 14th century in a misguided attempt to subjugate the fiercely independent locals of the wild and moun-

tainous area of Sfakia and was subsequently used by the latter in resisting
the Turks.

A monument commemorates an 1828
battle in which hundreds of Sfakians
died. The fact that their ghosts are still
said to haunt the area has not discouraged
flocks of tourists from descending upon
its fine beach in summer to camp and
party. Recently, several rooming houses
and a taverna-bar have been erected, but
the area is still basically unspoilt, although one is warned to look out at night
for farmers' trucks, parked with dangerous casualness in the middle of the
road as if the possibility of oncoming
traffic was inconceivable.

From Frangokastello, the road to the
west continues on to the fishing village of
Hora Sfakion, from which it is possible
to take a regular caique to **Agia Roumeli,**
the fishing village at the southern mouth
of the **Gorge of Samaria.** The road north
from Hora Sfakion leads to the New
Road along the coast between Rethimno
and Hania.

The Southeast Route

Instead of turning off the main north-
south route towards the southwest, the
traveler can continue along this road towards Agia Galini. The first stop en
route, the picturesque hillside village of
Spili, lies on the main road just 7 km
south of the eastern turn-off towards
Preveli and Plakias.

Anyone accustomed to the aridity of
Greece in summer will be both
astonished and delighted by the torrent of
water continually gushing out of the
mountainside in the center of the village.
There it is channeled through a **Venetian
fountain** and drinking trough, its 19
spouts marvelously fashioned in the form
of marble lions' heads. Spili is, needless
to say, a wonderfully refreshing place to
stop on the way south. On the left you see
the **Kedros range** (1177 m). To climb
up, it is best to start in Kendrahori or in
Ano Meros in the Amari Valley.

The lovely fishing village of **Agia
Galini** is some 25 km further to the

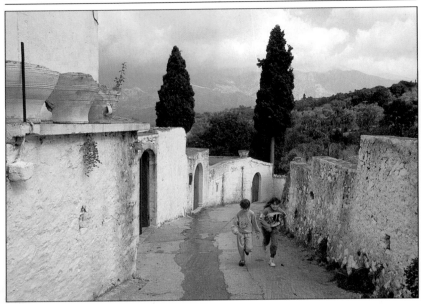

south. Like similar villages in France and Italy, it has long been discovered and overrun by tourism; however, the village still clings picturesquely to the side of a cliff face, its main street making a winding descent down from the headland to the sea. Throughout the village, especially along and near the spacious concrete pier, are numerous cafés, restaurants and tourist shops, as well as a small beach around the rocky point to the east of the harbor. From above Agia Galini, the main inland road offers a connection northwards through the lovely Amari Valley (see below) or continues curving eastwards through a fertile farming valley and the commercial center of Timbaki to the spectacular beach of Matala.

The wonderful Minoan excavations at Agia Triada and Festos are only a matter of minutes away, along the main road leading north to Knossos and Iraklio.

Above: Village life in the Amari Valley. Right: What does this ass have to do with Mitsotakis?

AMARI VALLEY

Situated only 30 km southeast of Rethimno, the **Amari Valley** is one of the most beautiful in all of Crete: A soft and fertile Shangri-La tucked away between the rugged ranges of Kedros to the west and Mount Psiloritis to the east.

To reach the valley, you turn off the new road 3 km to the east of Rethimno, and follow the sign to Amari. From here it is an approximately 27-km drive to the village of **Apostoli**, which stands at the northern approach to the valley. Along the way, a worthwhile detour is to the village of **Hromonastiri** and its church of Agios Eftihios. The remains of the rare 11th-century frescoes are meagre but superb and are considered the oldest on Crete. Beyond Hromonastiri can be seen the peak of **Mount Vrissinas**, the highest in the area and site of one of the finest Minoan peak sanctuaries on Crete.

From the village of **Apostoli**, Amari Valley extends some 50 km south to the main road linking the port of Agia Galini with the beach of Matala and the archaeological site of Festos. As there are roads running along both its sides, a complete circuit of the valley from north to south and back to Rethimno – about a 120-km drive – is easily possible in one day.

The valley, fertile and well protected from marine landings from the north and south, used to be one of the most important in Crete, particularly during the Byzantine periods, and is thus sprinkled with numerous churches, castles and various other edifices from other epochs. Take a trip south along the eastern side of the valley. About 1 km beyond Apostoli, with its 14th-century church, the tiny village of **Agia Fotini** offers a view of the whole valley. East of here is the village of **Thronos** in the center of which stands a 14th to 15th-century church and, on an acropolis 10 minutes' walk above the village, the remains of the Greco-Roman city of **Sybritos**, with its magnificent view of the valley.

˙ Some 5 km further on, near the turn-off to the village of Amari, is the former **Monastery of Asomaton**, now an agricultural school. Just outside the charming village of **Amari** is the church of Agia Anna with frescoes dating from 1195 to 1225, the earliest found on Crete. At **Vizari**, there are remains of a Roman town and a Christian basilica (eighth century).

At **Fourfouras,** the jumping-off point for walks in the Psiloritis range, is a church (14th-/15th-century) with the remains of some frescoes of the period, while above the nearby village of **Platania** there are three caves: Digenes (820 m), Kissospelios (1000 m), and the Cave of Pan (1750 m). Just north of the village of **Apodoulou** are, on the right, the Church of St. George (Agios Giorgos), with mid-14th-century frescoes by the monk Anastasios and, up the hill on the left, Late Minoan *tholos* tombs.

Just after Apodoulou, the road divides. A left or eastward turn leads along a secondary road through the village of **Ka-**

mares with its cave and eventually joins up with the main north-south route to Iraklio. A right turn leads south to a juncture with the road running up the western side of the Amari Valley. From here, one can either return to Rethimno via the western side or continue south to the lovely port and beach of Agia Galini, and then drive back to Rethimno via the mountain village of Spili (see above).

The western Amari route skirts the slopes of **Mount Kedros** and, for those not driving, offers superb views to the south and west of the valley and the Psiloritis range. There are also fine churches and frescoes at the villages of **Agia Paraskevi**, **Kardaki** and **Meronas**, with the latter offering a rare fresco of the Christ Child as the Eucharist and a 14th-century one of the Virgin Mary that is one of the earliest on Crete.

East of Rethimno

Another rewarding trip to the east of Rethimno offers the opportunity to visit,

Above: A cove near the little fishing village of Bali on the northern coast.

in one day, a mountain village famous for its potters, an ancient Dorian city, a prehistoric cave, and a charming fishing village on the north coast between Rethimno and Iraklio.

Margarites is the village, about an hour's drive (27 km) east along the New Road to Iraklio and then south up into the foothills of Mount Psiloritis via the Old Road. A typical Cretan mountain village that would be worth visiting in its own right, it has a long tradition of pottery making that has in recent years seen a vigorous revival, much of it due to the presence of foreign buyers. During summer, shops selling local wares are open in the mornings and evenings and some all day long.

The remains of the ancient Dorian city of **Eleutherna**, inhabited from the ninth century BC until the Middle Ages, lie just outside the village of **Prines**, about five minutes' walk from a parking area (200 m to the north). While little systematic archaeological excavation has been done since the 1920s, the site, on a promontory between two river beds, is superb. The antique **bridge**, which dates to Greek times, is another 20 minutes' walk to the north and a marvellous specimen of its kind.

The large, many-chambered and wonderfully stalactited **Cave of Melidoni** is located directly south of the village of Melidoni, about 10 km east of Margarites, on the Old Road southeast of the trade center of Perama. To reach the cave, follow the signs through the village and out to a small chapel just to the right of the cave's entrance.

In ancient times the cave was said to be the habitat of Talos, King Minos' giant, bronze, bull-headed guardian of Crete. In the Hellenistic period (300-67 BC), the cave was the site of worshippers of Hermes. Today, just inside the entrance, there is a stone altar commemorating yet another martyrdom of Cretans at the hands of the Ottomans. In 1824, several hundred people, escaping from marauding soldiers in nearby villages, were trapped in the cave by the Turks, who blocked the entrance with brushwood and set fire to it, thus suffocating the lot.

The pocket-sized fishing village of **Bali** is just a 7-km drive north across the new costal road and down a rather precipitous road to the sea. Bali (the name comes from the Turkish word for honey) has considerable charm, a small beach and plenty of picturesque tavernas and cafés to accommodate the stream of visitors that has increased steadily in recent years. Its beautiful natural setting and rustic warmth remain, however, as yet unspoiled.

Our final tour east of Rethimno is one which might best be taken on a trip which continues to Iraklio. Some 53 km (about a two- hour drive) over the Old Road east of Rethimno and into the mountains is the village of **Anoghia**, yet another site of Cretan martyrdom, this time at the hands of the Nazis.

It is here that the German commandant, General Kreipe, was briefly hidden after being kidnapped by British and Cretan resistance fighters. As a result, the Nazis killed every male in the village and razed all of its buildings, except the church of St. John the Baptist, hence the rather unpicturesque, poured-concrete look of the village today.

Nevertheless, it houses a thriving tourist industry, producing numerous handicrafts and holding various music festivals. In addition, it is one of the main jumping-off places for a journey to the upper slopes and peak of **Mount Psiloritis** (Ida). Its famous cave is said to have been the birthplace of Zeus.

Most of the 20-km journey from Anoghia to the **Cave of Ideon Andron** can be covered by car over a winding asphalt road which passes through a landscape dotted with picturesque stone cheese huts (*mutata*). Some of these are hundreds of years old and still serve shepherds not only as repositories for curing goat's cheese but also as refreshingly cool summer sleeping quarters.

The road up to the slope of Psiloritis ends at the tourist pavilion on **Nidha Plateau**; from here, it is only a 20-minute walk to the cave. The cave's immense entrance (about 27 m wide by 9 m high) and the size of some of the interior chambers (the largest being 34 m by 36 m) explain why it is thought of as the birthplace of Zeus.

Archaeological evidence, traced to the 8th and 9th centuries BC, demonstrate that young Cretans used to perform weapons dances in front of the huge entrance to honor Zeus. One of their shields can be seen in the Archaeological Museum in Iraklio.

Offbeat Beaches

Plakias, close to Frangokastello, is a calm area with a long beach fairly littered right near the town but cleaner as one walks to the west. The little settlement attracts young wayfarers many of whom camp out on its beaches. The setting is lovely, backed by flowering shrubs and herbs and jutting mountains. The beach has a few hotels and tavernas. At the end of a gorge at **Preveli**, you will also find a splendid beach.

Three lesser known beaches, known as **Damoni**, lie along the coast in the sparkling water of the eastern section of Plakias Bay. The middle one is nudist. A little further is **Ammoudi**, a dignified family beach with a taverna and rooms to rent. Ammoudi is close to the inland village of **Lefkogia** which offers a few rooms to rent. East of Rethimno are three coves embraced by large, flat rocks, and with sandy beaches. Paradise Beach is the nicest. **Bali** is a small resort with the Bali Beach Hotel offering rooms to rent. East of Rethimno there are nice beaches at **Panormos**.

THE SKOULAS FAMILY: PAINTERS AND MUSICIANS

On the way to Psilioritis, a picturesque village nestles in the mountainside. **Anogia** is justly proud of its exquisite woven articles and handicrafts. However, its main attraction is a 75-year-old primitive artist, Emmanouil Skoulas.

The self-taught painter and sculptor was originally a shepherd, but at the age of 37, he sold his flocks and devoted his life entirely to his art. He started to draw quite accidentally, imitating an artist whose work he saw in Iraklio. Talent clearly ran in the family. Another older Skoulas named Alkiviadis started painting at the age of 65. His naive style has attracted quite an international crowd of admirers. Emmanouil's son Vassilis is one of the best *lira* players in Crete.

Skoulas admits that he knows nothing about technique and is not even remotely

Above: Tableau by the native painter Alkiviadis Skoulas from Anogia.

interested in learning. "I like to have my own personal style," he says. "I've lived what I paint; I've seen it with my own eyes." And the dignified old man has certainly seen a great deal with his own eyes. His paintings are a vivid and colorful depiction of Crete's history and village life, executed in naif style. The topics range from war scenes to weddings and other typically Cretan events such as parachutists, a Cretan couple drinking a glass of wine and the gun-powder explosion at Arkadi. The sizes vary greatly from small pictures to enormous wall paintings. The very large ones are not for sale. Also a skilful sculptor, Skoulas carves any pieces of wood he can find, using the form to determine the subject matter. Skoulas's son sells his work since the proud old artist shies away from haggling over prices. "I'd like to give them away for free," he maintains. "I paint so that my grandchildren will see my work and thus keep alive things of the past. When I work I forget about everything. It makes me feel happy and fulfilled."

RETHIMNO

Access / Local Transport

FLIGHTS: For airplane tickets: **Olympic Airways**, Rethimno, Tel. (0831) 22257, 24333.
BUSES / FERRIES: There is transportation between the airport and the harbor of Hania. Buses run hourly connecting Iraklio and Hania. Bus services run to all local villages, beaches, etc. Various bus companies offer sightseeing tours, including day trips to Knossos and the Gorge of Samaria. Travel agents also sell ferry tickets.

Accommodation

LUXURY: **Creta Star**, Rethimno, Tel. (0831) 21896. **Rithimna Beach**, Rethimno, Tel. (0831) 29491. **Kalypso Cretan Village**, Plakias, Tel. (0832) 31296. **El Greco**, Rethimno, Tel. (0831) 71102. **Rethimno Bay**, Rethimno, Tel. (0831) 27512. **Oassis**, Perivolia, Tel. (0831) 44705.
MODERATE: **Adele Beach Bungalows**, Rethimno, Tel. (0831) 71047. **Amnissos**, Rethimno, Tel. (0831) 71502. **Kriti Beach**, Rethimno, Tel. (0831) 27401. **Rea**, Agia Galini, Tel. (0832) 91390. **Neos Alianthos**, Plakias, Tel. (0832) 31280. **Bali Beach**, Bali, Tel. (0834) 94210. **Xenia**, Rethimno, Tel. (0831) 29111.
BUDGET: **Golden Beach**, Adele, Rethimno, Tel. (0831) 71012. **Ionia**, Rethimno, Tel. (0831) 22902. **Steris Beach**, Rethimno, Tel. (0831) 28303. **Livikon**, Plakias, Tel. (0832) 31216. **Miramare**, Aghia Galini, Tel. (0832) 91221. **Miramare Beach**, Rethimno, Tel. (0831) 24118.

Restaurants

SEAFOOD : All restaurants in the Venetian harbor offer delicious seafood dishes.
BASIC GREEK: **Tasso's**, beachfront, Tel. (0831) 24615. **Socrates**, Rimondi Fountain, Tel. (0831) 24365. **Pantheon**, beachfront, Tel. (0831) 29026.

Museums

The new **Rethimno Archaeological Museum** is in the former prison, opposite the entrance to the Venetian Fortress. Open 8 am to 3 pm, Sundays 9.30 am to 2.30 pm, closed on Tuesdays and national holidays.
The museum at the monastery of Arkadi. Open 8 am to 7 pm every day (closed 1 hour at various times for midday break).

Local Festivals

Epiphany (January 6) is celebrated with the blessing of the waters, in the Venetian harbor by the Bishop of Rethimno. A *Carnival Parade* leads down the main Iraklio-Hania road past the Public Gardens, three Sundays before Lent, the dates changing every year relative to the moveable feast of Easter. *Feast Day Of St. John the Theologian* at the Preveli monastery, May 8. *Anniversary Of The Battle Of Crete*, May 19-22, with a wreath-laying ceremony in the suburb of Perivolia on May 21. Also on May 21 is the *Feast Day Of Sts. Helen and Constantine* at the monastery of Arkadi. At Hora Sfakion, the *Anniversary of the 1821 Revolution against the Turks* is celebrated on May 26-27. In July, Rethimno holds both its biennial *Cretan Handicrafts Exhibition* and the *Rethimno Wine Festival*, the latter is a joyous two-week affair in the Public Gardens from 8.30 pm to 2 am, with much eating, drinking, dancing and entertainment. August 15 is the feast day of *The Annunciation Of The Virgin Mary*, the second biggest religious holiday of the year outside of Easter. On November 7-9, the monastery of Arkadi commemorates *the 1866 Gunpowder Room Explosion* with ceremonies taking place at Arkadi and Rethimno.

Caves

Idaion Andron (Nidha Plain), Melidoni, Sentoni (Zoniana), Marathospilios (Margarites), Spiliostou Digeni (Platanias), Kraneos Ermis (Patsos), Tripiti (Ano Meros), Gerani.

Cinema

Kartalion, Voulgaroktonou St., **Oassis**, Georgiou St., **Pantellis**, Potaliou St.

Hospital

State Hospital, Rethimno (behind the Public Gardens), Tel. (0831) 22261.

Monasteries

Arkadi, Preveli, Arseniou, Roustika.

Post / Telegraph / Telephone

General Post Office (ELTA), Koundouriotou Street.
Central Telephone / Telegraph Office (OTE), Moatsou Street. Long distance dialing phones are also available at many cafés and cigarette kiosks.

Rent a Car

Avis, Arkadi St. 196 (Tel. 29409). **Kaklidakis**, 4 Martirion Pl. (Tel. 28316). There are numerous automobile & motorbike rental agencies in Rethimno.

Shopping

Handicrafts: For good buys try the shops on Nearchou Street off the Venetian harbor and Arkadiou, Platanos Square near the Nerantzes Minaret.
Leather goods: Giorgos Psathakis, at the Rimondi Fountain.
Jewelery: Cretan House, 222 Arkadiou Street, and Gamma Gold-Silver, 81 Eleftherios Venizelou Street.

Taxis

Martirion Place, Agostou Statioti Place, Dimitrakaki Street.

Tourist Information

The **Greek National Tourist Organization (EOT)** is situated on the beachfront, Tel. (0831) 24143, 19148.

SEA OF CRETE

Hania
Rethimno
Iraklio
Sitia
Lassithi
Gavdos

IRAKLIO

IRAKLIO CITY
KNOSSOS
ARHANES / MOUNT IOUHTAS
TILISSOS / FODELE
SOUTHEAST OF IRAKLIO
THE SOUTH / MESSARA PLAIN
FESTOS / MATALA / THE EAST

IRAKLIO CITY

Iraklio, the biggest city in Crete and the island's capital, brims over with a noisy vitality that helps compensate for its sprawling, unplanned outskirts and the endless traffic jams in the alleys inside its Venetian walls. Its population, swelled over the past 20 years by migration from the surrounding villages, is now over 130,000, making it Greece's fourth largest city. The province of Iraklio is among the richest in the country in terms of per capita income, thanks to traditional agricultural products such as olive oil, sultanas, table grapes and wine, and a healthy tourist industry that brings more than one million visitors a year to Crete.

In Minoan times the settlement served as a port of Knossos, and the Greeks called it Heraclium, after the legendary point of Hercules' landing. The Saracens arrived in the ninth century and called it Rabd-el-Khandak. Under the Arabs, Iraklio became a major Mediterranean slave market. But Byzantine rule was restored in AD 964 after a long siege by the army of Nikiforos Fokas. The name changed to Handax for a while, and then to Candia

Preceding pages: Fishing nets drying on the docks of Iraklio. Left: Detail of the 17th century Lion Fountain.

when the Venetians bought Crete in 1210 and sent colonists to establish feudal rule over the rebellious islanders. For more than four centuries, Crete was the jewel in the crown of imperialist Venice.

As the island's capital, Candia was a flourishing port on the galley routes to the Levant and an export center for Cretan produce – timber, sweet wines, cheese and even table grapes. One medieval traveler, Canon Pietro Casola, who stopped off in Candia in 1494 wrote: "Candia is a very large, strongly walled city situated in a plain. It has beautiful houses, although they are flat-roofed in the Eastern fashion. It has a fine port, which is somewhat dangerous at the entrance, especially for larger ships."

To face the growing threat from Ottoman Turkey, the fortifications were rebuilt in the 16th century, enclosing a wide expanse of gardens and orchards within the city. Every citizen was expected to contribute both funds and labor. When the Turks eventually attacked Crete in 1648, they quickly overran the island but were stopped short by the massive defences of Candia. A 21-year siege followed, one of the longest in history, before General Francesco Morosini surrendered to the Ottoman Grand Vizier in September 1669 and sailed back to Venice with the remnants of the defend-

121

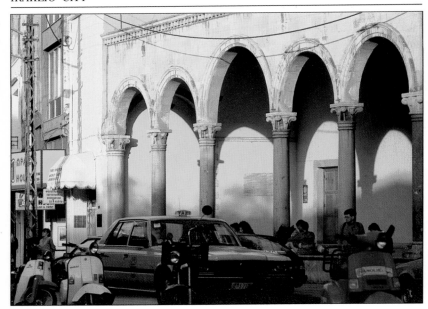

ing force and the city archives. Under Turkish rule, Iraklio was governed by a pasha and known as Megalo Kastro (the Great Fortress). When Crete won autonomy in 1898 with the help of the Great Powers – Britain, France, Russia and Italy – Candia became Iraklio and quickly developed into the island's most important commercial port.

Getting Around

The best starting point for exploring Iraklio is officially called **Plateia Venizelou** but is known to residents as *ta liontaria* (the lions), after the marble lions decorating the 17th-century **Morosini Fountain**, one of the city's main landmarks. Fed by an aqueduct that carried water from the springs on Mount Iouhtas, 15 km away, it was originally topped by a

Above: The Church of St. Mark (Agios Markos), often the site of art exhibits. Right: Winter rains and the sea's swell hammer at the walls of Koules fortress.

larger-than-lifesize Roman statue of the sea-god Neptune. The square is filled with cafés, newspaper stands, bookstalls and souvenir shops. This is the place to pick up a map, guidebooks, a copy of *Zorba the Greek* (available in several languages) and cassettes of Cretan music. It also boasts a renowned *bougatsa* shop where you can try a creamy custard- or cheese-filled pie, served warm from the oven.

Sitting at one of the cafés beside the fountain, you look across to the **Church of St. Mark** (Agios Markos), built by the Venetians in the 13th century and named for the Serenissima's patron saint. It is used now for staging concerts and art shows. The 50-room **palace** of the Duke of Crete, a bureaucrat sent from Venice to govern the island for a two-year period, survived into Ottoman times, but all that can be seen of it now are the vaulted ceilings of the shops opposite the fountain. The **Vikelas library**, the biggest in Greece outside Athens, replaces another set of Venetian administrative

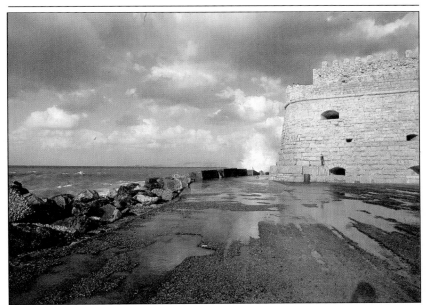

buildings to the south of the square. The recently restored **Loggia**, a kind of colonial clubhouse for the Venetian nobility on the island, designed in elegant near-Palladian style by the architect Francesco Basilicata in the early 17th century, stands around the corner on August 25th Street. It was heavily damaged during the Second World War, and was almost entirely – and authentically – rebuilt in the 1980s. From its balcony the Duke of Crete issued proclamations and presided over festivals and processions. Adjoining the Loggia is the former Venetian Armory, now the **City Hall**. The battered statue of a woman set in its north wall is thought to be a personification of Crete.

To the left, heading down to the harbor, is **El Greco park**, with a post-office caravan conveniently positioned at one side. On the far side of the park is the **"OTE"** telephone office. On the right, set back from the street, stands the **Church of St. Titus** (Agios Titos), the patron saint of Crete, who is credited with converting the islanders to Chris-

tianity in the first century AD following the instructions of St. Paul.

The church has been rebuilt several times since its foundation soon after Nikiforos Fokas recaptured the island. It was the seat of the Orthodox archbishop of Crete, then of the Roman Catholic archbishop during the Venetian period. After the siege, the Grand Vizier ordered its conversion into a mosque. It was re-dedicated to St. Titus after the Turkish minority finally left the island in 1923, and the minaret was replaced by a belfry. It was not until 1966 that the mitre-shaped reliquary containing the skull of St. Titus was returned from Venice, where it had been taken by General Morosini shortly before the taking of the city. It can now be seen in a chapel to the left of the entrance. A patch of cranium is just visible, surrounded by silver and gilt, and a steady stream of Irakliots passes in and out to say a prayer and kiss the glass case that protects it.

Continuing down the street past shipping offices, car rental and travel agencies, you reach the **inner harbor** where yachts moor, the fishing boats land their catch and fishing nets are repaired.

One of the favorite meeting places of the youth of Iraklio is the **Café Marina** where you should enjoy a Greek coffee or a delightful, cool frappée (whipped and frozen Nescafé) and admire the fishing boats bobbing at berth and the nets spread on the wall. Looking out toward the city you will see the great vaults of the **Venetian arsenal**. A series of high, vaulted tunnels are all that remains of the arsenal, once a busy shipyard where galleys were repaired and re-equipped. Each was designed to hold one vessel.

The squat miniature fortress standing guard over the inner harbor was built by the Venetians but is known nowadays by its Turkish name, **Koules**. Now restored, it is a remarkable piece of 16th-century military architecture, with more than 20 thick-walled chambers and a store-room still filled with cannonballs. A ramp leads up to the battlements.

The roof terrace offers a panoramic view of the city stretched out at the foot of the Ida range, with its labyrinth of modern housing, toward the left the new port where the big ferries anchor, and a good view of the coastline on either side of the city. The pointed mountain on the western horizon is known locally as *stroumboulas*. The fort's upper level is used as an open-air stage for plays and concerts in summer. (Franco Zeffirelli's version of Verdi's *Othello*, starring Placido Domingo, was filmed here rather than in Cyprus). The exterior walls carry three carved reliefs of the lion of St. Mark, the symbol of Venetian power emblazoned on monuments throughout the eastern Mediterranean.

From the fortress, you can walk along the inside of the modern harbor wall, which encloses an increasingly busy port handling passengers and containers bound for Cyprus, North Africa and the western Mediterranean. The low-lying is-

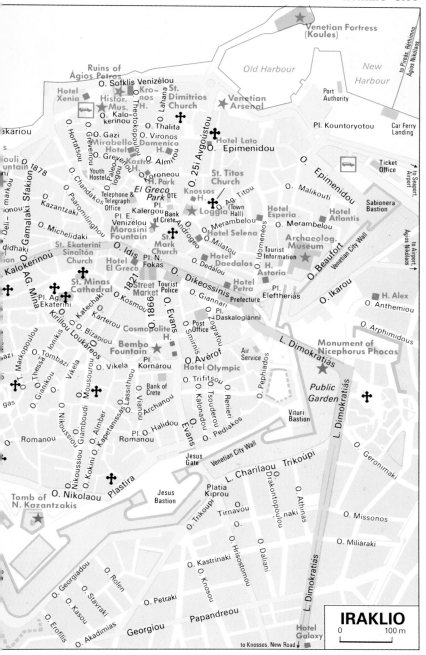

Venetian Fortress (Koules)

to Piréas, Réthimno
Agios Nikolaos

Old Harbour

New Harbour

Ruins of Ágios Petros

St. Sofklis Venizélou
Hotel Xenia
Histor. Mus.
Kro- nos H.
St. Dimitrios Church
Venetian Arsenal

Port Authority

akariou

O. Kalo- kerinou
O. Lahana
Pl. Kountoryotou
Car Ferry Landing

Theotokopoulou
O. Gazi
O. Thalita
Hotel Lato

Hortatsou
O. Grevenou
O. Vironos
O. Epimenidou
Ticket Office

iouli untain ni

1878
Mirabello Hotel
Domenico H.
Grevenou
O. 25í Avgoústou
O. Epimenidou
to Seaport, Airport

O. Chandakos
Kastro H.
Almr.
St. Titos Church
O. Malikouti
Sabionera Bastion

Kazantzaki
Youth Hostel
Oroneou
Knossos
O. Merambelou
Hotel Esperia
Hotel Atlantis

O. Psaromilinghou
Telephone & Telegraph Office
El Greco Park
OTE
Ag. Titou (Town Hall)
O. Merambelou
Archaeolog. Museum
O. Beaufort
Venetian City Wall

O. Michelidaki
Pl. E. Venizélou
Kalergou
Loggia
Merambelou
Tourist Information
to Airport
Agios Nikolaos

Gamalaki Sfakíon
Kalokerinou
AG. Mina
didhaki ion
St. Ekaterini Sinaïtôn Church
Morosini Fountain
Bank of Crete
St. Androgeo
Hotel Selena
O. Milatou
Idomeneos
H. Astoria
O. Ikarou

O. Idis
Hotel El Greco
Pl. N. Fokas
St. Mark Church
Hotel Daedalos
O. Dedálou
Hotel Petra

St. Minas Cathedral
1821
Street Market
Tourist Police
O. Dikeossinis
Pl. Eleftherias
H. Alex
O. Anthemiou

Pl. Ag. Ekateríni
Katechaki
O. Kosmou
1866
O. Giannari
Prefecture
O. Arphimidous

Markopoulou
Kirillou Loukáreos
Karterou
O. Bizaniou
Evans
O. Daskalogiánni
Zografou

Tombazi
Vikela
Cosmopolite H.
Post Office
O. Smirnis
Air Service
O. Pephiados
Monument of Nicephorus Phocas

O. Thessa
O. Gianikou
Mousourou
Bembo Fountain
Pl. Kornárou
O. Avérof
L. Dimokratías
Public Garden

Nikoussiou
Giamboudi
Vianou
Lassithiou
O. Vikela
Hotel Olympic
O. Trifitsou
O. Tsouderou
Renieri
Vituri Bastion

O. Romanou
Kokini
Almber
Kapetanássas
Archanou
O. Kalonadou
O. Pediakos
Evans

Plastira
Pl. O. Halidou
Romanou
Jesus Gate
Venetian City Wall
L. Charilaou Trikoúpi
O. Geronimaki

Tomb of N. Kazantzakis
O. Nikolaou
Jesus Bastion
Platia Kiprou
O. Trikoúpi
Tirnavou
Drakontopoulou
naki
O. Athinas
O. Missonos

O. Georgiadou
O. Rolen
O. Stavraki
O. Petraki
O. Kastrinaki
O. Hisostomou
O. Daliani
O. Knosou
L. Dimokratías
O. Miliaraki

O. Kasou
O. Erofilis
O. Akadimias
Georgiou
Papandreou
Hotel Galaxy

to Knossos, New Road

IRAKLIO
0   100 m

land in the distance is **Dia**, uninhabited now and a sanctuary for the *agrimi*, the long-horned Cretan wild goat.

Back at the roundabout, a right turn takes you past the skeleton of the medieval church of **St. Peter**, badly damaged in the 1941 bombing of Iraklio which preceded the German airborne invasion of the island, and past the bus station for Rethimno and Hania.

Opposite is the **Historical and Ethnographical Museum**, housed in a neoclassical mansion dating from the early 1900s. It is a pleasantly cool place to linger on hot afternoons, and moreover, has a number of interesting exhibits that offer much insight onto Crete's past.

The garden contains relics of war: Venetian cannons and a pile of cannonballs as well as several unexploded bombs from World War II. Inside, the collection ranges from early Christian

Above: Entrance to the Historical and Ethnographical Museum. Right: Even in the hectic city there are peaceful spots.

and Byzantine stonework in the basement (**Room 1**) to a handsome display of hand-woven Cretan textiles in **Room 11** on the top floor.

Rooms 2 and 2a contain Venetian sculptures, including a rebuilt fountain dating from around 1600 and a lion of St. Mark from the Agios Dimitrios fortress outside the city walls, with a Latin inscription saying: "I protect the Kingdom of Crete." There are stone reliefs from the Franciscan monastery which stood on the site of the Archaeological Museum and was destroyed in the Turkish siege.

Room 3 holds inscriptions from the Venetian period. **Room 4** is devoted to the Turkish times, with Ottoman sculptures, among them some elegant tombstones of Turkish officials, decorated with stone turbans, as well as attractive 18th century tiles taken from a mosque. In the corridor are wallpaintings from a Turkish house, showing Iraklio in a romanticized Cretan landscape.

On the ground floor to the right of the entrance, **Room 5** contains early Chris-

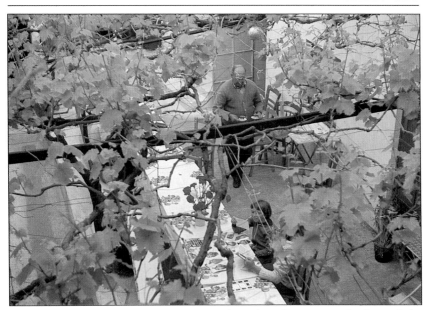

tian and Byzantine ecclesiastical items, as well as Byzantine and Venetian jewelry and a collection of gold and bronze coins. There are impressive icons from the Savathiana monastery above the village of Fodele and the church of Panagia Gouverniotissa on the way to the Lassithi Plain, together with richly embroidered vestments from the Asomatos monastery in the Amari valley in western Crete and a carved wooden lectern from the Valsamonero monastery on the slopes of Mount Ida. In the hall, a partly rebuilt Byzantine chapel displays 13th- and 14th-century frescoes.

To the left of the entrance, **Room 7** holds the historical collection, dominated by items from the island's bloody revolutionary struggle for independence from the Turks and memorabilia of the independent Cretan state of 1898-1913, administered by Prince George of Greece and, from 1906, by Alexandros Zaimis. There are portraits of Cretan warrior chieftains, a fine array of their weapons, historic photographs and a flag of the in-dependent Cretan state. In front of the staircase is a banner proclaiming *Eleftheria i Thanatos* (Freedom or Death), the Cretan rebels' rallying cry. It belonged to a chieftain from the Argiroupolis district of Rethimno. On the first floor landing are more photographs dating from the days of independence, and a series illustrating the 1941 Battle of Crete.

On the left is **Room 9**, which reproduces the study of the Cretan writer Nikos Kazantzakis, (1883-1957), author of *Zorba the Greek* and *The Odyssey: A Modern Sequel*. The desk, book collection and other memorabilia come from his house on the island of Aegina.

Another room on the same floor commemorates the Cretan-born statesman Eleftherios Venizelos, who dominated Greek political life for 20 years after the island was united with Greece, and another Cretan-born prime minister of Greece, Emmanouil Tsouderos. He took office as the Germans invaded northern Greece in April 1941, and later escaped to Egypt.

The **second-floor rooms** contain a spectacular collection of textiles, many in the brilliant scarlet that characterizes much Cretan handwork. Embroidered motifs on silk, linen and cotton include dragons, mermaids and elaborate floral designs, while the woven blankets are sometimes decorated with lively historical scenes. **Room 10**, containing the ethnographic collection, is fitted out as a well-appointed domestic interior from the turn of the century.

Back at *ta liontaria,* the narrow pedestrian way across the street, **Odos Dedalou**, follows the outline of the city's first fortification wall and emerges close to the Archaeological Museum. Besides souvenir shops, jewelers, bookshops and newsvendors, Dedalos Street is peppered with restaurants offering typical Greek fare. Alternatively, a right turn beside the fountain takes you up to the traffic lights

and across **Odos Kalokerinou**, the corso or main thoroughfare of Venetian days, into the market street, **Odos 1866**. Butchers' shops jostle groceries filled with Cretan produce, cheeses, honey, wines, olives in brine and pungent herbs, along with old-fashioned barber shops, and stores selling leather goods and the distinctive Cretan knives. Smells of roasting meat drift out from the covered alley filled with tavernas which opens off the east side of the street.

At the top of the street, on **Plateia Kornarou**, is the **Bembo Fountain**, put together from fragments of ancient marble, including a headless Roman statue which its architect, Zuane Bembo, hauled all the way from Ierapetra on the southeast coast. The polygonal stone kiosk in front of it is a Turkish fountain house.

The main road to the right, **Odos Kirillou Loukareos**, leads round to the huge 19th century cathedral, **St. Minas** (Agios Minas). In its shadow stands the church of **St. Catherine of Sinai** (Agia Aika-

Above: Wines, fresh and dried fruits, nuts: all products of Crete. Right: Peddler and priest in Iraklio – a bargain for redemption.

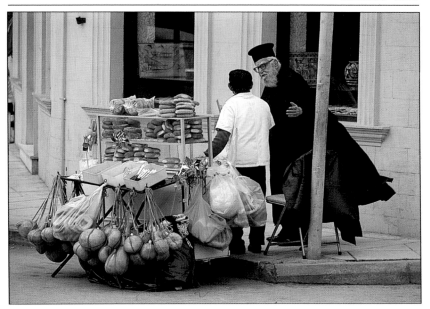

terini Sinaiton), an appealing mixture of Byzantine and Venetian architecture which dates from 1555. It contains a magnificent collection of Cretan icons. After the fall of Constantinople to the Turks in 1453, the Agia Ekaterini college in Iraklio, a dependency of the monastery of the same name in the Sinai desert in Egypt, became a renowned center of learning and artistic life as dispossessed Byzantine intellectuals arrived in Crete on their way to a new life, spreading Classical thought and literature across western Europe.

Cretan icon painting was especially important at this period, with painters traveling to and from Venice, where they absorbed the elements of the early Italian Renaissance. The church contains six icons by Mihail Damaskinos, a 16th century painter who worked in both Byzantine and Western styles. The icons used to hang in the Vrondisi monastery in the foothills of Mount Ida. Now they are displayed on the western wall of the church and are numbered 2, 5, 8, 9, 12 and 15.

Walking due south from Cathedral Square through a maze of narrow streets, you quickly reach the **Martinengo Bastion** where Nikos Kazantzakis is buried. An alternative route is to head back to Plateia Kornarou, going up Odos Evans and turning right onto Odos Nikos Plastiras, which follows the line of the Venetian walls from the Jesus bastion. The Martinengo Bastion is the next one along the way. **Kazantzakis' grave** is a stone slab, marked by a tall wooden cross. An inscription taken from his writings reflects the spirit of his admired friend, Zorba: "I fear nothing. I hope for nothing. I am free."

The **fortifications**, designed by the Venetian military engineer Michele Sanmicheli, enclose the inner city in an angular semi-circle cut by seven heart-shaped bastions and four gates. Two of them, the Hania Gate to the west and the Jesus Gate to the south, have survived. You can walk along the western and southern ramparts, which are as much as 40 m thick in places. The moat now contains a

soccer pitch and two outdoor theaters where performances are staged during the city's annual summer arts festival. Behind the children's playground outside the **Vituri Bastion**, at the southeast corner of the fortifications beside Leoforos Dimokratias, you can inspect an *agrimi* at close quarters: There are several of them living in an enclosure at the base of the ramparts.

The Archaeological Museum

Built on the side of the medieval Catholic monastery of St. Francis, a prominent landmark in wood-cut illustrations of Iraklio in Venetian times, the Archaeological Museum is situated just off **Eleftheria** (Freedom) **Square**. Across from the museum is the **tourist information office**. Freedom Square is the largest in

Above: The camera of this photographer on Eleftheria Square might also land in a museum. Right: The discus of Festos (ca. 1650 BC).

Iraklio and a favorite spot for a rendez-vous on Sundays and summer evenings, with its numerous tables and chairs under the shade of planes. People often meet here for a walk in the dusk (known as a *volta*) or to go to one of the movies lining the square. The many photographers with their old-fashioned equipment are one of the square's curiosities. Various events also take place here, from concerts to demonstrations and political speeches.

In summer, it is best to visit the museum early in the morning, since the galleries quickly get overcrowded. As scarcely any Cretan antiquities are to be found in museums abroad, the Bronze Age collections provide a unique guide to Minoan art and lifestyles.

Gallery I: The finds from the Neolithic and early Minoan period (5000-2000 BC), before the great palaces were built (and before the advent of the potter's wheel) illustrate the highly developed skills of early Cretan craftsmen in metalwork, pottery and in carving stone vases and sealstones. Case 7 con-

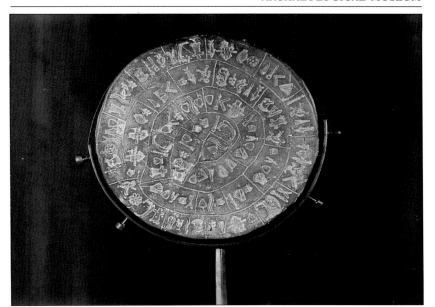

tains fine stone vases from an early cemetery at Mohlos, an islet off the nothern coast, in use from about 2600-2100 BC. Their shapes are designed to set off the striped limestone and marble. A *pyxis*, or small box, in soft serpentine has a lid with its handle carved in the shape of a reclining dog. Case 10 has a four-wheeled cart dating from around 2000 BC, the earliest evidence for wheeled transport on Crete, and a flat-bottomed boat, both from Palekastro on the eastern coast. Case 16 contains a sealstone which is carved in the shape of a crouching monkey. Case 14 includes early mould-cast daggers in copper bronze and occasionally silver. Cases 17 and 18a contain fine jewelry from Arhanes in gold, rock crystal, carnelian, ivory and faience, a kind of glazed clayware.

Gallery II: Finds from the early palaces (dated to 1900-1700 BC, the Old Palace or Protopalatian period), include the Town Mosaic from Knossos, a collection of faience plaques showing miniature house façades in varied architectural styles. The same case holds tablets in hieroglyphic script (not yet fully deciphered) and a bronze dagger from Malia with a gold hilt in a latticework design.

Gallery III: Distinctive pottery from the Kamares Cave, high on Mount Ida and overlooking the palace of Festos, comes in an amazing array of colors and designs. Delicate cups in what is known as "eggshell ware" are perhaps the most attractive, with some angular in style, imitating metal shapes. Larger vases from Festos, like the fruitstand with its toothed rim, or the punchbowl with appliqué flowers are spectacular creations with a hint of the Rococo exaggeration that Minoan artists sometimes indulged in when they moved away from the miniature scale which seems to have suited them best. The Festos disk in Case 41, made of clay with characters stamped in spiral bands on both sides, has not yet been deciphered, although it has been suggested that it records an early hymn. It was found in a context dated to around 1700 BC.

Gallery IV: The finds of the period of the later palaces (1700- 1450 BC) include some of the most remarkable Minoan artworks known. Case 49 contains a jug decorated with a delicate pattern of waving grass and a rhyton, or vessel pierced for pouring libations to a god, decorated with marine motifs in the naturalistic style developed by potters at Knossos in the final years of the Minoan palace civilization.

Case 51 holds the famous bull's head rhyton, made of dark serpentine with eyes inlaid in red jasper and clear rock crystal. Its horns – now restored – were of gilded wood. A double axe is incised on its forehead. It was found in the Little Palace at Knossos.

In Case 59 is the Lioness Head rhyton, made of white limestone and found in the Central Treasury at Knossos. Case 56 contains an ivory acrobat with arms outstretched, perhaps a bull-leaper. Long ceremonial bronze swords from the palace at Malia are displayed in Case 53, including one with an ivory hilt and rock crystal pommel.

The two bare-breasted snake goddesses wearing elaborate flounced skirts in Case 50 are made of faience. They were found, like many of the treasures in this gallery, in two stone-lined pits beneath a floor in a Knossos palace shrine, known as the Temple Repositories. Case 55 contains reliefs in faience from the same find, among them a realistic cow suckling her calf. The richly decorated Gaming Board in Case 57 has an ivory frame inlaid with gold and silver leaf, lapis lazuli, rock crystal and faience, and four accompanying ivory gaming pieces. It comes from a corridor in the palace and is dated to around 1600 BC.

Gallery V: The exhibits mostly come from Knossos in the Neopalatian period (1450-1400 BC), when it apparently was

Left: The snake-goddess suggests how people were clothed back then.

ruled by Mycenaeans from mainland Greece. Case 62 contains tall stone lamps made from reddish marble, imported from southern Greece, and some Egyptian objects found at Knossos, including the bottom half of a 13th-century BC statuette of an Egyptian named User, perhaps an envoy to Crete.

In Case 69 are rectangular clay tablets from several sites inscribed in Linear A, the Minoan script, which still remains undeciphered. The long narrow tablets from Knossos are in Linear B, the earliest form of Greek, and record farm production and storage from year to year during the period of Mycenaean influence. They survived accidental incineration in the fierce fires which destroyed these sites.

Case 66 contains stone vases from Knossos, including the huge, flat alabastrons made of gypsum which were found in the Throne Room and may have been used in a last-minute religious ritual intended to avert destruction of the palace. The appealing clay house model in Case 70, found at Arhanes, illustrates several features of Minoan architecture: small windows to keep out both heat and cold, more light provided by an interior courtyard, columns tapering downwards, and an upper-floor terrace.

Gallery VI: The finds come from graves of the later palace and post-palatial periods and include some spectacular jewelry and weaponry. The Royal Tomb at Isopata contained a series of striking Egyptian alabaster vases displayed in Case 72.

An unusual horse-burial from Arhanes is on show in Case 75a: The animal was sacrificed and ritually dismembered. Case 84 contains bronze weapons belonging to the Mycenaean warriors, buried in graves north of Knossos, among them spearheads used for thrusting and short swords designed for fighting at close quarters.

Case 85 holds a bronze helmet with large cheek-pieces. A reconstructed helmet made of pieces of boars' tusk, once sewn on to a leather skull-cap, is displayed in Case 78. This kind of helmet is discribed in Homer's *Iliad* as part of a warrior's equipment. It is also illustrated on an amphora from Knossos in Case 82.

Superb goldwork is displayed in Cases 86, 87, and 88, notably the large gold ring from Isopata showing a ritual dance with a goddess and worshippers in a flower-filled meadow and a pair of earrings in an stylized bull's head. Each gold granule was applied separately using a highly skilled technique.

A circular bronze mirror from Arhanes has an ivory handle. In Case 79a is an elaborately carved ivory pyxis showing a bull-catching scene. Three huge bronze cauldrons from Tilissos stand against one wall, each big enough to stew a whole sheep at a feast or celebration.

Above: Stucco of a bull's head from the north entrance of the palace in Knossos. Right: Religious idols of the Minoans, a clay image of a bull.

Gallery VII: Finds from villas of the later palace period and from sacred caves are dominated by the giant double axes, an important Minoan religious symbol. They come from the coastal villa at Nirou Hani and are displayed on restored poles. Case 89 holds bronze figurines of men worshipping, their right hands pressed to their foreheads in a kind of salute. One realistic, larger piece shows an older man with a protruding stomach in the typical stance of a worshipper. Case 93 contains material from the villa at Agia Triada, including several fine marine-style vases, as well as vessels containing carbonized barley, millet, beans and figs from fire-destruction levels at Festos and Palekastro in eastern Crete.

Cases 97 and 98 display bronze swords and small gold double axes left as offerings in the Arkhalohori cave in central Crete. In Case 101 is one of the great masterpieces of Minoan goldwork: a pendant of two bees apparently storing a drop of honey in a honeycomb. It comes from the Chrisolakkos cemetery at Malia

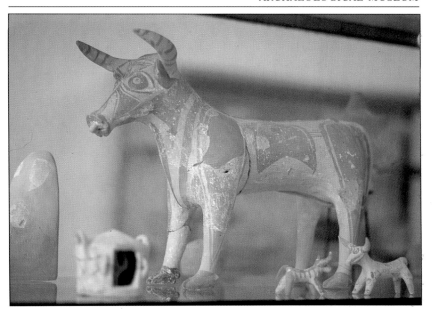

and is dated to around 1550 BC. Three other masterpieces, stone vases of steatite with remarkably lively relief scenes, are shown in separate cases. All were found at Agia Triada.

The heavily restored Boxer rhyton features scenes from boxing and wrestling matches, with the fighters wearing what look like leather helmets, as well as bull-leaping acrobats. On the Chieftain Cup, a Minoan official is seen receiving a consignment of animal hides. All three vases are thought to have been made in a Knossos workshop around 1550 BC.

Case 99 contains copper ingots from Agia Triada in the shape of oxhides, each weighing around 29 kg. They were hauled by their protruding corners.

Gallery VIII: The items on display are all from the late palace-period and surrounding town at Zakros in eastern Crete. Case 109 contains an outstanding find: A rock crystal rhyton, with its handle made from rock-crystal beads which have turned green along with the bronze wire on which they are threaded. It was re-stored from more than three hundred fragments.The pottery from Zakros is of high quality: Case 110 contains a rhyton in marine style decorated with starfish and shells against a background of sea-weed and rocks. In Case 112 is another carved stone rhyton, made of chlorite, showing a mountain sanctuary complete with wild goats and flowers. It was originally covered with gold leaf.

Case 113 contains bronze ingots and a whole elephant tusk found in the palace store-rooms, discolored by the fire which destroyed the settlement at Zakros around 1450 BC. In Cases 114 and 118 are an extraordinary collection of stone vases, including tall rhytons in Egyptian alabaster, cups made from colorful striped limestones and several imported vases from Egypt. A bull's head rhyton in chlorite is displayed in Case 116, smaller than the one from Knossos, but just as finely crafted.

Gallery IX: Among the finds from a variety of neo-palatial-period sites in eastern Crete are a magnificent collection of sealstones in semi-precious stone displayed in Case 128, along with impressions and detailed drawings that reveal the Minoan miniaturists' lively imagination and ingenuity.

Cases 126 and 127 hold objects from the fishing town of Gournia on the northern coast, among them bronze tools and large limestone lamps. Case 122 contains pottery as well as stone lamps and vases from the island of Psira off the northeastern coast, including a striking vase in clay in a shopping-bag shape, decorated with double axes. Case 123 contains clay figurines of people and animals, including some horned beetles which were dedicated at a sanctuary at Piskokephalo south of Sitia. A real-life example, also on show, illustrates the accuracy of the Minoan potters' study of nature.

Gallery X: The decline of Minoan civilization is reflected in the finds from the Postpalatian period (1350-1150 BC),

Left: A small clay temple with a goddess.
Right: An Agia Triada sacrophagus detail.

mostly from houses built in the ruins of the Knossos palace and over tombs elsewhere on the island.

Case 133 contains several large clay "goddesses" from a shrine at Gazi on the western outskirts of Iraklio, one with three poppy pods in her headdress, suggesting that opium was not unknown to the Minoans. Another terracotta group in Case 132, from Palekastro, shows three women dancing, while a fourth, in the center, plays the *lira*.

The comparative poverty of the period is illustrated by the jewelry in Case 139: Necklaces are made of beads of glasspaste and semi-precious stones, rather than gold. In Case 143 are idols from a sanctuary at Agia Triada, including a figure on a swing.

Gallery XI: Life in Crete changed markedly from 1100 BC to 800 BC, as bronze tools and weapons were gradually replaced with iron – though bronze was still used for ceremonial objects. In the Sub-Minoan, Protogeometric and Geometric periods, new pottery shapes and styles of decoration come into use, and burial customs changed: Cremation became the rule and ashes were buried in large clay vases.

Case 155 contains a burial urn found at Knossos, decorated with a scene of two lions tearing a man apart. Case 148 displays a curious rhyton in the shape of an ox-drawn chariot, and clay goddesses with arms upraised from a shrine at Karphi above the Lassithi plain. Case 149 contains finds from a cave sanctuary of Eileithyia, the goddess of childbirth, at Inatos on the south coast. Among them are clay figurines of heavily pregnant women, some giving birth in squatting position.

Gallery XII: Items from the eighth and seventh centuries BC, the Late Geometric and Orientalizing period, reveal a new artistic liveliness, indicating that Crete was again in touch with both mainland Greece and other regions of the southeast Mediterranean. Case 159 contains cremation vases from Fortetsa near Knossos with brightly colored designs as well as gifts for the dead.

In Case 169 are some impressive bronze finds from the cave sanctuary of Zeus high on Mount Ida. Fragments from a tripod cauldron depict an oared ship with two standing figures aboard. It may represent the abduction of Ariadne from Crete by Theseus. A bronze quiver, bronze greaves and two semi-circular bronze mitrae worn below the breastplate to protect the stomach illustrate Cretan armorers' skills.

Case 170 contains a unique collection of ninth-century BC jewelry, mostly from the re-used Bronze Age tomb at Teke close to Knossos. It was found in two vases buried beside the tomb doorway, prompting suggestions that it may have been the family vault of a group of Knossos metalworkers with Near East origins. The hoard includes a gold pendant inlaid with crystal on a plaited gold chain, another crescent-shaped pendant,

a necklace of rock crystal beads and a gold strip with impressed decoration of warriors fighting lions.

Gallery XIII contains a collection of decorated clay burial chests and bathtubs, which were also used as coffins by the Minoans. The chest-shaped type probably imitates a wooden original.

Gallery XIV is upstairs and displays Minoan frescoes, many of them discolored by fire and quite thoroughly restored more than 40 years ago. But they still convey the Minoans' interest in elaborate religious ceremonial and their enthusiasm for nature as well as their exceptional artistic abilities. The frescoes were painted on wet plaster, sometimes molded in low relief to create a three-dimensional effect. They date from the later palace period, although some from Knossos belong to the period of Mycenaean influence.

At the top of the east flight of stairs is a wooden scale reconstruction of the palace at Knossos which gives an idea of its labyrinthine quality. Frescoes Numbers

2-5 are fragments from a religious procession of large figures and come from the Corridor of the Procession Fresco leading to the great entrance to the palace at Knossos.

The best preserved is the Cup-bearer, carrying a deep conical rhyton, who wears a sealstone on his wrist. Number 6 shows a griffin, a mythological combination of eagle and lion, discolored by fire. It comes from the Throne Room. The figure-of-eight-shaped shields in Number 7 were a popular motif also used on pottery and in ivory-carving: They are modelled on tall shields made of animal hides which Mycenaean warriors carried.

The Lily Prince, Number 9, wears an elaborate headdress of lilies and feathers and has been identified as the priest-king of Knossos, though some scholars believe he may be a boxer. The bull's head in low relief, Number 9, is thought to be all that remains of a bull-capturing scene from the north entrance to the Knossos palace. The Royal Ladies in Blue, Number 10, come from the east wing of the palace and the Dolphins, Number 11, from the Queen's apartments there.

The colored spirals, Numbers 12-13, also come from Knossos, while the Partridge Frescoe, Number 14, was found in a small building south of the palace, which the excavators named the Caravanserai.

The bull-leapers, Number 15, a young man turning a backwards somersault over a dappled bull, while two young women act as catchers is one of the finest depictions of this cultic competition. The Lily frescoes, Numbers 16 and 17, are elegant still lives from a villa at Amnisos, on the nothern coast just east of Iraklio.

A series of paintings from the villa at Agia Triada, near Festos, is blackened by fire: Numbers 18, 19 and 20 are all from the same room and show a kneeling

Right: A copy of the "The Captain of the Blacks" from Knossos.

woman, another woman at a shrine and a wild cat. Two procession fragments, Numbers 21 and 22, are next to a painted floor from Agia Triada with a design of dolphins, octopus and fish. In the center of the gallery is a painted stone sarcophagus, also from Agia Triada, dating from around 1400 BC. It is covered with plaster painted with scenes from a funeral ritual on one long side and, on the other, a bull-sacrifice. One short side shows a procession and the other two chariots pulled by griffins and driven by women.

Gallery XV: Displayed here are "La Parisienne", the haughty, long-necked priestess who seems to represent a Minoan ideal of beauty; and the fascinating miniature fresco depicting priestesses performing a ritual dance outdoors before a crowd of spectators who are segregated according to sex. The restored Camp Stool fresco, to which "La Parisienne" possibly belongs, shows seated priestesses and priests holding goblets and chalices.

Gallery XVI: The Crocus Picker fresco was originally restored showing a boy collecting blossoms: In fact it was a blue monkey. The Captain of the Blacks is a fragment from a scene showing a running white warrior followed by a group of black, perhaps Nubian, mercenaries. Three fragments from a Knossos town house show a bluebird among flowers, and scenes of monkeys in a garden. There are three small fragments, too, of olive trees in relief, painted in delicate pinks and grays.

Galleries XVII and **XVIII**, containing the Giamalakis collection, are normally closed. Back on the ground floor, **Galleries XIX** and **XX** are sometimes open: They contain stone and bronze sculpture from the archaic and Greco-Roman periods. In **Gallery XIX** are three bronze figures from Dreros in eastern Crete, made of bronze hammered onto a wooden core and secured with pins. They show Apollo, Artemis and Leto.

KNOSSOS

The road to the Minoan palace of Knossos, 5 km from Iraklio, is signposted from Plateia Eleftheria: Bear left at the cemetery and again at the turning for the coastal highway. (The No. 2 bus for Knossos leaves every 15 minutes or so from a stop next to the Morosini Fountain.) At the 3.5 km mark, a side-road forks right to the village of **Fortetsa**, from where the Grand Vizier's artillery bombarded the city during the great siege. To the left is the University of Crete's science faculty, built on the site of an ancient cemetery, where more than three hundred tombs were unearthed with burials covering more than a millenium, from the Sub-Minoan to the early Christian periods. Curiously, no major cemetery from the period of the Minoan palaces has yet been discovered around Knossos, which prompted the peculiar

Above: Northern side of the central court-
yard. Right: The room of the tall pithoi.

hypothesis that the palace complex was simply a vast funerary monument. However, a stroll around its buildings, which still evoke an atmosphere of domestic luxury, is likely to dispel such notions. The road passes through the Roman city of Knossos, of which there is virtually nothing to see, and drops down towards the Keratos valley.

To the right, a driveway leads to the **Villa Ariadne**, the house built by Sir Arthur Evans, the British archaeologist, who bought the site of the palace at the turn of the century and dug there for the next 30 years, though the bulk of the excavation was completed between 1900 and 1906.

A Cretan excavator, Minos Kalokerinos, was the first to dig on the Kefala hill in 1878, unearthing some of the store-rooms and a dozen *pithoi* or tall storage jars. He immediately identified the building as the palace of his namesake King Minos, the legendary king of Crete mentioned in Homer's *Iliad*. Later, an American journalist, William Stillman, broached the idea that the building might have inspired the origins of the labyrinth myth in Greek legend. Evans arrived on Crete in 1894, but it was not until after the island became independent under Greek suzerainty and an archaeological law was drafted that he was able to purchase the entire site. While the excavations were in progress, Evans also had substantial sections of the palace reconstructed in reinforced concrete, in order to preserve the architecture, notably of the living quarters on the east side of the complex. The restorations have been sharply criticized, both by professional archaeologists and aesthetic purists, but without them it would be next to impossible to gain an impression of the size and scale of the palace. A few hundred meters further on, a left turn leads to the village of **Makritichos**, straggling down the hill to the Keratos stream, which for years has provided skilled excavators to work at Knossos.

In mythology, Knossos was known as the home of King Minos and the prison of the Minotaur, the hybrid monster born of Queen Pasiphae's love for a white bull. Tribute owed to Minos by Athens came regularly in the form of seven maidens and seven young men, who were devoured by the Minotaur. Then Theseus, the Athenian king's son, arrived among a group of sacrificial victims and killed the monster with the help of Ariadne, Minos' daughter. She gave him a sword and a ball of red thread to help him find his way back through the labyrinth. The rest of the story is less happy: The labyrinth, by the way, had been designed by the Athenian craftsman Daedalus who later escaped from Crete with his son Icarus on wings crafted from wax and feathers. Ariadne eloped with Theseus, but he abandoned her on the Aegean island of Naxos and went home to Athens.

The site of Knossos, a low hill, was occupied in Neolithic times since at least 6000 BC. In the Early Minoan period the settlement grew steadily before the hill-

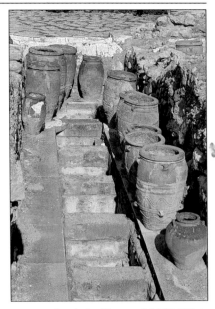

top was leveled off around 1900 BC to construct the Old Palace. After it was destroyed in a major earthquake around 1700 BC, the New Palace was constructed: Most of the restorations were done on the buildings from this period. The half-dozen imposing town-houses excavated around the palace, and the **Little Palace** next to the Villa Ariadne, were built around 1600 BC following another earthquake which damaged parts of the palace. At the same time, country houses and city mansions were built all over Crete, marking the peak of Minoan wealth and artistic achievement. Knossos was at its most densely populated, with town houses built close to the palace and buildings scattered over the surrounding hillsides. There is no evidence of a fortification wall. Estimates of the Late Bronze Age population of Knossos vary, but it is unlikely to have exceeded 20,000.

About 1450 BC, a major disaster struck the island: Palaces and villas were destroyed in fierce fires. Whether the cause was the eruption of the volcano of Thira (formerly Santorin), or invasion by armies from the Greek mainland is still the subject of heated discussions today. Only at Knosssos did life continue without a break, although there was some damage to the palace. 70 years later, however, the palace and its dependent buildings were razed in a fire that also cremated the old palace accounts that were written in Linear B (Old Greek) on clay tablets. The presence of the tablets, together with pottery in Mycenaean styles, suggests that in its final years, Knossos was the Mycenaean administrative center for the island. Parts of the palace appear to have been reoccupied around 1200 BC, but it was abandoned by the end of the Bronze Age and the site appears to have become a sanctuary. During the Geometric period, the town was situated to the north and west.

In later centuries, Knossos became a city state contesting power with Gortys in the south. But after the Roman conquest of AD 67, Gortys became the capital of the province of Crete and Cyrenaica – the area around Benghazi on the Libyan coast. Fine mansions decorated with statues and mosaic floors were built at Knossos during the Roman period: One, the **Villa Dionysos**, has been excavated but is not open to the public. In the early Christian period, Knossos was the seat of a bishop, and two basilicas, dating from the fifth and sixth centuries AD, have been excavated north of the Roman city. By the time of the Arab conquest in 824, Knossos had declined in importance. Iraklio, named Rabd-el-Khandak by the Arabs, became the island's capital.

The approach to the palace is from the west, past a bust of Evans, into a paved courtyard with raised walkways. To the left are three deep circular walled pits which may have served as granaries. During rebuilding at the end of the Old Palace period, they were stuffed with rubbish, including fine pottery fragments, and then paved over. Looking down into the central pit, you can see a staircase from an earlier house, dated to 2000 BC.

The courtyard is overlooked by the remains of the west façade, whose huge masonry blocks were once faced with gypsum, quarried south of the palace. In the southern corner is the **west entrance** and porch, which led through heavy wooden doors – the sockets for the doorposts survive – into the **Corridor of the Procession Fresco**. Paved with gypsum flagstones, it turned left and left again around the southwest corner of the palace complex to the **central court**. Part of the corridor has disappeared through erosion of the hillside, so you have to enter through a reconstructed doorway.

Passing a downwards-tapering column you reach the **South Propylaea**, an imposing roofed gateway, supported by four impressive columns, which has been partially restored. (Minoan columns were made of wood, but no satisfactory explanation has been given as to why they taper in reverse.) The fresco reproduction is a detail from the Procession Fresco displayed in the Iraklio Archaeological Museum. A pair of stone horns of consecration on a wall to the right once decorated the top of the south façade of the palace. The large *pithoi*, looking rather out of place in such a grand entranceway, date from the period of resettlement in the ruins of the palace around 1200 BC.

Climbing a monumental staircase you reach the **Upper Propylaea** leading on to the **Piano Nobile**, as Evans called the floor where the state reception halls were probably located, borrowing the term from the Italian Renaissance. This floor was restored on the evidence of architectural remains which collapsed onto the floor below when the palace was destroyed. The lobby, Evans' porticoed vestibule, leads into a large hall with a small room to one side which held a large number of **stone rhytons**, including the

1 West Porch
2 Processional Corridor
3 Central Court
4 South Propylaia
5 Staircase to Piano Nobile
6 Throne Room
7 Pillar Crypt
8 Room of the Tall Pithos
9 Grand Staircase
10 Hall of Double Axes
11 Hall of Colonnades
12 King's Megaron
13 Queen's Megaron
14 Bathroom
15 Queen's Toilet
16 East Portico
17 Court of the Stone Spout
18 Magazines of the Great Pithoi
19 Royal Pottery Stores
20 East Bastion
21 Magazines of the Medallion Pithoi
22 North Entrance
23 Pillar Hall
24 North-East Magazines
25 Lustral Area
26 Theatre Area
27 West Court
28 Walled Pits
29 Altar
30 Lower Corridor
31 Lower Magazines
32 Old Keep
33 North-East House
34 South-East House
35 House of the Chancel Screen
36 South House

KNOSSOS

0   10   20   30   40m

Lioness Head rhyton in the Iraklio Archaeological Museum. A long upper corridor on a north-south axis had rooms opening off both sides, but a gap was left in the reconstruction so that you look down into the **corridor of the magazines** immediately below and the long, narrow storerooms opening off it. Originally there were 23, some with additional storage space in stone chests beneath the floor, some of them lined with lead. Poles topped with double axes would have stood in the pyramid-shaped stone blocks left in the corridor, like those from the Nirou Hani villa on display in the museum. The huge *pithoi* in the magazines held oil, wine and grain: According to one estimate there was room for at least 400 jars with a total capacity of more than 75,000 liters of oil or wine. To the left of the **upper corridor** are two large

Above: Life as it might have been in the room with the Dolphin fresco. Right: The room with the Dolphin fresco reconstructed in modern Knossos.

inter-connecting rooms which Evans partially restored. Across the corridor are smaller rooms, one of which contains copies of several frescoes now in the museum, among them the Bull-leaper, the Captain of the Blacks and two panels of the miniature frescoes. One shows a tripartite shrine of the kind found in the palace. Five columns surround a lightwell, the main source of light and ventilation for the inner rooms of the palace.

To the left, a small staircase leads down to the **central court** near the Throne Room. A rounded corner at the bottom of the stairs is a left-over from the Old Palace. The court, about 50 m long and 25 m wide, was once paved and is aligned northeast and southwest like those at Festos and Malia. Scholars are divided over whether it was used for bull games: Evans believed they were more likely to have been held outside the east wing of the palace, beside the Keratos stream. An antechamber, equipped with a replica stone seat and a purple stone basin which was found in a nearby passageway, leads to the **Throne Room**. It is now fenced off, but from the doorway you can inspect the original throne, made of gypsum with a tall wavy back, and flanked by twin stone benches. The fresco of heraldic griffins in a field of lilies, dating from the period of Mycenaean influence, adds formality to the small room. Evans found overturned jars and large stone alabastrons on the floor, which he interpreted as part of a last-minute ritual to avert the disaster that led to the palace's destruction. Opposite the throne, steps lead down into a lustral basin, one of the small gypsum-paneled spaces that still baffle archaeologists. They are generally thought to have been used for religious rituals. Off the Throne Room was a small shrine.

Just south of the Throne Room, past a staircase leading to the Piano Nobile, is a **Tripartite Shrine**, similar to the one pictured in the miniature frescoes, where the sanctuary lies behind a façade of twin columns standing on either side of a central section supported by a single column.

Beside the shrine is the **Lobby of the Stone Seat**, from which you can peer into one of two dark **pillar crypts**, thought to have been used for religious rituals, perhaps involving sacrifices. Troughs sunk into the floor at the base of the pillar may have been used as receptacles for liquid offerings.

The Lobby leads into the **room of the tall pithoi** and the **Temple Repositories**, named for the two large chest-shaped pits in the floor, which originally had lids. A smaller one between them was inserted at a later date. The outer chest contained the faience figures of the snake goddesses and other shrine equipment now displayed in Gallery IV of the Iraklio Archaeological Museum. The other large chest was robbed: Evans found only a few fragments of gold leaf. Heading back to the south end of the Court, you find a copy of the priest-king figure from the Procession Fresco, looking out towards the open space.

Crossing to the right-hand side of the Court, you go down the elegant **grand**

145

staircase leading to the Domestic Quarter, originally built into the side of the hill. Four flights of gypsum steps survive and there may have been a fifth. They are lit by a deep lightwell. This part of the palace shows off Minoan architecture at its best: The rooms are divided by pier-and-door partitions to ensure warmth and privacy when closed, or an airy coolness in summer. Three smaller staircases linking the different storeys and corridors between the rooms contribute to the labyrinth atmosphere.

The reproduction of the **Shield Fresco**, of animal hides stretched on a frame into a figure-of-eight shape, may have decorated the hall of the double axes below, just along the corridor from the hall of the colonnades. It is named for the double axe masons' marks on the blocks of the adjoining lightwell, but is also known as the King's megaron. The room was divided by double doors and had a sheltered L-shaped portico at one end.

A passage leads southwest into the **Queen's megaron**, decorated with copies of the lively **Dolphin Fresco** and colorful rosettes, and furnished with stone benches. An old palace floor with irregular paving is visible below the later floor level. Beside the Queen's megaron is a **bathroom** fitted with a clay tub. Beyond, a narrow corridor leads to a **toilet** with a drainage system to allow for flushing. Grooves in the wall and floor suggest that a wooden seat was fixed above the drain. An eleborate drainage system channeled waste water down to the Keratos. The **court of the distaffs**, also named after the mason's marks found on its wall, provides light for this area. Leaving the living quarters from the Queen's veranda and then turning left, you go by the terrace flanking the hall of the double Axes to the **east portico**. This is the area of the palace workshops. A parallel corridor

Right: Relief of a bull and rebuilt Minoan columns.

leads past a narrow storeroom containing pieces of lapis lacedemonios, a speckled green stone found only in the southern Peloponnese region of mainland Greece and used for making stone vases and seals. It appears to have been a carver's workshop and some of the lumps show traces of work in progress. To the north is a room with a stone bench, which may have been a potter's workshop. Continuing north, you arrive at the **court of the stone spout**, which can be seen high up on the west wall and apparently channeled rain water to a cistern outside the court. Ahead are the **magazines of the giant pithoi**, part of a storeroom complex of the Old Palace: The huge vases date from around 1800 BC. Further north are the **royal pottery stores**, also a survival from the earlier palace, where fine pottery from Kamares was found.

A staircase leads down to the **east bastion**, marking the east entrance to the palace. Beside the steps is a stone water channel, descending in a series of parabolic curves interspersed with settling basins – the Minoan equivalent of a storm drainage system. Climbing again, you pass the giant pithoi and arrive in the **corridor of the chess board**, where the richly decorated gaming board in Gallery IV of the Iraklio Archaeological Museum was found. A line of tapering clay pipes, part of the drainage system, can be seen beneath the corridor, before you reach the **magazine of the medallion pithoi**. From here, you can return to the grand staircase by way of the **corridor of the Beys**, or go back to the central court up a staircase to the right.

From the central court, you head right for the **north entrance passage**. To the left was a series of rooms where the Saffron Gatherer and miniature frescoes were found. Beneath them were deep, stone-lined pits from the Old Palace period, which may have been granaries, or, as Evans suggested, dungeons. The entrance itself is guarded by a copy of a

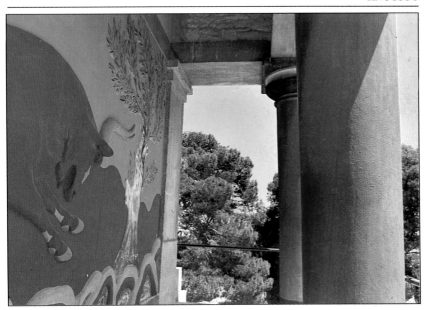

relief fresco of a charging bull in an olive grove, perhaps a scene from a bull catch. Evans thought that this fresco may have remained above the ruins for a long period after the destruction of the palace. If so, it must have helped embed the legend of the Minotaur in popular memory. The entrance was narrowed when the later palace was built and the **north pillar hall** was added, with a double row of gypsum pillars. According to one theory, the palace banquet hall was located above the pillar hall. Domestic utensils were found in the neighboring northeast magazines. To the left, past the north portico, is the **North Lustral Basin**, the biggest of the lustral basins at Knossos. Evans thought, visitors to the palace underwent a ritual cleansing and anointing before being admitted.

Outside the palace, to the northwest, is the paved **theater area**, overlooking a flight of steps leading down to the Royal Road to the west. This may have been a reception area. The road continued west into the Minoan town and branched north

to the Little Palace. It was lined with houses: In one of them Evans found fresco fragments from around 1600 BC that were pieced together to reconstruct the Bluebird scene. On the opposite side of the road was a building that was identified as an armory. Of the surrounding sites, the south house, the house of the sacrificed oxen and the house of the fallen blocks, where a pile of collapsed masonry from the south façade of the palace illustrates the force of the earthquake that destroyed the Old Palace, are most accessible, lying south of the main complex. Further on down the valley is the **caravanserai** (now closed to the public) where visitors from the south stopped before crossing a viaduct across the Vlichias stream and approaching the southwest entrance to the palace.

The **Little Palace**, where the bull's head rhyton displayed in the Archaeological Museum was found, and the unexplored mansion (which was eventually excavated in the 1970s), lie on the other side of the road from Iraklio, but are also closed to visitors. To the west, further excavations in the Minoan town revealed a house of the New Palace period which apparently was used as a cult center. In a basement room, the bones of at least three children were found: ten per cent of them were marked with cuts from a knife indicating that the flesh had been deliberately removed. The find, which stirred considerable controversy among archaeologists, has been interpreted as an isolated instance of ritual cannibalism in Minoan religion, but it does raise doubts about Evans's picture of life at ancient Knossos as orderly, peaceful and relatively carefree.

ARHANES AND MOUNT IOUHTAS

Leaving Iraklio by the Knossos Road, you pass the palace and Spilia to take the right-hand fork for Arhanes at 9.5 km. One kilometer further on is a sharp bend, where in April 1944 two British officers, Patrick Leigh Fermor and Stanley Moss, along with a group of Cretan resistance fighters captured General Kreipe, commander of the German forces on the island, while he was driving from his headquarters in Arhanes to his quarters at the Villa Ariadne at Knossos. Kreipe was sent to Egypt aboard a Royal Navy submarine after an arduous 18-day trek through the mountains to the south coast, hiding in caves to avoid pursuit.

A flourishing village, **Arhanes** is famed for its wine and lamb chops, available in the local tavernas. Its wealth goes back to Minoan times. Sir Arthur Evans excavated a reservoir which may have supplied Knossos with water, while Dr. Giannis Sakellarakis and his wife have excavated three important sites around the village. There are remains of a palace-style building in the Tourkogeitonia

Right: From the summit of Mount Iouhtas you can see all the way to Iraklio and the northern shore.

area of Arhanes. It produced pieces of a miniature fresco and fragments of an ivory statuette of similar quality to the Knossos bull-leaper figure. At **Fourni,** a hilltop to the northwest of the village, a **Minoan cemetery** was found, including an ossuary, dated to the Early Minoan period (around 2500 BC), and an unplundered royal tomb – the first unearthed in Crete. It contained the body of a young woman, accompanied by more than 100 pieces of gold and jewelry, dated to around 1400 BC.

On the north slope of Mount Iouhtas, 3 km northwest of the village, a **Minoan shrine** was unearthed. A dirt track, the first turning to the right after passing the church on the way into the village, leads up past the local rubbish dump and on to the site. Of the three rooms, the central one contained a pair of lifesize clay feet, probably belonging to a wooden idol. The west room held evidence of a ritual sacrifice, interrupted when the building collapsed in the great earthquake of 1700 BC that destroyed the old palaces. But the bones found on an altar, along with a bronze knife, were those of a young man, indicating that in moments of crisis, the Minoans were prepared to carry out human sacrifice.

South from Arhanes, the road leads on to the Minoan villa of **Vathipetro**, destroyed around 1450 BC. It contained evidence of weaving and pottery making as well as wine and olive presses. Heading back towards Arhanes a left turn onto a dirt track takes you up **Mount Iouhtas**, which has a magnificent view over the north coast of the island. A Minoan sanctuary has been excavated beside the telecommunications relay station on the north tip of the peak.

From Iraklio to Kanli Kastelli

Leaving Iraklio by the Hania Gate, you turn left at the first traffic light outside the walls. The road passes through vine-

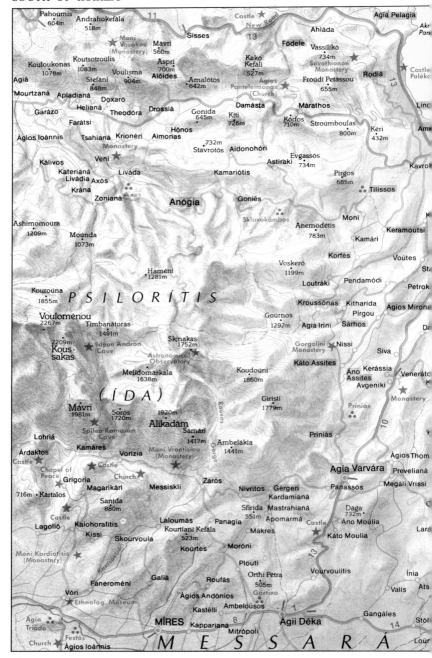

Pahoúmis 604m
Andrahokefála 518m
Sísses
Castle New Road
Ahláda
Agía Pelagía
Akr Pan

Moní Vosákou (Monastery)
Mávri 560m
Fódele
Vassilikó 734m
Savathíanon Monastery
Castle Palék

Koutsotroúlis 1083m
Kouloúkonas 1078m
Voulísma 904m
Aspri 700m
Alóides
Kakó Kefáli 527m
Ágios Panteleímonas (Church)
Froudí Petássou 655m
Rodiá

Agiá
Stefáni 848m
Amalótos 642m

Mourtzaná
Apladianá
Doxaró
Damásta
Márathos
Linc

Garázo
Heliana
Theodóra
Drossiá
Gónida 645m
Kíti 726m
Kórfos 710m
Stroúmboulas 800m
Kéri 432m
Am

Farátsi

Ágios Ioánnis
Tsahianá
Krionéri
Aimonas
Hónos
732m
Stavrotós
Aidonohóri
Evgassós 734m
Astiráki

Monastery
Káma
Kávro

Kálivos
Veni
Liváda
Kamariótis
Pírgos 685m
Tilíssos

Kateriana
Livádia
Axós
Krána
Zonianá
Anógia
Goniés
Sklavokámbos
Moní
Anemodétis 783m
Keramoútsi
Kamári
K

Ashimomoúra 1209m
Moúnda 1073m
Korfés
Voútes
St

Hameni 1281m
Voskeró 1199m
Loutráki
Pendamódi
Petrok

Kouroúna 1855m
P S I L O R Í T I S
Kroussónas
Kitharída
Pírgou
Ágios Miróna
Da

Vouloménou 2267m
Timbanátoras 1491m
Goúrnos 1292m
Agía Iríni
Sárhos

2209m
Kous-sakas
Ideon Andron (Cave)
Skínakas 1752m
Astronomical Observatory
Gorgolíni Monastery
Nissi
Siva

Melidomáskala 1638m
Koudoúni 1860m
Káto Assítes
Áno Assítes
Kerássia
Avgenikí
Veneráto
K

Mávri 1981m
Soros 1720m
1920m
Alikadám
Giristí 1779m
Priniás
Monastery

Lohriá
Spílea Kamáron Cave
Samári 1417m
Rouvas Gorge
Priniás

Árdaktos
Castle
Kamáres
Vorizía
Moní Vrontisíou (Monastery)
Ambelákia 1441m
Ágios Thom

Chapel of Peace
Castle
Church
Agía Varvára
Preveliana

Grigoriá
Magarikári
Messiskli
Zarós
Nívritos
Gérgeri
Kardamianá
Panassós
Megáli Vríssi

716m
Kártalos
Sanída 880m
Sfírida 551m
Mastrahiana
Apomarmá
Daga 732m
Áno Moúlia
Lará

Lagolió
Kaloharafitis
Kissi
Laloumás
Kourtíani Kefála 523m
Panagía
Mákres
Castle
Káto Moúlia

Skoúrvoula
Kourtés
Moróni
Plouti

Moní Kardiofisis (Monastery)
Faneroméni
Galiá
Roufás
Orthí Petra 505m
Vourvoulítis
Inia

Vóri
Ethnolog. Museum
Ágios Andónios
Gortína
Valis
Ats

Agía Triáda
Church
Festós
Ágios Ioánnis
Kastélli
Kapparianá
Ambeloúsos
MÍRES
8
Mitrópoli
Ágii Déka
Gangáles
14
Stöl
Loúr

M E S S A R Á

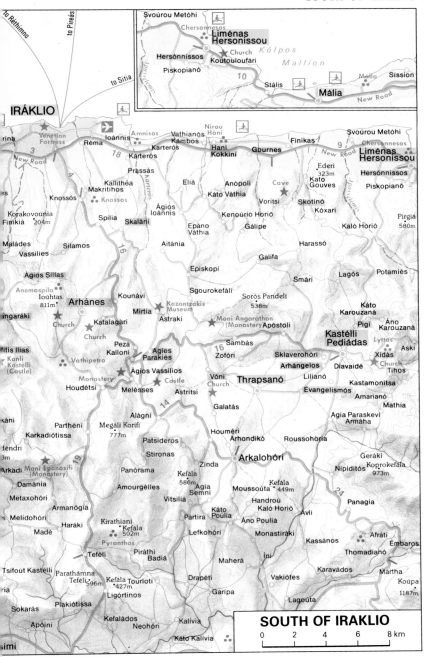

SOUTH OF IRAKLIO

0   2   4   6   8 km

151

yards and along a river valley before climbing to Tsangaraki and the village of **Profitis Elias**, 19 km away. It used to be known as **Kanli Kastelli**, the Turkish for "bloody castle" after a 1647 battle in which the Venetians severely defeated the Turks. On the rocky hill above the village is the castle of **Temenos**, built by Nikiforos Fokas after he had driven the Saracens off the island in 961. He intended to make it the center of a new inland capital, to protect the Cretans from pirate raids. But few islanders were willing to move away from Iraklio and Fokas was called back to Constantinople before he could build anything more than the castle.

The fortifications were restored in the 14th century and in the 16th century, when Muslim pirates again threatened Crete. From the top of the village, a path

Above: A vineyard in spring – the tender leaves are used to make dolmades. Right: Grapes are dried to raisins on strips of paper.

leads up to the fortress along the north side of the hill. The main north entrance is guarded by overlapping curtain walls. There are few visible remains on the summit of the twin-peaked hill, but the view is impressive. The road continues for 6 km to Venerato on the Festos road, or you can go back to Tsangaraki and turn right 2 km further on to Agios Syllas and Fortetsa and down to the Knossos road, with a left turn bringing you back into the city center.

TILISSOS

Leaving Iraklio by the Hania Gate, take the Old Road for Rethimno, turning off for **Tilissos** after 10 km. The road climbs another 3 km to reach the village, passing through the vineyards of the Malevizi district, famed in medieval times for its sweet grapes which produced the wine known in western Europe as Malmsey. In Minoan times, Tilissos straddled the route from Knossos to western Crete through the foothills of Mount

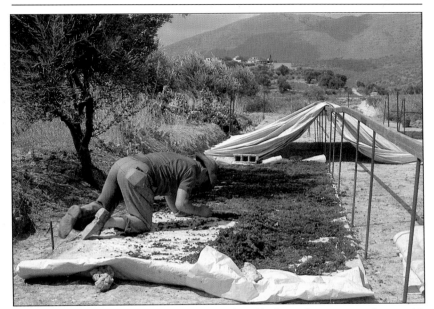

Ida (Psiloritis). Even its name is thought to be a survival from the Bronze Age: On Linear B tablets it appears as *Tu-ri-so*.

The complex of three Minoan villas, built at the same time as the later palace at Knossos, lies on the outskirts of the village. It was first excavated early this century after the three huge bronze cauldrons displayed in the Archaeological Museum were discovered by chance. House A, in the center, consists of two blocks linked by an open courtyard. It has all the architectural features of a wealthy two-storey Minoan house, including storerooms still containing tall storage jars. House B is built on a rectangular plan with few recognizable architectural features. House C has well-preserved walls standing remarkably high and a circular cistern built when the site was re-occupied in the post-palace period. A paved Minoan road runs along the length of its west side.

Beyond Tilissos, the road climbs through more mountainous country. 6 km further on it cuts across another Minoan site, this time a large country house with walls built of roughly hewn fieldstone rather than fine masonry. It overlooks the **Sklavokampos valley**, named after Slavs resettled there by the Byzantine Emperor Nikiforos Fokas in the tenth century. The road continues past the village of Gonies to reach Anogia, 32 km from Iraklio.

From Iraklion to Fodele

Leaving Iraklio by the Hania Gate, take the New Road west, which climbs above the broad sweep of the coastal plain. At 10 km, look right for the **castle of Palekastro** which was captured by the Venetians from the Genoese, and later rebuilt about 1573 as part of a massive program of fortification against the Turks. A stone lion of St. Mark in relief still looks out from the ramparts. 3 km further on, a dirt road leads right to **Ligaria bay**, a good place for a swim after a morning's sightseeing. Beyond lies **Agia Pelagia**, where a hotel complex is built over Minoan and classical remains.

A turning left leads up to the village of **Rodia** with a spectacular view over Iraklio bay. Some medieval houses survive, and 5 km beyond is the superbly situated **Savathianon Cloister**. The turning for Fodele comes at the 22-km mark, where the road winds into a narrow valley. In 1668, the beach opposite was the landing place of an Ottoman army under the Grand Vizier Mehmet Koprulu, which finally forced the Venetian defenders of Iraklio to surrender the following year.

Fodele is traditionally thought of as the birthplace of the painter Domenikos Theotokopoulos (1541-1616), better known as El Greco, although recent research indicates he was probably born in Iraklio. El Greco, who made his way to Toledo in Spain after first emigrating to Venice, like many other ambitious young Cretans in the Renaissance, is commemorated with a bust and an inscription in Greek and Spanish on a stone quarried in Toledo. It was erected in 1934 by students and faculty of the University of Valladolid, Spain.

From the center of the village, a track leads down to and across the stream and then up the opposite side of the valley to the fresco-decorated Byzantine **church of the Panagia**, built among the ruins of an eighth-century Christian basilica.

SOUTHEAST OF IRAKLIO

From Iraklio to the Kazantzakis Museum and to Kastelli Pediadas

Heading out of Iraklio, you take the Knossos road, passing the palace on your left and climbing up the hill past the early 19th-century aqueduct at the top of Keratos valley. At the 10 km mark, you branch left for the village of **Skalani**. A right turn just before the village, signposted for the Nikos Kazantzakis Mu-

Right: The potters of Thrapsano still practice their traditional art.

seum, puts you on the road for **Mirtia**, the modern name for Varvari, the village where the novelist's father, a prosperous Iraklio merchant, was born. (Kazantzakis senior appears, thinly disguised as the fervent drinker and patriot Captain Mihalis, in the novel *Freedom or Death*). From there the road continues south through rolling hills carpeted with vineyards. There are spectacular views across to the foothills of **Mount Ida** rising on the right and of **Mount Dikti** on the left. After 10 km, the road branches right into the village.

The **Nikos Kazantzakis Museum** is housed in a restored mansion overlooking the village square. It contains an interesting collection of photographs and memorabilia illustrating Kazantzakis' literary career, travels and political involvement, starting with his childhood in Crete, when the family fled the island more than once to escape Turkish reprisals after a rebellion. After law school in Athens and philosophical studies in France, Germany and Italy, he divided his time between Athens and a house on the island of Aegina. He served briefly as minister of education in 1945 before leaving Greece and settling in Antibes in the South of France. He died in Freiburg, Germany. One room is devoted to Zorba, his partner in a lignite-mining venture in the southern Peleponnese, who inspired his best-known novel *Zorba the Greek*. An upstairs section holds theatrical memorabilia, from productions of his own plays as well as adaptations of the novels as plays, musicals and films.

Beyond Mirtia, the road continues to **Agia Paraskevi** where you take a left turn. Continue for 6 km before taking a right to **Voni**. Bearing left just outside the village, then right a kilometer further on, you head for the village of **Thrapsano**, famed for its pottery-making tradition. The workshops specialize in those large storage jars known as *pithoi.* Each can take almost a week to make. At some

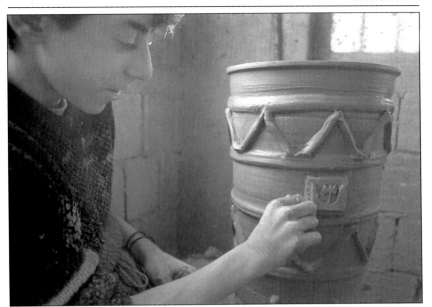

shops you can pay by credit card and have your *pithoi* shipped home by air. 3 km beyond Thrapsano on the road to Kastelli lies the village of **Evangelismos**, where the domed cruciform church of the same name has some rare 14th century fresco scenes from the Old Testament, including the Garden of Eden and the Creation. Ask for the key to the church, which is kept by *kiria* Katerina at the café across the street. Continuing towards Kastelli, you pass through **Arhangelos** before reaching **Sklavero**, where the church of Isodia Theotokou (known to villagers as the Panagia) contains some good quality frescoes, dating from the fifteenth century. They include a lively scene of St. George slaying a dragon and rescuing a princess.

Kastelli, the center of the **Pediada district**, is named after a Venetian castle which no longer exists. You follow the signs for Iraklio through the town, but when the road swings left, keep straight on for the village of **Xidas**, 3.5 km further on. There are few remains to be seen,

but the view over the Pediada district and up towards Lassithi is well worth the short climb up to the two churches that mark the site.

The simplest route back to Iraklio is to return to Kastelli and follow the signs for Iraklio. For **Agios Panteleimon**, a church with interesting frescoes of the 13th/14th century, turn right down a dirt track just under 1 km from the town. After 2 km you reach the church, which is flanked by two oak trees and a pleasant taverna, where the key is kept. (If it's closed, the key can be found at the village of **Pigi**, another kilometer down the track.) The church incorporates many fragments of ancient masonry and inscriptions. From Pigi, you head for the Lassithi road, 8 km away, and then turn left for the drive back to the coastal highway and Iraklio.

THE SOUTH

Leaving Iraklio by the Hania Gate, you turn left to Mires and Festos at the 2.5 km mark. A right turn 5 km further on is

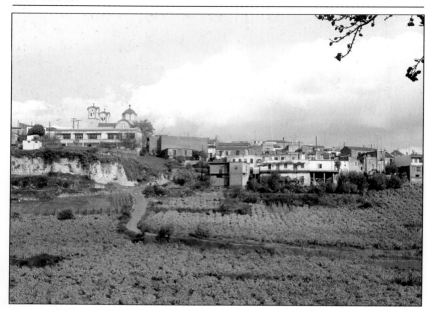

signposted for Agios Mironas. This is an alternative route, which is slower but has much less traffic. The road climbs past the new University of Crete hospital buildings, and the view opens out: You look back to Iraklio and the sea, and to left and right over valleys chequered with vineyards and olive groves.

At 13.5 km, you reach **Agios Mironas**, an attractive village complete with a statue of a local revolutionary hero, Giannis Makrakis, and a 13th-century church dedicated to (Saint) Agios Mironas, a third-century Bishop of Knossos, who suffered a martyr's death. In local legend, he was famed for killing a dragon that was devouring the faithful. On the way out of the village, you pass his hermitage on the left-hand side of the road, a grotto with icons and censers hung against a background of dripping rock.

Above: Autumn has settled in the vineyards around the village of Agios Mironas. Right: The Odeion of Gortina (Gortys), where the first Code of Laws was found.

Agios Mironas is the capital of the Malevisi district, renowned already in Venetian times for growing the grapes which produced a sweet wine.

At 19 km you reach **Kato Asites**. From here, a side road ascends to the Gorgoleni convent, 2 km away, with a magnificent view across much of central Crete. The road continues into the foothills of Mount Ida to **Sarhos** and **Kroussonas**, 8 km away, a noted weaving center, from which you can return to Iraklio through Korfos and Keramoutsi.

Continuing south, you pass **Ano Asites** to reach a flat promontory overlooking the main road to southern Crete, with a white chapel (**Agios Panteleimon**) built on its tip. This was the acropolis of the ancient city of Rhizenia. At 23.5 km, a path leads off to the site. Italian archaeologists excavating here found a Late-Minoan refuge site, dating from the end of the Bronze Age, with a sanctuary that remained in use into the seventh century BC. The main foundations of two seventh-century temples were also unear-

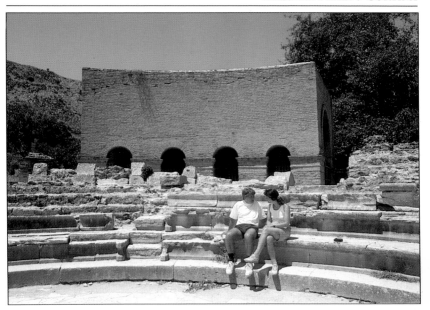

thed and the ruins of a Hellenistic fortress can be seen. The road passes through the village of **Prinias** and then joins the main Phaestos route at the village of **Agia Varvara**, said to lie at the exact center of the island.

THE MESSARA PLAIN

The **Messara Plain**, the rich agricultural heartland of Crete, comes into view as you continue south. It is filled with olive groves interspersed with hundreds of plastic-covered greenhouses where cucumbers and tomatoes are grown. Temperatures are noticeably warmer here than in the north of the island. The plain runs parallel to the south coast, but is separated from it by the arid **Asteroussia Mountains**. In Early Minoan times, this region was already extensively settled before Festos became the center of economic activity in around 2000 BC.

44 km further is the village of **Agii Deka**, named after ten early Christian martyrs who died, like Agios Mironas,

under the persecutions of the Roman Emperor Decius in the third century AD. A signpost leads around the village to the 13th-century church named after them. It was partly constructed – like many other buildings in the village – of re-used masonry from the Roman city of **Gortina** (Gortys).

The sprawling site of **Gortina**, the capital of Crete in the Roman imperial period, lies 2 km further on, among the olive groves to the left of the road. To the right is the **Basilica of St. Titus** (Agios Titos), the island's patron saint. This well-preserved church, dating from the sixth century AD, is supposed to be the burial place of the saint, who was asked by St. Paul in 67 AD to convert the Cretans to Christianity. To the north lies the **Odeion**, a small first-century-BC amphitheater rebuilt in the second century AD. Behind the Odeion is a brick shelter where the **Gortys Law Code**, inscribed on stone blocks, is displayed. It is the earliest of its kind in Europe, and dates from the first half of the fifth century BC. It is written in a Doric dialect and inscribed in boustrophedon style, in the way an ox ploughs a field: The lines read alternately from left to right and then from right to left. It is 600 lines long and contains detailed laws on marriage, divorce, assault and rape, inheritance, property and the status of slaves. The code is said to have inspired the lawgivers of ancient Athens and Sparta, Solon and Lycurgos, and was also much admired by Plato.

A **Venetian watermill** stands on the river bank just beyond the Odeion: Some of the law code blocks were found in the stream nearby. From the Odeion, a path climbs to the **acropolis** of Gortina, the heart of the city in classical Greek times, when it vied with Knossos for supremacy. Much of the Roman city is still unexcavated, but Italian archaeologists, who have worked here since the 1880s, recently completed a full topographical

Above: Sun reflecting on the hot-houses in the Messara Plain.

158

survey, and a detailed plan is displayed at several points on the footpaths signposted around the site. The remains include several temples, a well-preserved small theater and public baths. Gortina was destroyed in the seventh century by Arab raiders and never rebuilt.

FESTOS

Continuing through **Mires**, the market town of the Messara Plain, you reach the left turn for **Festos** (Phaistos) and Agia Triada at 59.5 km. Cross the Geropotamos river and climb the hill to the **Minoan palace**. It is magnificently situated with a panoramic view across the plain to the south and up to the twin peaks of Mount Ida, also known as Psiloritis. The site was occupied in the Neolithic and the Early Minoan times before the Old Palace was built around 1900 BC. Like Knossos, the palace was destroyed in a devastating earthquake around 1700 BC and immediately rebuilt on a grander scale. The later palace was razed around

Map labels (left to right, top to bottom):

TIMBÁKI · Fáneroméni · Galiá · Roufás · 505m Górtina · Vóri · Ethnolog. Museum · Ágios Andónios · Kastélli · Ambelóusos · Agía Triáda · MÍRES · Kapparianá · 8 · Ágii Déka · Festós · Mitrópoli · Kamilári · Ágios Ioánnis · Petrokefáli · M E S S A R Á · Houstoulianá · Church · Kalamáki · Platános · Gerop ótamos · Pitsídia · Sivas · Koussés · Péri · Alithíni · Flathiakés · Vagioniá · Pómbia · Apessokári · Listaros · Plóra · Vassiliká Anógia · Vigla 659m · Moni Apezanón (Monastery) · Kandila · Harkokefála 375m · Agios Kirillos · Megáli Korifí 546m · Vassiliki · Moni Odigitrios (Monastery) · Pigaidákia · A S T E R O Ú S S I A · Miamoú · Liondária 467m · Andiskári · Tsoúros 593m · Vigla 685m · Krótos · Plátia Peramata · Lamnassos 492m · Kalí · Kalógiros Liménes 287m · Papadogiánnis · Kefáli 391m · Léndas · Akrotíri Lithinó · Lebena · **WEST MESSARA** · 0 2 4 km · to Kókkinos Pírgos · Kommós · Mátala

1450 BC in the great wave of destruction that spread across the island. Festos was reoccupied at the end of the Bronze Age and went on to became a flourishing Greek city until it was wiped out by Gortina in the second century BC.

Festos has been excavated by Italian archaeologists since Frederico Halbherr started digging in 1900. Its plan echoes Knossos in many respects, with an imposing entrance from the west leading into the central court, shrines and storerooms side by side, reception rooms to the north, workshops in the northeast quarter and town houses built close alongside. But the monumental **grand staircase**, with shallow steps leading up to the **Propylaea**, is a unique feature. You enter down a flight of stairs leading into the west court, where the façade of the Old Palace has been exposed. Above it, the later palace façade is set 10 m back.

Climbing the grand staircase you pass through the Propylaea porch into a light-well and then take a narrow staircase down to the **central court**. Large *pithoi* are still in place in the storerooms of the later palace to the right. In front of the double row of store-rooms of the later palace was a square hall looking out to the court. Further right, the southern section of the palace has been eroded away, as has much of its eastern area. Along both long sides of the central court stone bases can be seen for wooden columns that supported a portico. The north side of the court is cut by an elaborate doorway flanked by wooden pillars and recesses where a guard may have stood. Their walls are painted with a simple diamond pattern in red on a white ground. Double doors opened onto another passageway, similarly painted, that led up to the reception rooms on the upper floor.

The passage leads to the **north court** and then to the **private quarters** which have been roofed and fenced off. Looking in, you see a room with pier-and-door partitions, similar to the king's Megaron at Knossos, with a portico to the east and a verandah to the north with a view of Mount Ida (Psiloritis). A dark smudge

159

beneath the right-hand peak marks the **Kamares Cave**, where the delicate multi-colored pottery displayed in Gallery III of the Iraklio Archaeological Museum was originally found. To the south, a smaller room with a gypsum bench and four columns resembles the queen's Megaron at Knossos. West of the larger megaron is a **lustral basin**, lined with fresh gypsum slabs, and a toilet connected to a drain in a separate complex of rooms. In the westernmost of these is a series of chests made of mudbrick: In one of them the Festos Disk was found in 1903. Returning by the stairs leading south you pass the **workshop area** along one side of the east court. A metalworking furnace is fenced off in its center. To the south are the rooms known as the east wing, including a main hall, a peristyle court, a bathtub and a colonnaded court that offers a stunning wiew across the landscape to the Asteroussia Mountains.

Right: The monastery of Valsamonero on the south slope of Mount Ida.

Agia Triada

The road to Agia Triada takes you past a church which once belonged to the **St. George Monastery** (Agios Georgios) and winds around the western edge of the ridge. (A footpath is signposted which takes you through orange groves to the site in about 30 minutes). The site has a spectacular view over the **Gulf of Messara**, with the **Paximadia Islets** at its center. **Agia Triada**, dating from the Later Palace period, was once thought to be a summer residence for the rulers of Festos, but recently scholars have argued that it consists of two separate but related villas, like those at Tilissos. The site was reoccupied after the 1450 BC destruction and the area of the lower town with its row of shops was constructed around 1200 BC.

On the upper level, the court was overlooked by Later Palace-era buildings laid out in an L-shape. The eastern wing had an elaborate drainage system and rooms decorated with gypsum slabs. A staircase

1 Corridor
2 Central Court
3 Shrine
4 Grand Staircase
5 Propylon
6 West Court, Theatre Area
7 Colonnade
8 North Court
9 King's Megaron
10 Queen's Megaron
11 Lustral Area
12 Workrooms

13 East Court
14 East Megaron
15 Stores
16 North-West Steps
17 Treasure Chamber
18 Pillar Shrine
19 Peristyle
20 Potter's Store

FESTOS
0   10   20 m

leads down to the lower court, enclosed to the east by a five-columned portico and to the north by a thick-walled building which may have been a warehouse. A Minoan road leading to the sea starts from the upper courtyard, passing along the north side of the L-shaped complex. To the left are the storerooms, some still containing huge *pithoi*. A gypsum staircase was totally blackened by the fierce fire that destroyed the building. The rooms in the western wing had a fine view of the sea. A hall with pier-and-door partitions led into two successive columned porticoes, then to the lightwell and a small inner room with gypsum benches around the walls. The gypsum slab in the center may have been a base for a bed.

One of the adjoining set of rooms to the north was decorated with frescoes depicting a woman in a garden and a cat hunting a pheasant that are now in the Iraklio Archaeological Museum. The famous stone vases fell from upper rooms in the west wing, while the bronze ingots

were found in a narrow treasury on the lower floor north of the porticoed hall.

Back in the lower court, you take the stairway down to the town, which mostly dates from the 14th and 13th centuries BC, although some buildings are constructed over houses of the Later Palace period. Opposite, on the right-hand side, is a line of shops, the only ones known from the Cretan Bronze Age. On the way out, the final building to the east is a 14th-century-BC shrine which had a frescoed floor with marine motifs, now in the Iraklio Archaeological Museum.

Vori, Valsamonero and Vrondisi

Returning to the main road after visiting Festos and Agia Triada, you turn left in the direction of **Timbaki**, an agricultural village being transformed into a wealthy market town thanks to the income from growing early vegetables in greenhouses. A right turning is signposted for **Vori**, 1 km away, where a beautifully arranged folk museum in a re-

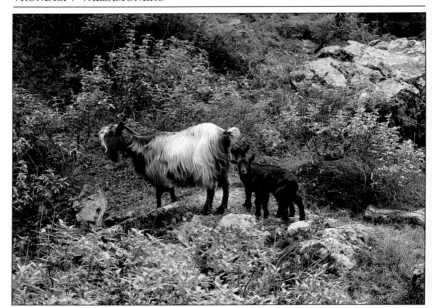

stored village house illustrates Cretan rural life and customs. Weaving, basket-making and smithing are all represented.

Heading back towards Iraklio along the main road, turn left for Zaros just before reaching Agii Deka. The road climbs gradually through the foothills of the Psiloritis Massif. At **Zaros**, a large village with springs that once supplied water carried by aqueduct to ancient Gortina, take the road for Vorizia and Kamares. At the 6 km mark, the **Monastery of Vrondisi** is signposted to the right.

A 15th-century Venetian fountain stands outside the monastery, decorated with battered figures of Adam and Eve. The twin-aisled church contains fine 14th-century frescoes, with a striking Last Supper painted in the apse of the southern aisle. 3 km further on, you reach **Vorizia**, where a left turning at the end of

Above: Mountain goats are curious but they keep their distance. Right: View of the snow-capped White Mountains from the Psiloritis (Mount Ida).

the village is signposted for **Valsamonero**. The *fylakas* will open the church of **Agios Fanourios** in the mornings: his house is down the hill on the way to the church, opposite a café. The oddly-shaped church is all that remains of the Valsamonero monastery. It has twin aisles and a third at right angles across the west end, decorated with outstanding 14th- and 15th-century frescoes. The drive back from Zaros to Agia Varvara through Nivritos and Gergeri offers a series of splendid views.

Hike to the Summit of Psiloritis

The **Psiloritis**, 2456 m, is Crete's highest mountain. It is said that every Cretan should stand at least once in his or her life on the mountain's summit, but few ever fulfil the pledge. It is also said that only goats and sheep can ever make it to the top.

The important role attributed to the Psiloritis by Cretans is obvious from the chapel that was erected on the range's highest summit, Timios Stavros. The mountains already had mythological significance before the Christian era. The **Kamares cave** on the southern slopes of the range served as a religious and sacrificial place for the early inhabitants of the island. The ceramics found there gave an entire epoch its name and are exhibited in the Archaeological Museum in Iraklio. Anyone who casts a glance from the entrance of the cave down onto the land and sea stretching below will suddenly understand the godly quality of this place.

The second major excavation site is the **Ida cave** in the eastern wall of the mountain above the Nida plateau. This is where the infant Zeus grew up, protected from death at the hands of his cannibal father, Cronos, by the ancient Curetes.

Several different roads lead to the summit of the Psiloritis, from the Arkadi Monastery, for example, from Kouroutes in the Amari basin, from Anoghia and from Kamares.

The shortest route, one that can be managed in a single day, is the climb be-

ginning at the **Nidha Plateau** (1370 m). The most beautiful path up to the summit is the Kamares climb because of the fascinating view of the Messara Plain and the southern coast below. It is, however, almost impossible to do the climb in a single day and one should plan for a night's stay in the **Kollita refuge** on the way up or down. Hiking in the upper regions requires considerable endurance and several things will be needed: Good hiking boots, sun protection, a large bottle of water, a sleeping bag or even a tent, flash lights, food for two days and seasonal clothes and/or a raincoat.

The trek begins at the eastern border of the village of Kamares by a supermarket where a gutter crosses the street. Climb the winding road and after a short while you will see another gutter made of cement that will be seen often on the way up. The trail is the mainstay of a number of travel agents and has therefore been given red markings. The higher you get the more fascinating becomes the view over the densely packed houses of the

163

village of Kamares to the rolling hills in the background.

It is worth starting the climb in the early morning but even then one soon begins to sweat and you will require frequent halts. The road leads by the edge of one gully and later to another. Then there is the gutter again which you follow for a while. After about one and three-quarter hours you arrive at a watering place and a sheep enclosure (**Mandra Kalamafka**). The road divides here: The left path leads to the Kamares cave. The way north leads to the summit of the Psiloritis. The road to the Kamares cave follows a water-pipe and eventually arrives at a reservoir known as the partridge reservoir *(perdikonero)*. A steep slope leads to the cave. The distance between Mandra Kalamafka and the Kamares cave is about one and three-quarter hours' walk.

Above: The south coast at Pitsidia not far from Matala. Right: The artificial caves of Matala are a particularly interesting attraction.

The trek to the Psiloritis from Mandra Kalamafka winds through some of Crete's wildest mountain landscapes. If you are lucky you may even spot some lammergeyers that have become quite a rarity. The path goes steeply alongside a deep gully.

After about one and a half hours one arrives at the **Vulture Source** (Skaronero) at an elevation of 1650 m. Unfortunately, too many of these birds of prey became the target of trophy hunters. You are more likely to find them shot, stuffed and covered in dust decorating the insides of taverns and cafés in spite of legal protection from nature conservationists. The Kollita refuge is about a three-quarter hour walk upward from the Vulture Source. You can spend the night in the modest little shepherd's hut if you would rather not sleep in a tent or outdoors. The summit is two and a half hours from the refuge.

The path leads in a northerly direction and soon meets up with the eastern trail (from the Nidha plain). A one and a half

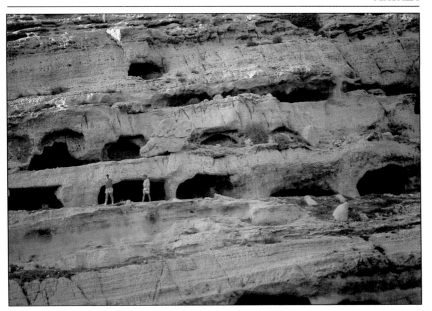

hour walk in northwesterly direction up a long cleft takes you to a crater-like gully that can be circumvented on the right. Continue in the same direction but on a saddleback offering a splendid view of the northern coast with Iraklio in the distance. From here trek westward on the eastern ridge all the way to the summit and chapel.

A word of warning: In spring, areas covered in snow and ice can be quite dangerous to cross. Should your equipment be inadequate we would advise leaving out the climb to the summit.

On a clear day the view from the top is fantastic. The sea sprawls at one's feet on two sides, and the view in the east and west is crowned by the high mountains of the Dikti and Lefka Ori ranges. In the south, the greenhouses of the Messara Plain glitter in the sun. The little stone hut in the southwest belongs to the mountain climbers' club of Rethimno.

If you don't wish to take the same way back to Kamares, take the southwesterly trail. It leads to **Kouroutes** or **Four-**

fouras in the Amari basin. A good sense of direction and an accurate map are both necessary.

MATALA

Returning towards Festos, turn right to take the lower road past the monastery church, which leads to Matala. A kilometer further on you pass the church of St. Paul (Agios Pavlos), set among cypresses and surrounded by a wall. It is said to be the oldest church in Crete, and was origianally just a cupola supported on four massive pillars. The nave was added later and the outer narthex dates from the Venetian period. After another 2 km you reach the main road from Mires to Matala and turn right for the village of **Pitsidia**.

One kilometer further on, a track to the right leads down to one of the best sandy beaches on the southern coast. It is overlooked by the Minoan site of **Kommos**, which, Evans thought, was an important harbor and customs post. A large admin-

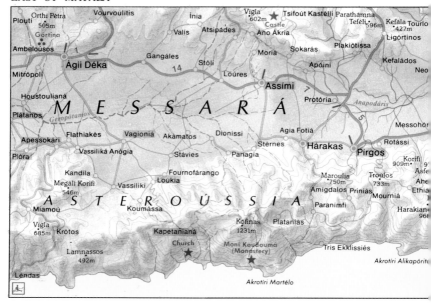

istrative building dates from the later palace period. Subsequently, a series of Greek temples were constructed over it: The first dates from the tenth century BC and is thought to be the earliest in Greece.

Back on the main road, you pass a series of hotels and rooms for rent to reach **Matala**, now a flourishing resort. The second-century-AD Roman tombs cut in the soft sandstone of the cliffs enclosing the cove, once the only accommodation in the village, are now fenced off. But there is a campsite above the beach for the "hippies," as backpackers are still known in Crete.

The significance of Matala Bay goes far back into the mythological past. This is where Zeus, in the guise of a bull, reached the coast of Crete carrying the beautiful princess Europa on his back. It is also where a part of Menelaus' flotilla drifted on its return from the Trojan war. His men narrowly escaped death when the waves smashed his ships onto the cliffs (*Odyssey* 3, 291). Matala first became significant as a harbor under the

Romans. The caves in the cliffs served as burial grounds in the early Christian era.

An excursion in a fishing boat around **Cape Lithino**, Crete's southernmost point, to the little fishing village of **Kali Limenes** is possible in calm weather. You can also reach it on foot via the monastery of Odigitrias. It is far less tiring to go by car, but beware – the road is in very poor condition.

East of Matala

Returning towards Festos, a right turning at the 2-km mark is signposted for **Sivas**, a pleasant village from which a dirt road leads to the Odigitria Monastery and the harbor of Kali Limenes. At the 4-km-mark you reach the village of **Listaros**. Beyond it, the landscape grows drier and wilder until you find the walled monastery compound at the 8 km mark. **Odigitrias** is the westernmost monastery complex in the Asteroussia mountains. The austere, burnt, hilly landscape runs along the southern edge of the Plain of

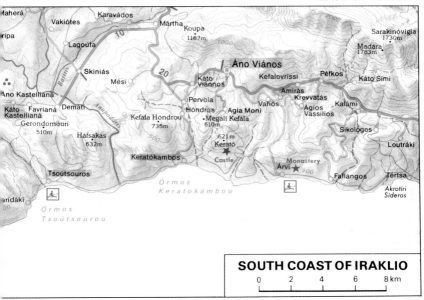

SOUTH COAST OF IRAKLIO

0   2   4   6   8 km

Messara and offers a natural defense against the redoutable winds that blow from North Africa. The highest peak is the **Kofinas** (1231 m). The starkness of the Asteroussia Mountains to find solitude necessary to meditation, and so it is no small wonder that one should find several remote monasteries here. The church contains fine icons, including one of Christ with the twelve Apostles in a branching vine, signed by the 15th-century painter Angelos. The door to the square tower is opened with huge iron key. In the 19th century, a Cretan rebel, an ex-priest, reportedly held off Turkish attackers by hurling beehives down from its top, but was eventually killed together with his family.

Other rooms in the compound room contain an old-fashioned grinder for olives and a press for extracting the oil. The track continues for another 4 km to reach **Kali Limenes**, with a fine beach on the Libyan Sea and pleasant tavernas. A better road leads there from Mires via Pombia and Pigaidakia (23 km). There is also

a daily bus in the late afternoon. Kali Limenes was mentioned in the Bible (Act 27,8) as the place where the apostle Paul stopped on his way from Cesarea to Rome. The former beauty of the bay has been rather spoiled by the huge oil tanks that stand on the islet of Agios Pavlos outside the bay. There is a chapel dedicated to the memory of St. Paul which stands to the west of the village.

Another dirt track leads east along the coast from Kali Limenes to the site of **Lendas**, 10 km away, but it is easier to reach from the main Festos road. A left turning just before the Basilica of St. Titus (Agios Titos) takes you through **Mitropoli** and across the Messara Plain to **Platanos** and **Plora**, where a right fork leads to the isolated **Monastery of Apezanon**, 10 km away.

The church of the monastery has been consecrated to St. Andonios Agiofarangitis. During the Turkish occupation of the island the monastery became an important place of learning and the maintaining of traditions. It possesses a num-

Above: The Kofinas is the most prominent elevation in the Asterousia mountains.
Right: Banking the coals in an ancient stove as it has been done for centuries.

ber of sacred relics and has an interesting library.

If you bear to the left you reach **Apeso-kari**, where domed graves from pre-palatial days were uncovered. At this point one turns right toward **Miamou**, a small mountain village that lies at an altitude of 480 m. Around 1900 the Italian School of Archeology conducted excavations in the region that turned up grave sites from the Neolithic age. Now the road climbs up into the **Asteroussia Mountains**. There are spectacular views on the descent to the sea. At 29 km you reach **Lendas**, the site of ancient Lebena and a famous sanctuary of Asklepios, the ancient Greek god of healing. In all probability the ancient name *Lebena* or *Levin* stems from a Phoenician-Semitic word for lion and refers in this case to the promontory that looks like some predatory animal about to jump into the sea. It reached its historical high point in the fifth and sixth centuries when it served as Gortys' harbor and became a mecca for pilgrims who came to take its healing waters.

The excavations on Lendas were carried out by the Italians. Only 100 m from the beach, between the foothills of Lendas and Psamidomouri, they discovered the remains of the holy shrine of Asklepios. Only two of the sixteen columns still stand. Under a mosaic floor in the nortwestern corner of the temple is an underground chamber that probably contained the precious objects given as offerings by the citizens of Gortina. This treasure was probably plundered during the Roman or Byzantine era. The pebble mosaic floor dating from the third century BC shows a seahorse framed by waves. Healing springs at the site were credited with curing sciatica among other ailments, and the buildings included a hostel where the pilgrims stayed.

The sanctuary was in use from the fourth century BC until Roman times, ac-

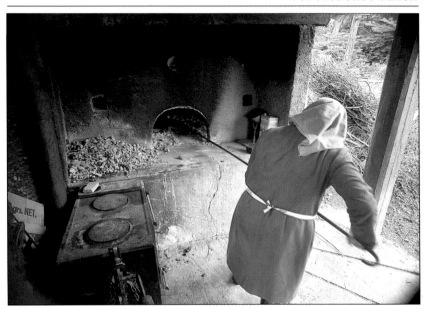

cording to archaeologists. People today still place a great deal of faith in the healing powers of the water. It is suppose to cure ulcers and wounds of all sorts and the ill come regularly from Athens and other points on the mainland to be cured.

The Asteroussia Mountains drop steeply into the sea east of Lendas. Surrounded by the sea, the **Koudoumas monastery** stands here, beneath the jagged peak of Kofinas (1231 m). To reach it you must follow the road from Agii Deka through Vagonia to the hamlet of **Loukia** (the terminus of the Agii Deka bus line). The dirt road at the southern end of the village winds its way for about 8 km through the arid landscape to the village of **Kapetaniana**, lying in a green hollow. From here the Koudoumas monastery is another 6 km over a very poor, very winding road. Nevertheless its unique and remote location makes it very much worth a detour if you have time.

There are no roads running along the coast in the southern foothills of the Asteroussia Mountains. In order to continue

the drive to the eastern part of the district of Iraklio, you must turn back to the southern section of the national road which has been under construction for years. 14 km after Agii Deka, the road leads to the town of **Asimi** and 12 km later to Pirgos. Another 15 km takes you to **Kato Kastelliana**, a little village on the eastern edge of the Messara Plain.

A dirt road leads from here in a southerly direction to **Tsoutsouros Beach**, renowned for its fine sand. Behind it is a valley that rises down gently away from the coast. A permanent stream runs through here and crabs of all sorts and sizes live in the dense oleanders growing on its banks. In Tsoutsouros there is a hotel as well as self-catering accommodations, *kafenions* and tavernas.

Another dirt road takes you from Tsoutsouros along the southern coast eastward to **Keratokambos**, another quiet resort with a beautiful beach, private lodgings and taverns. A road leads steeply from Keratokambos up to **Ano Viannos** (550 m) between the impressive

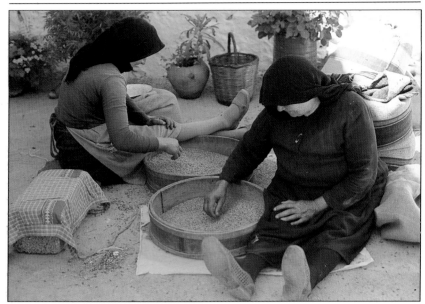

rocky crags of Kefala Hondrou and Megali Kefala. Ano Viannos is the capital of a district bearing the same name. Its white houses are arranged as in an amphitheater on the southwestern foothills of the Dikti chain. The luxuriant vegetation and the many fountains are quite remarkable.

The little village nestled amongst olive groves stands on the remains of the ancient city of Viannos, that once upon a time possessed minting rights. In 1954, excavations in **Galana Charakia** uncovered two large graves containing 30 burying *pithoi* and clay figures from the early and middle Minoan ages. A further Late-Minoan settlement was unearthed in **Kefala Hondrou** between 1956 and 1959.

Today, Ano Viannos has several medieval churches containing beautiful frescoes. The frescoes in the Agia Pelagia date to the 14th century; those in St. George (Agios Georgios) to the 13th century. About 7 km east of Ano Viannos, in the village of **Amiras**, a road leads down to the beautiful beach of **Arvi** (14.5 km). Dozens of thick, black plastic pipes carry water from springs on the southern slopes of the Dikti Mountains down to the greenhouses and banana plantations on the beach. There is also a monastery. Good accommodations and taverns make Arvi a favorite destination.

The most beautiful part of the trip begins east of Amiras. The elevated road offers a splendid view of the varying landscape. You leave the prefecture of Iraklio just before the resort of **Mirtos** from where a good road takes you to Ierapetra.

THE EAST

Start your trip from Iraklio by taking the old road that leaves from Plateia Eleftheria near the Archaeological Museum.

Above: Sorting out the grain requires a woman's patience. Right: Sitting on the shaded terrace of the cafenion, a job requiring man's patience.

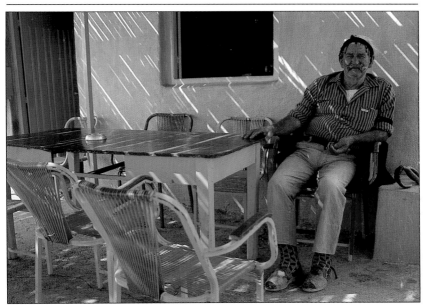

At 7 km you will pass the beach at **Karteros** and then after the riding center at 8 km you reach **Amnisos**, the most important port of Minoan Crete. This is where the Lilies fresco – now in the Iraklio Archaeological Museum – was found.

13 km east of Iraklio one reaches **Hani tou Kokkini**, the site of a Minoan villa covering an impressive 100-sq-m area. The villa, dating from 1500 BC, was discovered in 1918 and resembles the architecture of Knossos with some 40 chambers, two corridors and two courtyards being dug out. The complex is so generously proportioned, that some archaeologists argue it is a Minoan palace, probably a seaside resort for the higher castes living in Knossos.

2 km east of Hani tou Kokkini you reach the seaside village of **Gournes**, where a huge US communications airbase has been built. The installation is the site of frequent anti-American demonstrations, but Gournes has adapted to the needs of the servicemen. Further east, 26 km from Iraklio, one comes to **Limenas Hersonnissou**, a highly acclaimed seaside resort with an excellent beach and a popular spot for windsurfing. A number of bars, taverns and hotels accommodate the traveler although a room in the summer high season must be booked well in advance.

Limenas Hersonnissou was an ancient Minoan port, housing the huge temple of Britomartis (a deity in ancient Crete called sweet maiden) which has disappeared through the years. The area also served as a port for the Romans and traces of fountains and harbor works from that era can still be seen.

Malia

Malia is situated 34 km east of Iraklio, halfway to Agios Nikolaos. The village has one of the best beaches in Crete, but has lately lost some of its charm as huge new hotels overshadow the natural beauty. During the holiday season Malia never sleeps as tourists drink and dance the night away in bars and discos.

4 km east of town a narrow side-street leads to Malia's archaeological sites. As will be obvious at first glace, ancient Malia was situated in the midst of the best natural environment, situated between sea and mountain and engulfed by olive groves and fruit trees.

The Malia **Minoan palace** dates to 1900 BC and was built at about the same period as the palaces of Knossos and Festos. It was first discovered by Greek archaeologist Josif Hatzidakis in 1915, but a systematic study of the ruins was only begun in 1922 by the French Institute of Archaeology in Athens.

The first palace of Malia was ruined in 1650 BC. What is seen today are the remains of the second palace which survived until 1450 when it was destroyed by the same earthquake that also leveled Knossos and Festos.

A labyrinth of paved but narrow roads, starting from the palace's northern end,

Above: A storage jar from Malia. Right: Just another village conversation.

lead to the **central court**, a huge open area measuring 48 m from north to south and 22 m from east to west. In the middle of the court a pit served as a sacrificial site to the gods and the slaughtered animals were then roasted in a ceremony attended by the high priest. The sacrificial altar is a unique feature of the Malia palace not found in any other Minoan palaces on the island.

The central court was also used for bull-fights, as evidenced by a series of holes and columns on its perimeter to protect the spectators, among them the king himself who watched the events from the second floor of a building at the court's west side. The ground floor communicated with the palace's upper level via a main staircase at the court's northern side, where the main kitchen was situated.

The rooms on the south side of the court were used as **workshops** while the whole east side is covered by a series of long and narrow chambers that served as granaries. The **royal apartments** were

1 West Court
2 West Magazines
3 Loggia or Throne Room
4 Central Court
5 Staircase
6 Pillar Crypt
7 Sacrificial Pit
8 South Entrance
9 Walled Pits
10 South-East Entrance
11 Colonnade
12 East Magazines
13 Pillar Hall
14 Court of the Keep
15 Royal Apartments
16 Lustral Basin
17 North Court
18 North-East Entrance
19 North-East Magazines
20 North Entrance

MALIA

0   10   20   30m

situated on the palace's northwest corner and resemble typical Minoan architecture – separate rooms for the king and the queen, but a common bathroom. The Malia palace housed a total of about 350 chambers and is the third largest in Crete after the ones in Knossos and Festos. A complete tour of this magnificent complex takes more than an hour to go through numerous corridors, storage magazines and various other rooms used for religious purposes.

Excavations in the 1960s around the palace have revealed a number of structures (houses, benches, tombs, roads) indicating the existence of a large Minoan town. The most important find is 500 m east of the palace, close to the sea shore. Here a huge tomb, 40 m long and 30 m wide, served as the burial site for the royal family. The place is called *crisolakkos* (pit of gold) and indeed brought to light a number of gold treasures, the most famous being a gold honeybee pendant now housed at the Iraklio Archaeological Museum.

Offbeat Beaches

The steep slopes west of Iraklio hardly offer any opportunity to swim. A few kilometers beyond city limits lie the beaches of **Linoperamata** and **Ammoudara**. 21 km along the national highway, shortly beyond Rethimno is the fork leading to the bay of **Agia Pelagia**. Another swimming hole is a few kilometers further near the fork off to Fodele.

East of Iraklio are several beautiful beaches: **Amnisos**, **Nirou Hani**, **Hersonissos** and **Malia**. Unfortunately, tourism has made heavy inroads here which might not be to everyone's taste.

For idyllic coves and beaches with modest lodgings, a few taverns and *kafenions*, head for **Pitsidia** and **Matala** on the southern coast of the prefecture of Iraklio. Mass tourism has also spared the beaches of **Kali Limenes**, **Tsoutsouros**, **Lendas** and **Arvi**. The beaches located on the Libyan Sea are sunny and warm even in the winter months and attract many globetrotters all year round.

IRAKLIO

Access / Local Transport

FLIGHTS: Frequent flights to Athens from Iraklio Airport on Olympic Airways. Terminal: Platia Eleftherias, Tel. (081) 282-285.

FERRIES: Ferry boats to Piraeus daily from the East Quay, operated by Minoan Lines (central ticket office: 78, August 25th Street, opposite Agios Titos church, Tel. (081) 229602 and ANEK (central ticket office) 33 August 25th Street, Tel. (081) 222481. One-day cruises to the islands of Santorin and Ios in the Cyclades are available in summer. There are regular sailings from Iraklio to Alexandria, Egypt, and Venice with the Adriatica Line (Tel. Athens (01) 322-3693), for Limassol, Cyprus with the Stability Line and for Kusadasi, Turkey with Marlines, Tel. (081) 226-697, Arabatzoglou Travel Agency, 54 August 25th Street.

BUSES: The long-distance bus station for east Crete is east of the traffic circle at the bottom of Beaufort Street, Tel. (081) 282637. The bus station for Festos, Gortina and southwest Crete (also Tilissos, Anogia and Fodele) is outside the Hania Gate to the right, Tel. (081) 283-287. The Station for Hania and Rethimno is opposite the Historical Museum, Tel. (081) 221-765. The bus station for Thrapsano, Varvari and other villages in central Crete is outside the Venetian walls close to the New Gate.

Accommodation

LUXURY: **Galaxy**, Leoforos Dimokratias 67, Tel. (081) 238812. **Xenia**, 2 Sofoklis Venizelou Street, Tel. (081) 284000/4. **Astoria**, Platia Eleftherias 11, Tel. (081) 229002. **Knossos Beach** (mainly bungalows), Hani Kokkini, Tel. (081) 761204. **Creta Beach**, Ammoudara, Tel. (081) 252302.

MODERATE: **Atrion**, 9 K. Paleologlou Street, Tel. (081) 229225. **Kastro**, 22 Theotokopoulou Street, Tel. (081) 285020. **Marilena**, Ammoudara, Tel. (081) 2543112.

BUDGET: **Kronos**, Sofoklis-Venizelou Street, Tel. (081) 282240. **Dedalos**, 15 Dedalou Street, Tel. (081) 224391. **Olympic**, Platia Kornarou, Tel. (081) 288861/4. **Tsangarakis Beach**, Ammoudara, Tel. (081) 251768.

Staying in town is more convient, given the traffic jams around Iraklio, but can be stifling hot in summer. Few moderately priced hotels are fully air-conditioned (the Atrion is a welcome exception). The beach hotels west or east of the city are not always prepared for the individual traveler (half-board is the rule), but are well-equipped for water sports.

Restaurants

Hotel restaurants in Crete generally serve bland meals: eating out is a better alternative.

Kyriakos, Leoforos Dimokratias, close to the Ga-laxy Hotel; a sophisticated Cretan taverna serving good meat dishes and excellent wines. **Ippo-cambos**, Mitsotakis Street. An *ouzeri*, or informal eating place, where hot snacks, or *mezedes*, accompany *ouzo*, wine or beer. (There are other *ouzeris* worth trying in the pedestrian zone off August 25th Street, near the Agios Dimitrios church). **Gla-koumis** is the best of the tavernas in "meat alley", the arcade off Evans Street near the butchers'shops. **Nea Ionia**, a traditional lunching place on Evans Street, has good baked dishes.

Museums / Sites

Iraklio Archaeological Museum, off Plateia Eleftherias (Tel. 081/226092). Daily from 8 am-6 pm except Mondays, when it opens at 12 noon.

Historical and Ethnographical Museum, Eleftherios Venizelou Street, opposite Xenia Hotel. Open 9 am-1 pm and 3 pm-5.30 pm. Closed Sundays and public holidays.

Agia Ekaterini Icon Collection, next to Agios Minas Cathedral. Open 9.30 am-1 pm Mondays through Saturdays, and 5 pm-7 pm on Tuesdays, Thursdays and Fridays. Closed Sundays and public holidays.

Iraklio Harbor Venetian Fortress (Koules). Open 8.30 am-12 noon and 4-6 pm Monday through Saturday, 9 am-3 pm on Sundays.

Knossos Archaeological Site. Open 8 am-6 pm daily except Mondays from 12 noon onward. During winter it closes at 5 pm.

Local Festivals / Events

In July and August, the outdor theaters in the Venetian moat feature plays and concerts, usually with an emphasis on Cretan music and theatre. Foreign performing arts groups often combine appearances at the Athens Festival with a show in Crete.

Art and photography exhibitions are shown almost year-round in the Loggia near the Morosini Fountain. Cretan *lira* players perform at some tavernas - there are several on the Knossos road, which are also good places to see genuine Cretan dancing.

Hospitals

Apollonion General Hospital, Alber and Markou Moussourou Streets, Tel. 081/229713, 287411. **Venizeleion Hospital**, Knossos Street, Tel. 081/ 231931, 237502.

Post / Telegraph / Telephone

Iraklio: Area code 081.

Main Post Office: Plateia Daskaloyianni. Open 8 am-8 pm, Monday through Friday.

Main Telegraph office, OTE, El Greco Park.

Rent a Car

Most car-rental agencies are in 25 August Street. **Avis**, 25 August St. **Hertz**, 25 August St. **Hellas Cars**, 25 August St. **Vallilakis**, Airport. **Byron**, A. Titos St. 10. **Giatromanolakis**, 4 Ikaros St. **Kret-**

car, 25 August St. **Ida**, 62 Martyron St.144. **Inter-rent**, 62 Martyron St.117.

Shopping

The traditional Cretan red woven blankets, shoulder-bags, embroidered tablecoths and pillowcases have becomme antiques, but can still be found in a few shops in August 25th Street and around the Museum. Contemporary versions are easily found. Woolen floor rugs come in a variety of designs. You can also find heavy sweaters made from wool that still contains natural oils.

Silverwork is of good quality: a stroll down Dedalos Street gives an idea of what is available.

Cretan knives are good value, whether ornamental daggers or plain kitchenware.

A pair of black leather kneeboots made to measure will last for years.

Tourist Information

National Tourist Organization Office (EOT): 1 Xanthoudidi Street, opposite the Archaeological Museum. Tel. (081) 225636. Opening times 8 am-6 pm (weekends and winter until 2 pm).

Information desk at Iraklio Airport (4 km east of the city). Opening times 9 am-9 pm.

Tourist Agency: Solmar: Beaufort 8, 227702.

CENTRAL CRETE

Acommodation

AGIA PELAGIA: Capsis Beach, Tel. (081) 811112. **Penninsula**, Tel. (081) 811313. **Panorama**, Tel. (081) 811002.

AMNISSOS: Prince of Lillies, Tel. (081) 225822.

ARVI: Ariadni, Tel. (0895) 22312.

GOURNES: Erato, Tel. (081) 761277.

GOUVES: Creta Sun, Tel. (0897) 41103. **Byron**, Tel. (0897) 41130.

KOKKINOS PIRGOS: Filippos, Tel. (0892) 52002. **El Greco**, Tel. (0892) 51182.

LENTAS: Lentas, Tel. (0892) 22272.

LIMENAS HERSONISSOU: Paradise, Tel. (0897) 22115/30. **Belvedere**, Tel. (0897) 22010/5. **Hersonissos Palace**, Tel. (0897) 22777. **King Minos Palace**, Tel. (0897) 22781/2. **Nana Beach**, Tel. (0897) 22706. **Zorbas Village**, Tel. (0897) 22604. **Chrissi Amoudia**, Tel. (0897) 22971/3. **Dedalos Village**, Tel. (0897) 22515. **Maragakis**, Tel. (0897) 22405. **Voula**, Tel. (0897) 22097. **Antinoos**, Tel. (0897) 23142. **Golden Beach**, Tel. (0897) 22391. **Millotakis**, Tel. (0897) 23081.

LINOPERAMATA: Apollonia Beach, Tel. (081) 821602.

MALIA: Ikaros Village, (0897) 31267/9. **Sirens Beach**, Tel. (0897) 31321/3. **Grammatikaki**, Tel. (0897) 31560/1. **Frixos**, Tel. (0897) 31941. **Malia**

Mare, Tel. (0897) 31809. **Minoikos Ilios**, Tel. (0897) 31106. **Sofokles Beach**, Tel. (0897) 31348. **Bananies**, Tel. (0897) 31203. **Roussakis**, Tel. (0897) 31464. **Ibiscus**, Tel. (0897) 31313.

MATALA: Kapetan Nikolas, Tel. (0892) 42780. **Eva-Marina**, Tel. (0892) 42125. **Pringipissa Evropi**, Tel. (0892) 42113. **Chez Xenophon**, Tel. (0892) 42358. **Sofia**, Tel. (0892) 42134.

MIRES: Olympic, Tel. (0892) 22777.

PALEOKASTRO: Rogdia, Tel. (081) 821373.

PISKOPIANO: Edelweis, Tel. (0897) 22631.

STALIDA: Ilissia Pedia, Tel. (0897) 32090. **Alklyonides**, Tel. (0897) 31558. **Palm Beach**, Tel. (0897) 31666. **Cactus Beach**, Tel. (0897) 31319. **Heliotrope**, Tel. (8097) 31515/7. **L'Amour**, Tel. (0897) 31615. **Pelargos**, Tel. (0897) 61324. **Stalis**, Tel. (0897) 31246.

TIMBAKI: Agios Georgios, Tel. (0892) 51678. **ZAROS: Idi**, Tel. (0894) 31302.

Camping

Caravan Camping, Limenas Hersonissou, Tel. (0897) 22025; persons 108, tents 36. **Creta Camping**, Gouves, Tel. (0897) 41400; persons 270, tents 90. **Iraklio Camping**, Ammouda, Tel. (081) 2509868; persons 858, tents 283. **Pitsidia-Matala Comm. Camping**, Matala, Tel. (0892) 42340; persons 300, tents 100.

Restaurants

There are few restaurants to be found in the villages of central Crete, but simple, tasty dishes are often available at *cafenions*: salad, omelettes, beans, and fruit, along with local cheese and wine, or *raki*, the Cretan firewater. In the evenings, spit-roast meat and grill can be found at local *kentra* on the outskirts of most villages.

Museums / Sites

Kazantzakis Museum, Mirtia, open daily from 9 am-1 pm and 4-6 pm except on Tuesdays, Thursdays and Fridays. In winter it is only open in the morning.

Tilissos Archaeological Site. Open daily from 9 am-3.30 pm, Sundays from 10 am-3 pm.

Agia Triada Archaeological Site. Open Mondays through Saturdays from 9 am-3 pm, Sundays from 10 am-2.30 pm.

Festos Archaeological Site. Open daily from 8 am-6 pm, in winter until 5 pm only.

Gortina (Gortys) Archaeological Site. Open daily from 8 am-7 pm, in winter until 5 pm.

Vori Ethnological Museum. Open daily from 10 am-6 pm.

The siesta hours (2.30 pm-5 pm) should be avoided, even in winter, when looking for the keys to locked Byzantine churches, or visiting monasteries. This time is sacrosanct to Cretans, and during the hot season you might also wish to use this time of day to get out of the sun and relax.

SEA OF CRETE

Hania
Hania

Rethimno
Rethimno

Iraklio
Iraklio

Sitia
Sitia

Lassithi

Gavdos

LASSITHI

**LASSITHI PLAIN
AGIOS NIKOLAOS
ELOUNDA / SPINALONGA
KRITSA / LATO
GOURNIA / IERAPETRA
VAI / KATO ZAKROS
VALLEY OF THE DEAD**

LASSITHI

The Lassithi prefecture occupies the eastern part of Crete. It covers an area of 1818 sq km, and it has a population of about 85,000.

Lassithi is engulfed by two mountain ranges – Dikti (2418 m) to the west and the Sitian mountains (1476 m) to the east. The Cretan Sea forms the wonderful Gulf of Mirabello on the northern coast, and the Libyan Sea to the south washes Ierapetra, Greece's southernmost town.

Despite its relatively scant archaelogical remains, Lassithi endured domination by all the peoples who invaded the island. The area flourished during Minoan times and successively passed to Roman, Byzantine, Venetian, Turkish, German, Italian and Greek hands.

Up until the 1960s, Lassithi was largely unknown to foreigners and its first regular visitors were hippies enjoying beautiful sites, sandy beaches, cheap accommodation and Cretan hospitality. But the area which is now prowdly described as the "Cretan Riviera" was destined to become one of the most visited parts of the country. In the summer months;

Preceding pages: Windmills above Lassithi Plain. Left: Safe from the sun in the shadow of one's home.

Lassithi's population more than triples and some 80 percent of the locals derive income from tourist services. Where rocks once stood, luxury hotels have been erected and all major credit cards are accepted in an area where, not so long ago, mules were the main means of transportation.

But progress came with a cost. Lassithi and mainly its capital town Agios Nikolaos have lost their calm charm as disco music, noisy motorbikes and empty beer bottles mar the high summer season. Still, Lassithi is relatively untouched in comparison with other parts of Crete. The Gulf of Mirabello and the entire area close to Ierapetra provide beautiful sandy beaches, exceptional views of the sea and traditional tavernas. On its eastern end, the Carpathian Sea washes Europe's unique palm forest of Vai.

The Lassithi Plain, overlooked by Mount Dikti, is one of Crete's most fertile areas producing top quality fruit and vegetables for export mainly to northern Europe. For around six centuries, the plateau has been irrigated by thousands of windmills (and more recently Diesel-run pumps) pumping water without a stop for almost two centuries. Lassithi farmers were the first in Greece to built an extensive network of hothouses which, with the aid of the mild climate, yield a variety

179

of agricultural products all year round. Temperatures in Lassithi range in the winter between 12 - 26 degrees Celsius while in the summer they can go up to 42 degrees with the southern *sirocco* wind blowing from the Sahara in June and July. The northern *meltemi* wind, on the other hand, brings cooler temperatures in late August.

Agios Nikolaos provides the best of Cretan culture in the summer months with festivities of various kinds taking place around the town's bottomless pool where according to legend the goddess Athena used to bathe.

From Malia to Neapolis

After passing Hersonissos and Malia on the National Road from Iraklio to Agios Nikolaos you arrive at a wild ravine featuring the exceptionally beautiful monastery of St. George Selinaris (**Agios Georgios Selinaris),** 43 km east of Iraklio.

Built into the mountain rock the monastery, which has now been turned into a retirement home, is the most frequent stopover for travelers bound for Agios Nikolaos. Enjoy lunch in one of the many cafés and restaurants offering a variety of Greek cuisine but mostly the traditional *souvlaki* and spring water straight from the rock. The monastery attracts a huge crowd on April 23, the name-day of Agios Georgios (St. George).

If you choose to stay on the new road, nothing now stands between yourself and Agios Nikolaos to the east. But if there is time spare, the old road from Selinari leads to some other archaeological sites worth a short visit.

On the old road 49 km east of Iraklio, turn left to **Milatos**, a small village that took its name from the Doric city of Milatos which reached its peak in 1400 BC. Milatos is associated with Sarpedon, brother of King Minos, and is mentioned in Homer's *Iliad* as one of the seven Cre-

Akrotíri
Agios Ioánnis
Mironikitas
Gallou
Selles Trouli
Koudoúmalos Ágios
Georgios 331m
Amigdaliá Valtos Skiniás
Vrouhás
Agios Andónios Loúmas
Milatos Tsambi
Milatos Kounáli Moní Aretiou
(Monastery) Pláka Spinalog (Castle)
áno Síssion Frathiás Nofaliás Koutsoúra Spinalónga
Anginaras 760m Karidi 701m
307m Vathi Doriés
Moní Xera Xila Lakaki Epáno
Selinari (Monastery) Kouroúnes Pinés
Vrahássion Stavrós Káto Pinés
Latsida 794m Epano Eloúnda Mavrikianó
Deti Voulisméni Dreros Eloúnda
Church Kastri Fourni (Shisma)
619m Neápolis Kastélli Olous
Tsekoúra Arkolaki Nikithianós Ágios Ioánnis Eloúnda
998m 915m Limnes Agia Pelágia
Vrisses
Houmeriákos
e n a Anginaras
577m Drákos Elliniká
Maherá Káto Ágios Konstandínos
1487m Amigdáli
Exo Potami Amigdáli Karterides
Zénia Adrianós Éxo Lakkónia Ágios Nikólaos
ni Áno Amigdáli Fioretsides Marnéllides
Xeropótamos Skisma
Vitsiliás Tápes Flamourianá Hamilô
1234m Kefala Lato
assitháki Katharo Tsivi 564m
1564m Thílakas
Varsámi 521m Amoudara
1545m
Giannitsi Church Kólpos
Katharó Kritsá Kroústas Mirabéllou
(Avdeliákos)
Platia Korifi
1485m Istron
Pírgos Pahiá
Kouréli Halasménos Kaló Horió Ámmos
1386m 1392m Gournia
Giannou Prina
Korifi 665m Moní Fanetoménis Vassiliki
Kefala (Monastery)
Máles Megali Korifi 729m Messeléri Monastiráki
Hristós 1141m Kalamáfka Castle
vigla Moní Panagías Makriliá Stavrós Castle
Metaxohóri Exakoústis Episkopi Papadianá
(Monastery)
Estavroménos Kefala Epanohóri
951m 321m Katohóri 802m
Anatoli Katalímata
Mithi Karávi Kalógeri
Riza 550m Mourniés Kendri
Vainia
áki Gdóhia Stómio Gra Koutsounári
Kólekto Ligiá
300m Mírtos Néa Ammoudáres Néa Ierápetra
rtsa Mírtos Anatoli
deros

WEST OF LASSITHI

0   2   4   6   8 km

tan cities which sent troops to Troy to aid King Agamemnon. The ruins of the Doric city can still be seen but nothing important has been found. Sarpedon fled to Asia Minor from Miletos after he was defeated by Minos in a series of wars. There, he built a new city also named Miletos, which later became the greatest commercial center in Asia Minor.

Coming back on the new road you wind down to **Neapolis** 5 km east of Iraklio. The town was, until 1904, the capital of the Lassithi prefecture, now administrated from Agios Nikolaos. Neapolis is one of the most advanced towns in Crete with a fine Technical School of Domestic Science and other educational institutions. In 1340, a boy by the name of Petros Philargos was born in Neapolis. An orphan with no money he was raised by Venetian monks in the area. Philargos grew up to become Pope Alexander V in

Above: View over the fertile Lassithi Plain.
Right: Windmills are used in thousands to pump water from deep wells.

Rome. A road from the town's main square leads to **Kremasta Monastery** after 3 km. The complex housing some 170 monks was built in the late 1600s and achieved fame during the Ottoman occupation when it served as the residence of the Turkish governor of Lassithi, Kosstis Pasha, who in 1868 named Neapolis the capital of Mirabello and constructed a number of roads and public buildings.

A left turn from Neapolis leads to the ancient city of **Dreros**. The site was an ancient settlement with an acropolis and a small temple dedicated to the god Apollo Delphinios, dating to the seventh century BC. Apollo is portrayed as a dolphin that led Greek sailors in their quest to establish new colonies. Apollo Delphinios is also linked, according to Plutarch, with the Ionian city of Miletos in Asia Minor (mentioned earlier) which leads to the conclusion that the people of Dreros played an important role in the establishment of this Cretan colony. The temple also yielded three bronze figurines known as the **Triad of Dreros**

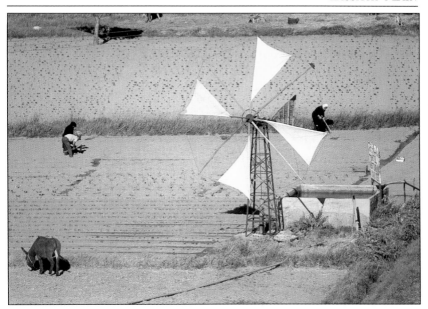

showing Leto and her two children Apollo and Artemis. It is now in the museum in Iraklio. Dreros is also representative of the classical period with a temple which was later turned into a Catholic chapel by the Venetians. The town remained strong up to the Hellenistic period and was then destroyed at about 220 BC in a series of wars with nearby cities. Finally, digging revealed two bilingual Eteocretan-Greek inscriptions which proved crucial in the eventual deciphering of the Eteocretan language, one of the oldest in the world.

THE LASSITHI PLAIN

Before proceeding on the main highway to Agios Nikolaos a right turn from Neapolis leads through a group of villages to the flat farmland of the **Lassithi Plain**.

Many tour buses head for Lassithi Plain so that their passengers can glimpse the picturesque "Valley of the Windmills." Yet few tourists actually explore the area on foot. Those who do find it easy to traverse, pleasantly unspoiled and incredibly fertile. Its flora is lovely and the borders of the fields and orchards are carpeted with wild flowers later in the spring than lower-lying areas. The Lassithi Plain sits at a height of about 866 m and is surrounded by the greenish peaks of Mount Dikti, making it blissfully cool during the scorching heat of summer.

Measuring 8 km long and 6 km wide, the plain is one of Crete's most fertile areas producing grain, potatoes, apples and rare wild orchids. But what makes the plain a spectacular site today are some 10,000 windmills used for decades to pump water for irrigation. As mentioned at the beginning of the chapter, however, nowadays the locals prefer Diesel-run pumps.

A number of villages lie on the road ringing the Lassithi Plain, and from them one can hike to monasteries, peaks and caves. On the eastern side is the village of **Tzermiado** and just east of it is the **Cave of Trapeza**, largely interesting because it was identified as the earliest settlement on the Lassithi Plain by Sir Arthur Evans and John Pendlebury. Its tombs had remains dating to the Neolithic Period but nothing much is left today.

Marmaketo, a little further along the road, was the birthplace of Manolis Kazanis, a hero of the Greek resistance against the Turks. The house where he was born is one of the buildings of the ethnological museum, showing a charming recreation of life in former years on the plain.

The **Kroustellenia Monastery**, which can be reached in a two-hour walk on a side road near **Mesa Lassithi** and **Mesa Lassithaki**, soars high above the southeastern side of the plateau. It was founded in 1543 by two sisters who were part of a group of refugees escaping the Turks in the Peloponnese.

In a two-hour walk from the monastery, one reaches the **Katharo Plateau**, scattered with a few villages inhabited only in the summer. The plateau is situated at a height of 1100 m and surrounded by the peaks of **Mount Dikti** (2148 m) and **Mount Lazaros** (2085 m). In a four-hour walk you can reach the village of **Kritsa** which is linked by a dirt road with Katharo Plateau. For more isolation, walk for one more hour to the **Horeftes**, an idyllic retreat with the romantic name *neraïdokolimbio* or "The Swimming Pool of the Nereids."

The most popular stopover in the area is the small village of **Psihro**, situated at the plain's southern end. Psihro was founded in the 15th century, taking its name from an icy spring nearby (*psihro* means cold). Every one of the village's inhabitants at some point will tell you the sad story of the Papadakis brothers. The two boys, Manolis and Antonis, fled to Egypt in 1823 when Turkish General Hasan Pasha devastated Lassithi. Manolis later enrolled in the Egyptian army

Right: The slopes of the Dikti massif rise up in the south of Lassithi Plain.

and after becoming an officer, he was sent back to Lassithi in 1867 to aid the Turkish governor Omer Pasha to suppress the Greek revolution against the Ottoman Empire. During one of the battles he was killed. In the meantime Antonis had left Egypt, found fame and fortune in Russia, and provided arms to the Cretan revolutionaries. When he heard of Manolis' death, he was deeply shocked and exclaimed: "My brother was killed by one of my weapons!"

Psihro is situated next to the mountain Dikti (2,418 m) and is a base for visiting **Dikteon Cave**, traditionally known as the legendary "birthplace of Zeus." A twenty-minute climb from Psihro brings you to the cave's entrance. But do not go alone or without a flashlight, good clothing, and steady shoes as it is cool, slippery and dark inside. At the end of the descent a huge stalactite cavern opens to the left. Its floor is covered by water and you will be overwhelmed by the breath taking view of hundreds of bizarre stalactites and stalagmites.

Myth has it that the ancient god of gods, Zeus, was born in the cave where his mother Rhea found refuge after escaping the wrath of her husband Cronos. Cronos, the master-god of the earth, ate the rest of his children, being afraid that they would steal his glory.

In modern times, the cave was excavated by British archaeologists in 1900 and revealed a number of offerings to Zeus including bronze double-axes and statuettes. The cave also features a number of stalagmites and stalactites giving it spectacular natural beauty.

Adventurers who want to ascend Mount Dikti can do so in about eight hours from Psihro. For the breathtaking walk you should take water with you. Rooms are available en route in village houses in **Limnahoro**.

If you choose you can spent the night at Psihro or go back to Neapolis and continue east to Agios Nikolaos.

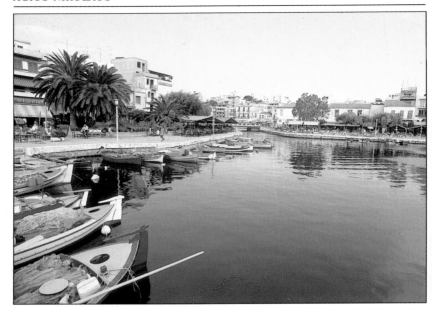

AGIOS NIKOLAOS

With a population of only 6000 people, Agios Nikolaos has become more of an international tourist attraction than any other Cretan town. Its hospitable people, well developed infrastructure, mild climate and crystal-clean beaches make it one of Greece's top vacation sites.

Situated 67 km east of Iraklio, the town overlooks the spectacular Gulf of Mirabello, which includes Crete's best known sand beach. Here, apart from swimming and water sports, one can enjoy fresh fish in a number of traditional tavernas with a view of sea and mountains, and exciting night life in discos and bars.

Agios Nikolaos takes its name from the small Byzantine chapel of St. Nicholas, on the port's nothern side. The village was founded in the year 1870 by settlers from Kritsa and Sfakia. During Venetian times the site was called Porto

Above: A narrow channel connects Lake Voulismeni with the sea.

di San Nicolo, the saint of seafarers. The chapel becomes the center of activity every December 6, when the saint's feast day is celebrated.

The port itself was linked in 1870 through a man-made channel with the small inland freshwater **Lake Voulismeni**. The lake is 60 m in diameter and 64 m deep although legend has it as the "bottomless pond" where goddess Athena bathed 3000 years ago. During the summer months the lake becomes a center of cultural festivities sponsored by town authorities. Travel agencies often organize Cretan nights with local food specialities, dances and songs. The municipality organizes annual festivities named *lato* which include folk dances from around the country and abroad, film presentations, exhibitions of art, Cretan handicrafts and swimming competitions.

On even years (1990, 1992 etc.), the town lights up with spectacular fireworks over the harbor to celebrate the Greek Naval Week which also includes water-skiing, swimming and windsurfing com-

Map legend:
1 Youth Hostel
2 Tourist Police & Information Centre
3 Post Office
4 Olympic Airways

AGIOS NIKOLAOS
0   100m

petitions. During Easter week, on the eve of the Resurrection, a puppet in the likeness of Judas is burnt on a platform in the middle of the lake. The event dates to the 18th century and becomes even more exciting as spectators light up candles to brighten the night. On New Year's Eve, decorated fishing boats enter the harbor to symbolize the arrival of the new year and when the clock chimes twelve, the sky lights up with colorful fireworks. A walk around the lake and on the port's periphery is highly recommended for the natural beauty they offer.

In Minoan times the place was called *lato pros kamarai,* as the harbor of Lato, and as *Kamara,* it was more important than the city itself. Kamara was fortunate as it suffered little from continuous wars among other Cretan cities during the Post-Minoan period and a single dispute with nearby Elounda (called *Olus* at the time) over the temple of Aris (God of War), situated between them, was settled after the intervention of Knossos which ruled that the temple should be shared.

Little is known about the city's fate under Roman, Byzantine and Arab rule. It then became a Venetian colony with the rest of Crete in the 13th century. The Venetians named the gulf Mirabello (lovely view) as well as the spectacular castle on the port (very few ruins to be seen today) which was erected in 1206 by architect Enrico Pescatore of Genoa. The **Mirabello castle** was one of 14 which Pescatore built or reconstructed in Crete. The castle was probably ruined in an earthquake and never reconstructed.

Agios Nikolaos, as seen today, was mostly built in the mid-1800s by local immigrants and has little to offer for the archaeologically inclined visitor. The **town's museum**, situated a few blocks away from the lake, has a collection of Minoan and post-Minoan artifacts up to the Middle Ages. The most important collection includes findings from some 250 Minoan graves at Agia Fotia dating back to 3000 BC. In the gold section is a splendid Minoan diadem, decorated with the figures of three *kri-kri*, the Cretan

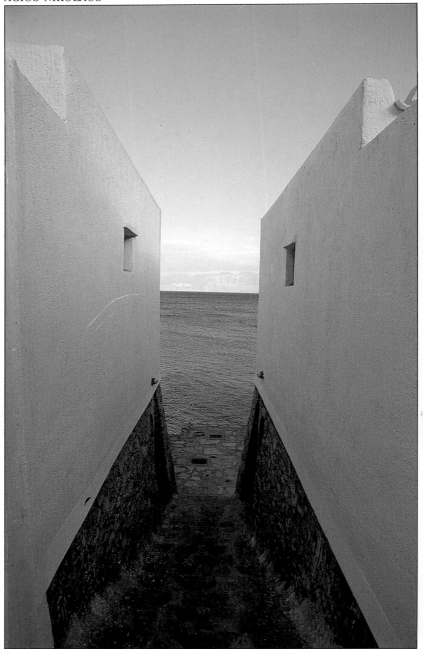

long-horned goat. The piece was discovered on the islet of Mohlos in the Gulf of Mirabello along with a hairpin shaped like a daisy, a lily-shaped bead and various other bits of jewelry used by Minoan women. The museum has an important pottery collection of some 700 vases from the Early Minoan period, used for storing oil and other goods.

The museum also features three "dedalic" statuettes dedicated to Dedalus, the legendary craftsman, who worked for King Minos in the seventh century BC. Finally, there is a big collection of Mycenaean pottery and ivory objects from the Bronze Age.

Shopping around in our times, Agios Nikolaos offers good leather buys and handmade pottery by local craftsmen.

ELOUNDA AND SPINALONGA

The next important destination in eastern Crete must be **Elounda**. Situated 11 km north of Agios Nikolaos, this small fishing village has become the most visited beach resort on the island. Originally called *Olous*, it was a Minoan town which flourished commercially. In Post-Minoan times it was conquered by Romans, Venetians, Turks, English and during World War II by Italians and Germans. In 1937, the French Institute of Archaeology unearthed an early Christian church decorated with spectacular mosaics which can still be seen today.

Elounda was one of few Greek settlements that minted its own coins, suggesting the independence of the city. The coins featured on one side the head of the goddess Artemis and on the other the head of Zeus with the word *Olontion* (Elounda). Nowdays Elounda is occupied by tourists and has lost most of its calm and charm. The beach is furnished with some of the most acclaimed luxury hotels

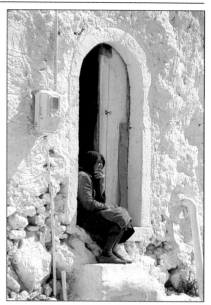

Left: Bungalow complex on Elounda beach.
Right: Old woman in front of her house.

in southern Europe, offering a wide range of accommodations (see hotel section).

At the entrance to the bay of Elounda lies the islet of **Spinalonga**. The name of the islet, separated from the mainland by a narrow isthmus, was given by the Venetians whose presence is still felt in the ruins of a magnificent **fortress** built in 1579 by the then governor Jacopo Foscarini. Spinalonga was conquered by the Ottoman Turks in 1715 who used the castle to protect their ships in the harbor. They also established Turkish village. In 1823, Turkish general Mohamed Berbantis slaughtered about 1500 Greek revolutionaries who were captured in the Milatos cave where they sought refuge from Turkish troops. In 1903, the Cretan authorities ruled that Spinalonga should be turned into a leper colony until its abolition in 1957. This period is recalled in an inscription whose text is culled from Dante's *Inferno:* "Every hope is lost to those who enter this place."

Nowadays of course, the risk of leprosy has been banished and Eloundra

189

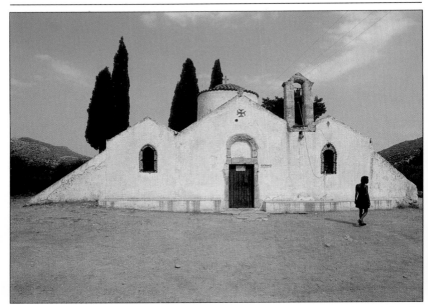

has become an attractive village for tourists. An especially fine view of the place is from across the isthmus. A number of *kaiki* (fishing boats) shuttle back and forth between the isthmus and the mainland. A final word on Spinalonga is that the Greek shipping tycoon Aristoteles Onassis once planned to turn the island into a casino.

KRITSA AND LATO

Another popular excursion from Agios Nikolaos is to **Kritsa**. To approach the village, leave Agios Nikolaos via the road leading out to Sitia and Ierapetra and 1 km out of town follow the sign to Kritsa, 12 km from Agios Nikolaos. Just before entering the village you come across the whitewashed chapel of **Panagia i Kera**, the best example of Byzan-

Above: The Byzantine Panagia i Kera Church dating from the 13th century. Right: Monks in the village of Kritsa, waiting for Godot perhaps...

tine art in Crete, built in the middle of a charming olive grove.The church, which dates to the 13th century, consists of three naves, with corresponding semicircular apses. Buttresses and tambour were added at later dates.

Adorning the church's interior are superb frescoes from the 14th and 15th centuries which are considered major ensembles of Byzantine paintings during the Paleologus era. The central nave is dedicated to the Assumption of the Virgin Mary with restored paintings from the life of Jesus Christ, the beheading of John the Baptist, the last supper and the crucifixion. The south nave honors St. Anne, the mother of the Virgin Mary, with paintings from their lives as told in the bible. The north nave is dedicated to St. Anthony and portrays the Second Coming of Christ, paradise and the weighing of the souls. A number of saints and martyrs complete the magnificent interior. The church can be visited every day from 9 am to 3 pm (in summer until 6 pm) and on Sundays from 9 am to 2 pm.

2 km further on, the main road leads to **Kritsa**. The village, clinging to a mountain side, was the site where the film version of Kazantzakis' *Christ Recrucified* was made with the participation of local inhabitants in minor roles next to the French and Greek actors chosen by French-born American director Jules Dassin who later directed the film *Never on Sunday*. Kritsa is also known for its traditional textile handicrafts which can be bought at bargain prices.

Just before entering Kritsa, a signposted dirt road to the right brings you to **Lato**, an ancient Doric city founded in the Post-Minoan era which flourished around the fifth century BC. Lato was excavated by the French Institute of Archaeology in 1900 and brought to light remains of a prosperous city with an amphitheater, a market place *(agora)*, fortifications, houses, roads, two acropolises and a temple, dedicated to the God of Light, Apollo. A walk to the north acropolis gives a fantastic view of the Gulf of Mirabello.

GOURNIA AND IERAPETRA

Your next tour from Agios Nikolaos is 19 km southwards on the way to Ierapetra at the village of **Gournia**. The site is especially appealing for its archaeological treasures, presenting a unique Minoan town complete with remains of streets, houses and of course an ancient palace.

Gournia was excavated in the early 1900s, and the findings indicate that the city flourished in about 1600 BC before being destroyed by the same earthquake that hit Knossos. The ancient town resembles a typical large Cretan village today with narrow streets and small crowded houses. The town's main street extended from north to south and was the site of intense commercial activity evidenced by the huge number of artifacts, tools and other items unearthed. Gournia was never inhabited after the Bronze Age and was completely forgotten. The town takes its present name from the stone washing basins *(gournes)* found outside every house during the excavations.

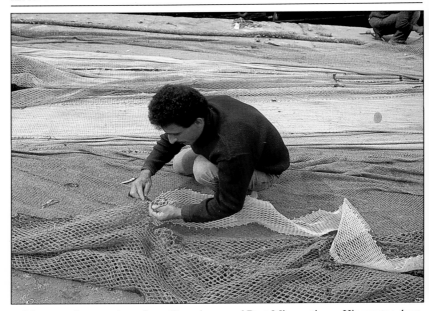

Most travelers continue from Gournia further south to **Ierapetra** via Pahia Ammos, Vasiliki and Episkopi villages. Ierapetra, 38 km from Agios Nikolaos, was until 1960 a place offering little more than a spectacular view of the Libyan Sea, good local wine and golden beaches. But in the last 20 years this town has flourished. Local farmers were some of the first in Crete to introduce hot-houses to raise their crops, produced year-round for markets abroad. Ierapetra was discovered by the hippies who made it one of their main sites with its cheap accommodation, mild climate and welcoming people. Minoan excavations in the nearby village of **Mirtos** brought in more traditional visitors forcing the area's rapid growth.

Ierapetra, the fourth largest town in Crete, took its name from the ancient port of *Hierapytna* which served as a junction between the island and Africa in Minoan

Above: This fisherman in Ierapetra is fixing tears in his nets.

and Post-Minoan times. Hierapytna dominated southeastern Crete about 145 BC. It fell into Roman hands in 67 BC but continued its growth in the Byzantine period and the Venetian occupation when it was renamed Ierapetra. During Roman rule the city had an impressive population of 120,000 and magnificent buildings which included a theater, public baths, and an aqueduct which stood until AD 1000. The Romans also used the city as a military port for their attacks against Egypt. The **Venetian castle** guarding the port was built in 1630 and is 50 m long from east to west and 25 m from south to north. It was armed with five large cannons and some 200 smaller guns. Ierapetra was conquered by the Turks in 1650 and from then on it fell from grace. The town's voyage through time can be seen at the local **museum** with a small collection of finds from each period.

These days, Ierapetra is occupied by discos, tavernas and hotels on excellent sandy beaches nearby. But avoid a visit during the middle of summer. Don't forget that you are only 300 km from the African coast and temperatures can get pretty high.

Ierapetra was the place where Napoleon stayed overnight on his way to and from Egypt. The ruins of the house where he slept can still be seen in **Kato Mera**. A caique trip 13 km to the south brings you to **Gaidouronissi**. The islet is deserted but the sea here is excellent for scuba diving. A short drive west from Ierapetra (15 km) lies the small village of **Mirtos** where British archaeologists brought to light a Minoan settlement dating to 2200 BC. The remains of a villa, built around 1600 BC, which served as the residence of the local Minoan governor, can still be seen. The villa was destroyed around 1450 BC probably by the volcanic explosion on Santorini and the earthquake that followed. About 90 rooms have been uncovered, containing a multitude of vases, sealstones, bronze utensils and tools.

From Ierapetra to Sitia

Leaving Ierapetra in eastward direction and then turning north, you will eventually reach Sitia. It is better, however, to avoid the route through the mountains and drive instead back north to **Pahia Ammos** (a small village next to Gournia) and then east on the coastal road. The stretch you now enter, from the village of **Kavoussi** to Sitia, is one of the most enjoyable Cretan rides through olive groves, orchards and villages overlooking the sea below. Locals call the area the "Cretan Riviera" which also includes the villages of **Lastros, Sfaka, Tourloti, Mouliana** (famous for its red wine), **Hamezi** (another Minoan and Venetian site), **Skopi** (known for its wedding celebrations), and eventually **Sitia**.

Mohlos

Mohlos, a tiny islet between Agios Nikolaos and Sitia on the stretch of coastline known as the "Cretan Riviera," was once connected to the cape on the eastern side of Mirabello Gulf.

Mohlos has recently attracted the attention of experts because of finds excavated by an archaeological team led by Nikolaos Platon. Mohlos is close to the larger islet of **Psira** and both can be reached by boat on excursions organized in Agios Nikolaos or by private caique from the mainland beach town of Mohlos, which has hotels and pensions.

Both Psira and Mohlos were ports trading with Egypt and other Middle Eastern countries during Minoan times. Traces of the harbor have been found in shallow water off the islet under what would have been the sandy spit connecting it to the mainland. Late Minoan houses are on the south side of the islet and can be seen from passing boats. Others are submerged in the sea.

The most significant artifacts in Mohlos were found in the tombs built up against the cliff. A rich cache of stone vases and jars, sealstones and gold jewto Iráklio

to Santorin

KRITIK

Akrotíri
Ágios Ioánnis

Mironikítas

Gallou
Sélles · Troulí
331m

Loúmas   Vrouhás

Pláka   Spinalog (Castle)

Spinalónga

Epáno
Pinés

Epáno Eloúnda
Mavrikianó

Eloúnda
(Shísma)   Olous
Eloúnda

Ellin' iká

Ágios Nikólaos

Amoudára

Kólpos

Mirabéllou

Psíra

Móhlos

Kálavros

Tourloti   Mirsíni

Méssa
Moulianá

Thólos

Sfáka

42

Orinó

Kapsás
1002m   Lástros

Koprokefála
1179m

Kavoússi   Mélisses
(Panagía)   Askordaliá
1237m

Bémbonas

Pírgos   Ístron

Kaló Horió

Pahiá
Ammos

Gournia

Thriptí

Hrissopigí

Lápithos

Moni Faneroménis
(Monastery)

Messeléri

Vassiliki

Papoúra
1011m   Thriptí

Afendis Kavoússi Orinó
1476m

Stávrohori

Ágios
Stéfanos

Castle   Castle

Monastiráki

Makriliá   Stavrós
Episkopí

Papadianá

Kefála
321m

Epanohóri
Katohóri   Katalímata
802m

Shinokápsala

Ágios Ioánnis   Kalivítis

Tsikkalariá

Koutsourás

Makrigialos

Análips

Kéndri

Vainía   Férma

Agía
Fotiá

24

Mávros
Kólimbos

Akrotíri T

Ierápetra   Koutsounári

Dragonáda

Gianissáda

to Rhodos

Akrotíri Síderos

LAGOS

Órmos
Ténda

195m
Mouros

ONLY FOR MILITARY

Ítanos

Vái

Órmos

Grándes

Akrotíri Faneroméni

eroméni
(stery)

Castle

Sitia

Petrás

Órmos
Sitías

Moní Tóplou
(Monastery)

Grándes

Palékastro

Mertidiá

Lídia Angáthia

Agia Fotiá

Módi Ágios Nikólaos
539m

Roussolákkos

opí
ládia

óri

Kimouriótis

Piskokéfalo

Káto
Episkopi

Roussa Ekklissia

Xirolímni

Petsofás
215m

Arnikó
Stavroménos
Krionéri

Mitáto

Langáda

Órmos
Karoúbes

Zoú

Káto Dris

Priniás
803m

Hónos

Vrissidi

Kellária

Hohlakiés

Máronia

Sfakiá

Katsidóni

Karidi Adravásti

Azokéramos
Traóstalos
515m

Épano Episcopi
os Geórgios
kriá

Sandáli

Praisós

Sitanos

Klissidi

Zákros

Ágios Spirídonas
Sikiá

Papaguiana

Néa Préssós

Kateliónas

Vígla Zákrou
711m

Káto
Zákros

Káto Zákros

Órmos
Zákrou

Vorí

Papagiannádes

Lamnóni

Akrotíri Avláki

Handrás
Etiá

Arméni

Ziros

Etianí Kefála
715m

Plágia
819m

Hamétoulo

Epáno
Perivolákia

Apidi

Xerókambos

Perivolákia

Kaló Horió

Agridomouri
628m

úlas

Agia Triáda

Agia Iríni

Kapsá
(bstery)
eró

Sárgou Kefála
539m

Goúdouras

Ather nolakós

Akrotíri Goúdouras

EAST OF LASSITHI

0   2   4   6 km

elry are now on display in museums in Agios Nikolaos and Iraklio.

Excavations in the early part of the 20th century by American Richard Seager turned up a settlement on Psira similar to Gournia and also flourishing during the Early and Late Minoan periods. Scant remains in the town, including a well, are reached via a long street with steps leading from what was the harbor. Two painted reliefs from houses on Psira are now in the Iraklio Archaeological Museum.

Sitia

Sitia (72 km from Agios Nikolaos), is the largest town in eastern Crete, and is still mostly untouched by the tourist storm which transformed Agios Nikolaos and Ierapetra. The town in the Minoan era was probably Eteia and it was known as the birthplace of Myson, one of the

seven sages of ancient Greece. Sitia flourished through the Roman and Byzantine times and took its present name after being occupied by the Venetians. In fact Sitia provided the name for the prefecture of Lassithi. "Lassithi" derives from "La Sitia," the name the Venetians gave to the region in the 15th century.

It was during that period that the town was devastated a number of times by earthquakes and attacks from the Ottomans. In 1651, the Venetians deliberately destroyed the town so that it would not fall to the Turks, who eventually made Sitia their provincial capital in 1870. The ruins of the Venetian fortress, overlooking the port, are worth a visit before lunch or dinner in one of the many tavernas serving fresh fish and local vegetables. A new museum has some notable pieces from the area's history and an airport will soon be built.

Sitia is famous for its *soultanines,* a sweet local raisin, which attracts huge crowds every August 30 to the "raisin festival," when producers celebrate the

Above: The tightly-knit houses of Sitia.

gathering of the year's crop with folk dances and Cretan music.

Sitia is a stopover for ships that pass weekly between Rhodes, Santorini, and Piraeus. The town's inhabitants are considered the most hospitable in Crete.

Toplou and Palekastro

Before proceeding to Palekastro and Vai make a stopover 7 km to the east at the village of **Agia Fotia** where a Minoan necropolis was discovered in 1971 thus providing the museum in Agios Nikolaos with its most important archaeological collection.

Continuing on the beach road east of Sitia, you arrive after 15 km at the Christian Orthodox **Toplou Monastery** which dates back to the 15th century. Today's building replaces an older church which was destroyed by an earthquake in 1612. The church was originally dedicated to St. Isidore (Agios Isidoros) but the name Toplou was given by the Turks in 1460. Toplou derives from the word for cannon and the building has the look of a fortress which was used as a refuge by Greek resistance fighters against the Turks or the Germans in World War Two.

The present monastery was built by the famous Kornaros family of Sitia. Vitsentzos Kornaros is the author of the Cretan epic poem *Erotokritos*, while Ioannis Kornaros painted, in 1770, the *Greatness of God*, an icon still considered to be a masterpiece of the Cretan miniature painting. The icon, which describes the universality of Christian healing. still adorns the monastery and is worshipped by locals as a miracle healer. Toplou Monastery is one of the richest in Greece as it owns most of the surrounding land.

A short drive (15 km) further east brings you to **Palekastro**. The village was excavated by the British School of Archaeology at the beginning of the century, unearthing a Minoan port town. It includes a palace with many rooms used

by the local prince and a central street lined with remains of houses and shops. The site has the usual acropolis of Minoan settlements and must have played an important role as a commercial port in Late Minoan times as it was one of few places on the island to be rebuilt after the great catastrophe in 1400 BC. Remains of more recent periods include an Archaic-Hellenic temple where a column (now kept in the Iraklio Archaeological Museum) is inscribed with a prayer to Zeus, many bronze and ivory items and a number of vases.

VAI AND KATO ZAKROS

Palekastro gives you the choice to head north to Vai and Itanos or south to Kato Zakros. **Vai** (9 km from Palekastro) has the only **palm forest** in Greece, which ends at a lovely sandy beach on the Carpathian Sea. The site is crowded by tourists in the summer, who often camp in the palm grove despite a police warning against it. Campers or not – the forest is

197

magical; during a full moon it resembles a tropical lagoon on a South Sea island. According to legend, Egyptian warriors created the forest in ancient times to honor a Pharaoh who believed that palm trees were the source of wisdom.

2 km north of Vai, near Crete's northernmost tip, lie the ruins of ancient **Itanos** near the easternmost part of Crete. Herodotus mentions the site in his *Histories*, explaining how a fisherman from the area guided a group of colonists from the island of *Thera* (Santorin) to the African coast in about 650 BC. The colonists went on to build the city of Cyrene whose ruins can still be seen in Libya. It is said that Itanos was originally founded by the Phoenicians but discoveries in the region indicate that the Minoans were there first creating yet another port which survived through Hellenic and Roman times but

Above: The unique palm beach of Vai is a nature conservation area. Right: This is all that remains of the great palace of the Minoan period in Kato Zakros.

198

was destroyed in the ninth century AD by pirates, and never rebuilt.

The south route from Palekastro leads through a group of villages to **Ano** and **Kato Zakros**, two of the loveliest villages in eastern Crete, overlooking the Carpathian Sea. The two villages are 7 km apart with Kato Zakros attracting more attention due to its impressive Minoan finds. The place was first excavated in the late 1800s and revealed some 15 houses of the Late Minoan period and finds from the Myceanaean age. In 1961, new digging took place after ancient objects were found in the area by local habitants and these excavations revealed a major Minoan harbor-town and a palace smaller only than the ones of Knossos, Festos and Malia. Archaeologists, who are still working on the site, now say that the settlement was a commercial center of Minoan civilization bringing in trade from Egypt and other countries in northern Africa and the Middle East.

The area was first inhabited about 2500 BC, a fact that is evidenced by

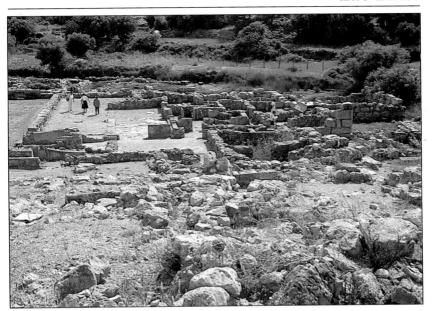

grave sites found at the north end of the village. The ruins have revealed the construction of a palace between 1600 BC and 1550 BC. The palace was badly damaged by earthquakes in 1500 BC, but was immediately repaired only to be totally destroyed 50 years later by the same catastrophic quake which ruined Knossos and Festos.

The palace, covering an impressive 6500 sq m, was a labyrinth of 300 rooms, similar in design to the ones in Knossos. The huge central court is engulfed by a number of apartments, storage halls, stairways and other structures while the area around the royal quarters was a well-planned harbor-town with large buildings and paved roads.

Recent findings indicate Kato Zakros had strong commercial ties with nearby countries. It brought copper from Cyprus, ivory from Syria and gold from Egypt. Its exports were oil, honey, wood, wine and various agricultural products.

Kato Zakros is the only Minoan settlement where, despite its destruction, so many finds were discovered in such good condition. Thousands of vases, metal and ivory tools, along with 35 giant containers, would be enough to fill up a small museum. Indeed, Kato Zakros has its own special place in the Iraklio Archaeological Museum, where the finds are exhibited.

Back in the palace, the royal apartments were placed on the eastern side with the king and the queen having different rooms. The biggest rooms of the complex lie to the west and communicate via a staircase to the upper floor where a huge chamber known as the **Hall of Ceremonies** is found. It was here that the king held political or diplomatic meetings with his associates or presided over religious ceremonies. At the palace's northern side an equally huge room surrounded by a maze of smaller ones served as the kitchen. Finally, in a separate area north of the palace where excavations still take place, blocks of small houses served as living quarters for lower-class people probably employed at

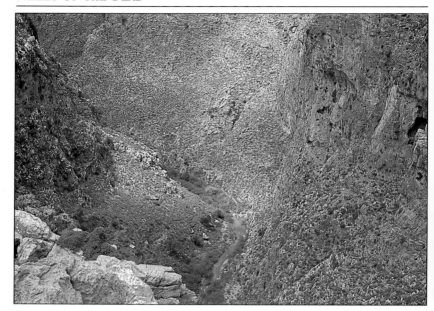

the harbor or the families of seefarers. Kato Zakros is the only Minoan settlement that offers a genuine idea of life during that era. It was never pillaged or remodeled. It has an exclusive room in the Archaeological Museum in Iraklio.

VALLEY OF THE DEAD

We shall begin this hike in the middle of Zakros. From the main square you turn into the street "Odos 25 Martiou," where a church stands. Take the path leading downward on the right of the church and go under the aqueduct, along a water canal until you reach the southwest end of the village. After about fifteen minutes the cement road gives way to a gravel covering which you must follow for about another 50 meters. At the fork you head left over the stream. Proceed amidst fields and vegetable gardens, up a cement

Above: A plunging view into Crete's version of Death Valley from the old road to Kato Zakros.

road, on a path alongside a water pipe in the direction of the valley.

Go through a gate and straight through a plot of land. After passing the fence, the road forks again. Do not go right down toward the stream, but left up a gentle slope leading above the tree-tops of the planes and oleanders lining the stream. About half an hour later you get a first glimpse of the opening to the gorge.

The path then leads in part along the stream in the shade of the plane trees. Another valley joins laterally from the left. At this point you can cross over to the stream's right bank and walk along an irrigation canal. The cliff above is dotted with little niches and caves. Some served as burial grounds for the dead in the pre-Christian era which is why the gorge has been called the **Valley of the Dead**.

About 500 meter further the path leads back to the stream which you can once again cross. You are now standing in a giant stone cauldron surrounded on all sides by cliffs. The path is in good shape; light shoes such as sneakers suffice. De-

1 South Entrance
2 Fountain
3 Cistern
4 King's Megaron
5 Queen's Megaron
6 Paved Court
7 Lustral Basin
8 Kitchen
9 Propylon
10 Magazines
11 Hall of Ceremonies
12 Workrooms
13 Treasure Chamber
14 Lustral Area
15 Central Court

KATO ZAKROS

0   10   20   30m

pending on the season the stream might be dry, in which case the splashing and murmuring of the water is supplanted by a deathly silence in the almost 200 m high cliff walls.

Finally the stream bed widens, the path becomes stony, oleanders join the shrubby blue summer lilac and out of nowhere the little stream reemerges. The reddish walls of the gorge appear ragged and hollow before disappearing altogether. A banana plantation is situated here.

A normal road crosses the stream bed at this point. This is the old road to Zakros, which you can take to get back to your starting point, and once again it offers a spectacular view of the gorge. First, however, make a quick excursion to the sea. The path to the left leads by the excavation site of the palace of Kato Zakros. The taverns along the beach are very inviting, and the bay can be an idyllic spot to bathe and sunbathe provided no tourist buses have stopped here. If you are tired of walking, try catching a ride back to Zakros, or use the old road leading upwards on the right of the gorge's exit.

South of Sitia

Sitia offers a base for a southern excursion towards the Libyan Sea through a purely Cretan territory of rigid cliffs with little cultivation, that has remained largely unchanged for thousands of years. A short drive (3 km) brings you to the village of **Piskokefalo**, founded in the 15th century during the Venetian occupation. In the surrounding area two minor excavations of Minoan sites dating to 1600 BC have brought to light a villa and a farming village with houses, storerooms, stables and a sanctuary.

7 km further south you reach **Nea Pressos**, built next to the ruins of ancient Pressos. The city was a major center for Eteocretans, a post-Minoan culture that survived for a millenium after the Greek invasion of Knossos and other Minoan centers, by taking refuge in the eastern end of the island. Four Eteocretan in-

scriptions dating to 600 BC were discovered in 1884 along with the remains of a Minoan villa and a Hellenistic necropolis. Pressos was destroyed in 144 BC after the long wars with Ierapetra.

Your next stop further south is the mountain village of **Ziros** dating back to Venetian times. The local **Church of Agia Paraskevi** is lavishly decorated with frescoes from the Cretan renaissance.

From Ziros, a secondary southern route leads to **Kapsas monastery**, dedicated to St. John the Baptist. Built in the 14th century by a group of monks, the original monastery was ruined by the Turks in 1471, but was rebuilt by the Venetians. A monk called Gerontogiannis (Old John), made news in the nineteenth century with his miraculous healings. His reputation attracted huge crowds from other villages who still come every August 29 when Kapsa celebrates his feast day. The monastery offers a unique view of the Libyan Sea and the nearby village of **Kalo Nero** (Good Water) has a wonderful beach.

Koufonissi, about 4 km off the southern shore of Crete near Atherinolakos, is the largest island in the archipelago, once known in antiquity as the *Leucai,* the White Islands. Evidence has been found of a settlement from the Early Bronze Age. The largest remains, however, including part of a theater built of stone, are from a prosperous Roman town. Excavations under the Greek Archaeological Service, which were begun in 1976, continue each summer.

The cultivation of a form of brilliant crimson dye, obtained from a gland in the shell of a spiny sea-snail, began in Minoan times. It was responsible for Kou-

Right: Crete's most luxurious hotel complexes can be found in Eloundra. Following pages: Seasonal fruits. A woman's hands at rest. A Cretan speciality: snails in olive oil, onions, tomatoes and spices.

fonissi's prominant position in the Mediterranean textile industry, known as the "purple trade," which was highly lucrative into the Roman era. An exhibit in the Sitia Museum illustrates the labor-intensive methods of harvesting the snails and obtaining the scant drops of the precious dye so highly prized by the Phoenicians, Greeks and Romans.

Offbeat Beaches

West of Ierapetra, the beach at **Arvi** is long enough to handle the crowds that gather there. The main virtue of the area is the fertile land around the beach on which fruit is grown. Take a stroll around the banana plantations.

Mirtos is a small village with some rooms for rent, a few tavernas and also good opportunities for swimming. During the last two decades an increasing number of big hotels have expanded throughout the area around **Ierapetra**. 24 km further on, just before the road branches off to inland Sita, you will reach the village of **Makrigialos** which has a beautiful beach. Along the coastline, to the east, at **Kalo Nero**, **Goudouras**, and near **Kapsas monastery** there are more rewarding beaches.

The beaches of **Kato Zakros** and **Palekastro** on the east coast of Crete are renowned for their tranquility, some friendly tavernas and rooms to rent. Undoubtedly the most scenic beach on the eastern coast, however, is the palm beach of **Vai** which is a protected area today where camping is prohibited.

The Istron Beach Hotel in **Istron** is on a cliff above a lovely beach, much nicer than the one at Kalo Horio. It is the best beach outside Agios Nikolaos.

Mohlos is a friendly village and a good place for diving. The posh hotels outside **Agios Nikolaos** have attractive beaches restricted to guests. At **Elounda**, people swim off the flat rocks at Olus or at the large pebble beach at **Plaka**.

THE CRETAN RENAISSANCE

Nothing really is known about Vitsentzos Kornaros, except where he came from and, of course, his name, which he mentioned in one of the verses of his Romanesque poem *O Erotokritos* (The Judge of Love), written around 1645. Sitia, his birthplace, reveals hardly any traces of this man, who was one of the greatest poets in the modern Greek language. But *O Erotokritos*, like his other works, has survived and maintained his reputation as one of the founding pillars of what came to be known as the Cretan Renaissance.

Most visitors to the island will not have the opportunity to dwell on the literary aspects of this Golden Age of Cretan culture, but the architectural testimonials of that time and, above all, its religious art, which blossomed during the Venetian era and evolved its own expressive form, are well represented. Between the 14th and the 17th century, that is until the darker days of Ottoman rule, Crete became a place where Byzantine traditions (with their elements of revived antiquity) fused with Western innovations, namely in the use of the Italo-Venetian medium.

Barring a few church façades, palaces and fountains, Cretan architecture from the days of the Renaissance can be discovered in remote backstreets of the old towns of Rethimno and Hania. The more visible examples of this art are the many chapels that dot the island, decorated with icons and frescos. Besides the names of the great Cretan poets of the Renaissance, such as Kornaros, Foskolos and Hortatsis, the names of many painters of the "Cretan School" of fresco working in the 15th century have been handed down through the ages: Ioannis Pagomenos, Pavlos Provatos and Konstantinos Paleokapas, among others.

The great master of icon painting, which experienced its Golden Age in the 16th century, was Mihail Damaskinos; but it was Domenikos Theotokopoulos, better known as "El Greco," who bridged the gap to western art. Not a single one of his works is to be seen on Crete.

AGIOS NIKOLAOS
Accommodation

LUXURY: **Istron Bay**, Tel. (0841) 61347/61325, on the beach, sea-water swimming pool, shopping arcade, private beach, tennis. **Minos Beach**, hotel and bungalows, Tel. (0841) 22345, on the beach of Ammoudi, pool, tennis, all bungalows with refrigerator and mini bar. **Minos Palace Hotel**, Tel. (0841) 23801, pool, refrigerator and mini-bar in all rooms, all bungalows with sea view. **Mirabello Village**, Tel. (0841) 28400, on the beach, two heated pools, indoor pool, sauna, three tennis courts, night club. **Hermes**, Tel. (0841) 28253, on the beach, pool, mini-golf, beauty parlor. **St. Nicholas Bay,** Tel. (0841) 25041, on the beach, pool, tennis court, pool bar.

MODERATE: **Ariadni Beach**, Tel. (0841) 22741. **Coral**, Tel. (0841) 28363 **El Greco,** Tel. (0841) 28894.

BUDGET: **Almyros Beach**, Tel. (0841) 22865. **Kera**, Tel. (0841) 28771.

Useful phone numbers
Area code: 0841. **Police**: 2225, **Tourist police:** 22321, **Harbor police**: 22312, **Hospital**: 22369.

ELOUNDA / SPINALONGA
Accommodation

LUXURY: **Astir Palace Elounda**, Tel. (0841) 41580, on the beach, pool, greek taverna, cinema, disco. **Elounda Beach**, Tel. (0841) 41412, on the beach, pool, tennis, all water sports, deep sea diving. **Elounda Mare**, Tel. (0841) 41102, 50 rooms and 40 bungalows with private pools, mini bar, refrigerators in all rooms. **Elounda Marmin**, Tel. (0841) 41535, 100 m from the beach, pool, tennis.

MODERATE: **Driros Beach**,Tel. (0841) 41238.

BUDGET: **Kalypso**, Tel. (0841) 41316.

Useful phone numbers
Area Code: 0841, **Police**: 41348.

IERAPETRA
Accommodation

LUXURY: **Ferma Beach**, hotel and bungalows, Tel. (0842) 61341, on the beach of Ferma, swimming pool, tennis court, golf. **Lyktos Beach Resort Hotel and Tennis Club**, Tel. (0842) 61280, on the beach, swimming pool, tennis courts, water sports, library, cinema and card room. **Patramare,** Tel. (0842) 23341, on the beach, swimming pool, hairdressing.

MODERATE: **Blue Sky**, Tel. (0842) 28264. **Minoan Prince**, Tel. (0842) 25150 **Porto Belisario Hotel**, Tel. (0842) 61358.

BUDGET: **Zakros Hotel**, Tel. 24101.

Useful phone numbers
Area code: 0842, **Tourist police**: 22560.

SITIA
Accommodation

LUXURY: **Sitian Beach**, Tel. (0843) 28821, on the beach, two pools, disco. **Sunwing**, Tel. (0843) 51621, beach club, pool, two tennis courts.

MODERATE: **Aldiana Club**, Tel. (0843) 94211. **Maresol Bungalows**, Tel. (0843) 28950.

Museums
AGIOS NIKOLAOS: **Archeological Museum** (Tel. 0841/24943), Paleologou St. 68. Finds from the excavation in eastern Crete.

SITIA: **Ethnological Museum.**

IERAPETRA: **Archaeological Collection.**

Archeological Sites
Gournia, open daily 8.45 am-3 pm. **Agia Fotia** (Proto-Minoan Necropolis), **Kato Zakros** (Minoan Palace) open daily 9.30 am-3.45 pm, Sundays from 9 am-2.30 pm. **Ierapetra** (archaeological collection), **Mohlos** (Proto-Minoan Necropolis), **Neapoli** (archaeological collection), **Palekastro** (Minoan settlement).

Festivals
Naval Week: Agios Nikolaos is probably the best place to be during Greek Naval Week taking place every June. The public is invited to go aboard warships anchored in the harbor, from where they can watch events connected with the sea. These include water sports, swimming competitions and varios exhibitions. A spectacular firework display is held on the final evening.

Lato-Kornaria: These are cultural activities organized in June, July and August in Agios Nikolaos, Ierapetra and Sitia. They include lectures, art exhibitions, folk and modern music festivals, track and field games and wine tasting.

Sultana Festival: The festival is held in Sitia by local raisin producers during the second fortnight in August. The event attracts many visitors who are invited to sample some 40 wine varieties and other local products. Folk music and water sports complete the festivities.

Beaches
Agios Nikolaos (Ammoudi), Ierapetra (east along the coast), Mirtos, Milatos, Anatoli, Lithines, Makri Gialos, Sitia, Palekastro, Vai.

Camping
Gournia Moon, from Agios Nikolaos on the road to Sitia, Tel. (0842) 93243; persons 165, tents 55. **Ierapetra Camping**, Tel. (0842) 61351; persons 123, tents 41. **Koutsoumari**, Agios Ioannis, Tel. (0842) 61213; persons 198, tents 66.

Monasteries
Selinari, Kremasta, Afetiou, Arvi, Krousteliana, Toplou, Faneromenis, Exakoustis, Kapsa.

Useful phone numbers
Area code: 0843, **Tourist police**: 22266.

FLORA AND FAUNA

Crete has a good range of common Mediterranean bird species with a number of rare ones, either residents or visitors, seen on their migratory route. The best time to see both is in the spring. Crete is on one of the main migratory routes for species that winter in East Africa but breed in northern Europe. The autumn migration is also a time to spot some species on their way south but the number of birds has greatly decreased in the past years.

Smaller songbirds are at greatest risk in Crete, often falling prey to overzealous hunters or collectors who cage them. Another hazard is the destruction of their habitat, a process that has taken place at an alarming rate in coastal areas and some of the flat interior. For this reason,

Above: "Live free or die," was the motto that almost led to the eagle's extinction. Right: Cretan hunters tend to shoot anything that moves.

the mountainous areas are home to some of the more fascinating smaller birds and a really impressive array of birds of prey.

The blue rock thrush and the rock Nuthatch are found on mountainsides. Colonies of noisy Alpine choughs are especially prolific near the Kamares cave on Mount Psiloritis.

Although some unfortunate magnificent predators end up as poorly preserved stuffed specimens decorating *kafenions,* many Cretan hunters are slightly more respectful towards larger birds, if not towards the laws that protect them.

Attempts have been made to restrict the indiscriminate use of pesticides sprayed from planes, or poisoned bait to exterminate unwanted animals. The use of these measures has been directly responsible for the dwindling numbers of many species.

During the warmer months, the mountains are home to long-legged buzzards, fairly langorous birds, the golden eagle and at lower levels Bonelli's eagle and bearded vultures. This extremely rare

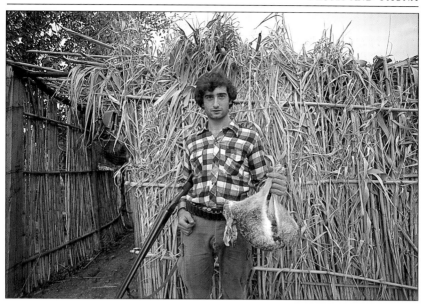

bird, one of Europe's largest and most majestic species, has its largest Greek population in Crete, particularly in the Samaria Gorge. In the winter, many of these birds fly down to the plains.

Most birds of prey breed in the early and mid-spring, although Eleanora's falcon, common on the rocky islets off Crete, nests in late summer. The vultures nest in winter. The vultures are also exceptional in that the male is larger than the female. In most vultures, which mate for life, the female is bigger and stronger.

The in-flight foreplay that precedes breeding is dazzlingly fanciful and agile. The birds soar over the area they have chosen for a nest, first playing with one another, then flying with interlocked toes. One of them will dive to the ground, at the last moment rising again. The male, as a finale, offers food to the female and she accepts it while making sounds similar to the calls of her young.

The griffon vulture, whose most abundant numbers are in Crete, is an ominous looking creature with a long neck, fierce

eyes and a huge hooked bill. Griffons are gregarious. They eat carrion and a few of them together can strip a large carcass in very short order.

The lammergier vulture, also a huge bird with a wing span of almost 3 meters, is distinguished from the griffon by its narrower wings and longer, wedge-shaped tail. It is extremely rare but more common in Crete than anywhere else. Occasionally, it may be sighted gliding over the Lassithi or Omalos Plains.

Coastal lagoons, marshy river deltas and wetlands are not common in Crete but afford good bird watching where they do exist. The river bed near Agia Triada in Iraklio is frequented by herons, egrets and sandpipers. Marsh harriers can often be seen drifting and darting over reedbeds near rivers, wings in open V-shape, looking for fish, frogs and snakes.

The marshes and reed beds near Agia Galini have nightingales and warblers. The river bed or hillsides near the Preveli Monastery may be the place to find the Sardinian warbler or the even rarer Ruppell's warbler, distinguished by a black cap and throat, red eye and white mustache. The chukar, a partridge reminiscent of those in the lovely Knossos frescoes, favors hillsides.

Adaptable kestrels and red-footed falcons, both predators, congregate in bushes or scattered trees in open areas or sometimes on telegraph wires on the edge of towns. Both are protected.

Two stunningly marked birds, the pink, black and white hoopoe and the yellow and black oriole, can sometimes be spotted in woodland or olive groves. Another frequent visitor to olive groves, as well as large gardens and old buildings near settlements, is the tiny insectivorous Scops owl. Its mottled markings adapt it perfectly for daytime snoozing against tree bark and if disturbed, it will freeze and raise its protruding ear tufts. Its most distinctive characteristic and one that for many symbolizes the atmosphere of the

Greek islands, is its powerful and persistant nocturnal call which sounds like "kook."

The hauntingly beautiful barn owl, whose shrill voice and preference for settling in old ruins has created the superstition that it is cursed, was the victim of hunting and pesticides around 1970. Its numbers were greatly reduced and consequently the rat population, part of its prey, rose significantly in Crete, illustrating the importance of birds of prey in the ecosystem.

The fauna is otherwise rather on the poor side. The *kri-kri,* Crete's wild goat, barely escaped extermination by being resettled on the islands off the northern coast. One still finds these stringently protected animals near the Gorge of Samaria and in some of the more remote mountainous areas. On the other hand, a fair number of smaller animals live on the island, including rabbits, swamp turtles (in Lake Kournas), weasels, snakes and lizards. There is no need to fear the snakes: Of the five types extant on Crete

Above: Crete is a wonderful place in spring, not only for sheep.

FLORA AND FAUNA

only one, the adder, is venomous, but not dangerous for humans because usually the snakes slither off at the slightest sound.

Trees and Shrubs

Crete had among the earliest of advanced civilizations in the eastern Mediterranean region. Deforestation of erstwhile dense woodlands in addition to climatic changes have resulted in the landscape as we know it today, consisting principally of lower vegetation, thorny undergrowth and hardy thickets. Man's hand, however, also played a role in importing new plants and trees from other parts of the world. Grapes and olive trees were already being cultivated during antiquity. Citrus fruits, agaves, opuntias and eucalyptus arrived on the island with the discovery of new continents.

The most common trees on Crete today are pines, cypresses, various oaks, planes, chestnuts and eucalyptus. In many places the landscape has been shaped by plantations of utility trees such as olive, orange, lemon, fig, almond, walnut and carob. Of more recent date are subtropical fruits including avocados, kiwis and bananas.

Among the most prevalent shrubs are broom, holly, oleander, myrtle and the Macchia's panoply of hardy growths. The lower vegetation – known as phrygana – includes a large number of medicinal plants and herbs such as sage, thyme and oregano.

Flowers

To see Crete in the early spring, blanketed in a colorful array of wild flowers and flowering shrubs, is a joyful experience for anyone, even those without a smidgeon of formal knowledge about the science of botany. For naturalists, the Cretan countryside, which boasts over 2000 species of plants, 130 endemic to

the island, is paradise and they may immerse themselves in the sighting and study of these forms, to the exclusion of everything else.

Crete is the only mountainous island to have all four of the major habitats which include the coast, cultivated land, low hillsides and mountains. In the lowlands, most plants are burnt out during the scorching heat between mid-July through late September, though the mountains still have some greenery. In the autumn, a second spring occurs, with many plants flowering between October to December.

The love of flowers goes back to the ancient times of the Minoans, whose art reflected the wide range of the flora, most of which is still blooming in Crete today. Pottery, drawings and frescoes of Minoan Crete show flowering plants such as the Barbary nut, an iris with bright blue flowers with white centers and yellow markings, the white, pink or yellow turban buttercup, crocuses, lilies, pale yellow sternbergias and clusters of sea daffodil.

The mythical and healing associations of Cretan plants are numerous. One of the most outstanding in this respect is the Madonna lily, one meter high with a few large funnel-shaped flowers of pure white, that is the most frequent floral motif of Minoan art. It symbolizes grace and purity, and both Greeks and Romans put wreaths of lilies and corn on the heads of those being married.

In Crete, the white lily is strongly associated with *Britomartis,* the "sweet virgin" who was pursued by Minos. She jumped into the sea and was saved from drowning by a fisherman drawing his nets. She later became called both *Dictyna*, "mother of the nets," and the Mother Goddess. To later Greeks, the lily was the flower of Hera who was the goddess of marriage and childbirth. The flower was said to have a magical power against witches and evil. The juice, or an ointment made from the bulb, is soothing for skin ailments and if pulverized with honey, makes an excellent face masque to remove wrinkles. The lily can be found in Crete on dry, stony slopes from May to July. Another variation, also a motif of Minoan art, is the brilliant scarlet chalcedonicum, found in woodland clearings on mountains from June to August.

A number of flowering plants must be eaten to release their powers. The sea daffodil, or *pancratium,* was believed to be a cure-all, as its Greek name (*pan* – all, *cratium* – strength) implies. Dioscurides describes the edible bulb as being good for a wide range of ailments from coughs to heart disease to chapped feet. It blooms on coastal sands from July to September.

One of the weirdest of the edible flowering plants is the mandrake, steeped in myth and magic because its shape often resembled a human figure and the plant is depicted as having a human head. It is a narcotic plant that is said to utter a shriek when dug up, the sound of which is harmful to men. Therefore a dog was used to extract the root from the soil. Besides being used in sorcery, the root was used as a painkiller during operations, and as a cure for gout, sleeplessness and as a love potion. It flowers in fields and stony places in both spring and autumn.

The white or pink-flushed peony, which blooms on stony hillsides from April onward, is also known to have powerful curative and magical properties. Theophrastus and Pliny suggested its root – said to cure convulsions, epilepsy and lunacy – should only be dug up at night for a person doing so during the day is in danger of losing his eyesight.

Cistus is a shrub with pink flowers that blooms from March until June in stony places. A gum, *ladanum,* exudes from the plant and is collected by pulling a leather-thonged flail through the plants in the hottest part of the day or it can be collected from the beards and legs of goats

Above: Beauty that pricks. Right: The fields are in full bloom during spring time.

feeding nearby. The gum is still used in medicinal plasters and perfumes, and a tea can be made from an infusion of the leaves.

Although the cultivation and development of land on Crete has interfered with the natural habitat of wildflowers, there are still more varieties in Crete than, say, in all of Britain. Those wanting a thorough and scientific guide to the Cretan wildflowers should consult Huxley and Taylor's *Flowers Of Crete.*

Mountainous and stony areas cannot be cultivated, so are especially rich in wildflowers. One logical way to see wildflowers is to combine looking for them with a visit to the ancient sites. The land has not usually been tampered with since ancient times, although unfortunately the use of pesticides has destroyed some flowers and harmed other sensitive species, especially the delicate orchids.

Polyrinia, a few kilometers south of Kastelli, is relatively unknown but has remains from Minoan to Byzantine times and, in addition, has a breathtaking panorama of the coastal plain and the sparkling sea. Above the white houses of the village on the crest of the hill, during March-June, there is a splendid profusion of the woody-stemmed shrub tree spurge, which has clusters of yellow flowers. In the midst of fortifications, ruined towers, and old walls are poppies, gladioli, crown daisies, Venus, looking glass, wild leek and feathery-leaved pheasant's eye.

Gournia, in mid-Crete overlooking the Bay of Mirabello, has paved floors in the ancient town that are covered in the spring with anemones, turban buttercups, star of bethlehem and widow iris. Outside the town walls grow impressive giant orchids.

At Festos, a cross-section of endemic Cretan spring flowers – anemones, irises and orchids, including the insect-imitating orchid *orphys cretica* - are enhanced by the appearance of the exotic blue-flowered love-in-a-mist. From Festos in

the south, one can see anemones, mandrakes and orchids. Also from Festos, it is an easy walk to Agia Triada, a smaller site with a wider array of orchids, Cretan ebony and anemones.

The originally Doric site of Lato, near Agios Nikolaos, has a view across vast alive and almond groves to the sea. Its floral highlights are a bright yellow form of turban buttercup, rock lettuce and *alyssoides cretica,* a much branched perennial with bright golden flowers.

Near Agia Galini, towards the cliffs to the west that rise among typical vegetation of phrygana or scattered scrubby bushes, growing on limestone, one might find tassel hyacinths, Jerusalem sage, and giant fennel, over 2 m high. An orchid with the name *orphys fuciflora* or the late spider orchid, with a distinctive blue pattern, grows here.

On the open hillsides near the Preveli Monastery grow spring flowers and aromatic herbs such as sage, rosemary, lavender or the Cretan dittany, a white woolly shrublet with pink flowers.

CAVES

Most visitors to Crete come in search of sun and surf but there are more and more individualists who will be happier delving into its darker depths in the form of caves. Probably the most famous "caves" at Matala are not really caves but rock-cut Roman tombs inhabited by a colony of free spirits during the 1970s.

Many Cretan caves have mythological associations, such as the **Ideon Cave** on the slopes of Mount Psiloritis, which was identified as the birthplace of Zeus in those days. The Psychro or **Dikteon Cave**, below Mount Dikti, is considered a rival to the Ideon Cave as the birthplace of Zeus, although most scholars believe it was the sanctuary of the Minoan mother goddess. It is also believed to have been the scene of the seduction of Europa by

Above: The entrance to the Melidoni cave near Perama. Right: The Bears' Cave at the Gouverneto Monastery on the Akrotiri peninsula.

Zeus, a union which produced Minos, the founder of the Minoan dynasty.

The **Kamares Cave**, at the southern foot of Mount Psiloritis, is thought to have been inhabited since Neolithic times. Excavations of the cave after its discovery by a shepherd in the late 19th century yielded the distinctive polychrome pottery with striking geometric designs now displayed in the Iraklio Archaeological Museum. The artifacts were votive offerings from the Festos rulers to the goddess Eileithyia who was worshipped in a sanctuary in the cave.

A well-paved road from Iraklio cuts through peaceful hamlets, surrounded by groves watered by abundant streams. The path to Kamares Cave begins almost opposite the cemetery in Kamares Village 56 km southwest of Iraklio. Ask the friendly villagers about hiring a guide because the steep ascent up the mountain side takes at least three hours and the path is marked sporadically with orange splashes. The cave nestles below the peak of the Dhigenis, at an altitude of 1524 m.

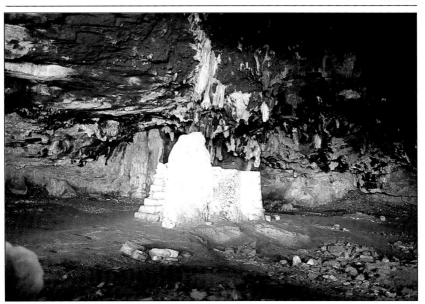

The **Skotino Cave** is a comfortable walk of 8.5 km from the main road running between Iraklio and Agios Nikolaos. The enormous cave is considered one of the most important sanctuaries on Crete. Skotino was first investigated by Sir Arthur Evans, then by French archaeologist Paul Faure, followed by Greek excavator Davaras. Faure speculated that the grotto was used as a religious sanctuary originally dedicated to Britomartis in the Middle Minoan period, when she was worshipped along with Artemis.

The area around **Elos**, south of Kastelli Kissamou, presents some possibilities for hiking through wooded hillsides and ravines, with several breathtaking views of the sea from the highest altitudes. Near the Koutsomatados Ravine, one of the most picturesque canyons on the island, the road enters a tunnel which leads to the **Agia Sofia Cave**. The cave has a chapel near the entrance and was inhabited in Neolithic times.

Melidoni Cave, northeast of Perama, an undistinguished town south of the Re-

thimno-Iraklio road, is known as the home of Talos, a bronze giant, notorious in mythology for hurling boulders at passing ships.

In 1824, several hundred people escaping from marauding soldiers in nearby villages, were trapped in the cave by the Turks, who blocked the entrance with brushwood and set fire to it, suffocating the villagers who all died. Melidoni is only a 5-km walk from Perama. From outside the entrance one has a lovely view across the Milopotamos Valley up to the Psiloritis mountain range.

Milatos Cave is 6 km from the coast to the east of Malia, on a side road that leads past the village of Sission. Milatos was the site of another horrific incident during the resistance in 1823. 3700 Greek children, women, and old men were besieged in the cave by 16,000 Turkish troops, before finally surrendering to Pasha Hasan. The old men were killed and the women and children sold into slavery. A memorial service is held each year to recall this gruesome event.

217

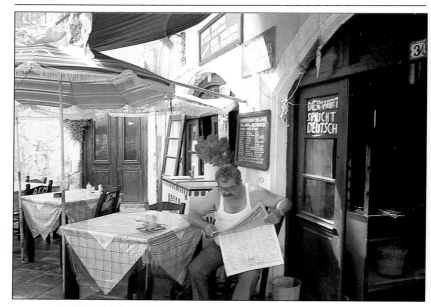

CRETAN COOKING

Traditional Cretan cooking is, to a degree, different from that of mainland Greece. Recent culinary "arrivals" such as feta cheese, *souvlaki, pastichio* and *doner kebab* were unknown on the island until relatively recent times. In many cases, basic ingredients and combinations resemble those of the mainland but there are a number of subtle differences determined by the addition of local ingredients or favored spices and herbs that betray contacts with, or influences from, the many different peoples who have either settled on the island or lived within its confines.

Cretan cooking is a blend of Greek, Roman and Byzantine traditions interacting within a relatively isolated region for over 2000 years. In the course of these

centuries Arabs, Slavs, Anatolian Greeks, Venetians and Turks have all lived for considerable lengths of time on the island. Moreover, many of their descendants continue to live there and culinary traditions whose origins are obscure. Today, people all over the world enjoy the cultural influences of other countries and poeples, and recipes travel from the land of their origin to be adapted and adopted into international cuisine. Until very recent times the diet of the Cretan people was very distinctive and many ancient Cretan recipes remain a jealously guarded secret. At least one factor that determines some of the peculiarities of Cretan cooking is the relative isolation that parts of the island enjoy due to mountains, valleys and plains. Village and urban life on the island have always been sharply poised against each other. Thus in Crete there is urban cooking, village cooking, that of the mountain areas and that more common to the plains and seacoast. Seasonal availability also plays its part in determining diet.

Above: Waiting for customers at a tavern in Rethimno. Right: Hospitality is one of the golden rules in the mountain villages of Crete.

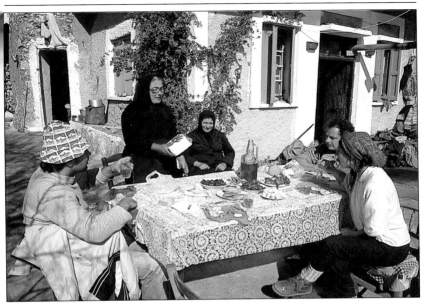

Cretan cheeses were famous in the Middle Ages – even in Europe. The most distinctive cheeses native to the island are *graviera, mizithra, staka, malaka* and *ladotiri. Graviera* is a more or less fresh and unripened cheese, mild and used widely. A salted and slightly aged version is *kephalotiri*. Both of these also are found in Greece. *Staka* is derived from the fats that accumulate while milk is being prepared for cheese making and is a great delicacy as is *mizithra* made from fresh sheep's milk. *Ladotiri* is almost always home-made and concocted from what remains after cheese making. It is preserved in oil *(ladi)* – hence its name.

Green Vegetables

Cretans are great vegetables eaters and the island has an abundance of them in the spring and even mid-winter. Some are boiled, some are specially set aside for pies or meat dishes. The former always incorporate cheese – either *graviera, mizithra* or *malaka*. The names of these vegetables invariably differ according to the various areas – *vlatzakia, stiphanos, radika, radikia, stamnangathia, maratho, staphilinakis, kokkoraki* and *askrolimbi* are but a few.

Pies

Cretan stone ovens were traditionally heated almost to incandescence and used during the cooling down period for the preparation of different foods. Bread went in first to be followed by meat (if used) and then pies. The latter would have been made of different kinds of dough depending on the nature of the filling. For meat pies stock and oil were incorporated.

Pies made of cheese, greens etc. on occasion use doughs prepared with *tsikoudia* – a native Cretan *raki* prepared from either the distilled lees from the wine press or mulberries (this is the most common). Sweet pies or doughs prepared for making desserts incorporate orange or lemon juice as well as raki.

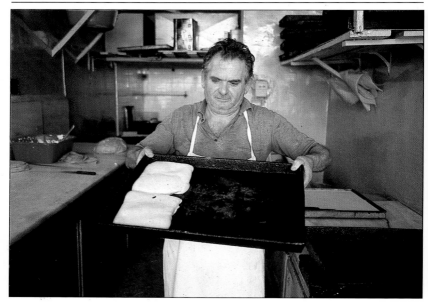

A very famous dish used to be prepared in the Sfakia/Selinos region of Crete when ibexes were still hunted for sport and food. This was prepared with an ibex kid that was stuffed with *mizithra*, *staka*, dill, various other herbs, greens, heavily peppered and then sealed in an earthenware pot with dough crust and baked in an oven. A modern variation is sometimes prepared using a whole kid or baby lamb.

Stews are very popular and varied. Some of these, such as fricassé, incorporate lemon sauce as well as different kinds of vegetables. Celery root is used widely with meat stews and the leaves of *maidano* (Italian parsley) are cut up finely with tomatoes to prepare sauces in which fish or meat are cooked. Artichokes are found in great abundance in Crete and are cooked with meat with or without lemon

Above: The best bougatsa – a farmer's cheese specialty – you will find at Kir Kors in Iraklion Right: An edible still life: bread, wine, olives, cheese, salad.

and egg sauces. It is said, that the Cretan diet is very healthy.

Meats

Traditional meats eaten by Cretans are baby lamb, kid, and hares or rabbits and pork in winter. Chicken, while eaten, was once considered to be almost the equivalent of a poor man's meat. An especially delicious way of preparing lamb calls for marinading it with lemon juice overnight and then placing it on a bed of thyme and (or) oregano sprigs. Heavily peppered, it is baked in a slow oven. Another recipe bakes the lamb in a sauce of yoghurt, eggs and melted butter.

Hare or rabbit is often buttered and fried. It is also incorporated in onion stews *(stifado)* flavored with orange juice (or rind), bay leaves, cinnamon and cloves. Snails are also eaten widely and appear in stews concocted with tomatoes, potatoes, and onions *(hohlious stifado)* or even baked in tomato sauce – usually laced with orange juice.

Seafood

Seafood is naturally most popular along the coastal areas of Crete and eaten grilled, stewed, baked or even raw. A favorite pastime among children is sucking out periwinkles and tiny crabs while on the look-out for sea urchins that were either eaten on the spot or taken home and eaten raw there.

The great variety of fish that once inhabited the seas around Crete has diminished due to foreign poachers, dynamite fishing and pollution. There are many varieties of bream, mullet both grey as well as red, and larger fish such as sword fish. Octopus is very popular and is cooked over charcoal, eaten in stews or as a seafood salad. The latter are also cooked with pasta in a very distinctive Cretan dish. Calamares are usually dipped in butter and fried. In winter, *baka-liaros* (imported dried cod) is often served. However, if you expect your seafood to be cheaper than at home, you will be sorely dissappointed.

Spices

Spices are greatly used in urban cooking in Crete. Hania and Rethimno were always known for their rich and elegant dishes, and these traditionally incorporated spices that were readily available in their markets. Crete, especially during Ottoman times, was a mid-way stop in the spice trade that ran from Alexandria and other North African ports to the southern shores of Crete. From here, goods were brought up to the northern coast and then made their way to Izmir and Istanbul. Cinnamon invariably appears in some meat dishes, sauces and sweets along with cloves. Hot chillis (grown on the island) are used in making the filling for small cheese pies called *skaltsounia*. They are also used in stews and salads. Cumin and coriander are used more widely than on mainland Greece and on occasion are dusted on grilled fish and used in sauces. Mint, dill, and parsley are used in a myriad preparations. Rosemary is used especially with fish.

ENTERTAINMENT

Tourists expect to find more than just a lovely beach and antiquies during their holidays. Entertainment is also expected, which is no problem on Crete. **Hania**'s bars and restaurants are far more varied than one would expect from a small town. *Kytaro* in the old town serves Chinese, vegetarian specialities and curries along with Greek dishes and lovely dry white wine from the Kastelli region. *Oleander*, in a restored Venetian mansion with tasteful antiques in the old Jewish quarter, serves pricey but good international cuisine. *Tamam*, on Zambeliou 49, has an outstanding menu. For authentic *mezedes* (appetizers), go to *Zorba's Café Ouzeria*, serving tasty tidbits to accompany your before-dinner aperitif. For simple taverna fare, *Jimmy's* opposite the

cathedral, or *Faka's* are real bargains. The owner at Faka's sometimes takes down a bouzouki and strums along to haunting *rembetiko* songs sung by the patrons.

Ideon Andron, in a lovingly restored Venetian building, pipes classical music into its charming garden café next to the *shadirvan*, or ritual fountain of the museum. *Palatzo*, behind the tourist mosque, is an ideal place to nibble on mezedes while watching the sunset.

Fagotto is a sophisticated club open in the summer when it plays recorded jazz interspersed with live performances. *Amaryllis* is a charming piano bar in a cosy restored hotel in the Jewish quarter.

Bars in Hania seem to attract particular types of customers. *Le Monde*, on Odos Kondilaki in the old town, is filled with tipsy American service-men having the time of their lives. Ladies will get a lot of attention here. *Ablomov* on the same street attracts a more sedate hip young set, while the *Cuckoo's Nest* is Hania's gay bar.

Above: Entrance to a night club in the old town of Hania. Right: Tavli means board and is played in a variety of fashions. Following pages: The dolphin fresco in Knossos.

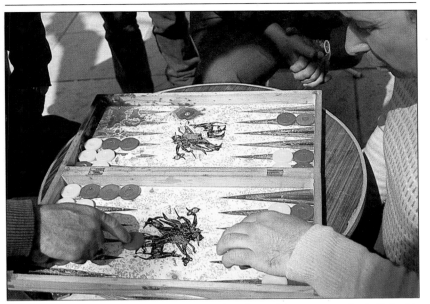

Those in the mood to dance might try the large *Ariadne* or *Estelle* discos. For traditional Cretan lyra music and folk dances, go to *Giorgos Drakakis' taverna* at the Venetian port. Larger *kentra* (nightclubs) such as *Lefka Ori* and *Zamania* operate in the summer on the outskirts of town and are the places Haniotes go to for a special night out.

Rethimno is smaller and less developed for nightlife. It used to have an abundance of clubs with live Greek music now found only at *Bar Retro*. Discos include *Fortezza* and Disco *Leski*. The wine festival in late July features electrifying live music and dance troupes, and is a good place to mingle with the locals.The *Knossos taverna* at the Venetian harbor is run by a friendly older couple, Josif and Anna, and is open all year. They serve reasonable local favorites –tiny olives, *paximadi* bread and *fava* (chick pea mousse).

Iraklio is the hub of traditional Cretan music and during the summer about a dozen places feature *lira* music and dancing. One of the most popular is *Psiloritis* on Akti Koundourou and the *Glass House* in the same vicinity. Iraklio also caters to foreigners and cosmopolitan Greeks in its discos such as *Babylon* on Doukas Bofor and the *Opera*.

In *Jam* on Dedalou you can listen to good recorded music in a large courtyard. In the same area are the *Curry House* and a Chinese restaurant. For more authentic and well-prepared fare, go to *La Parisienne*, a tastefully understated bistro run by a Belgian and his Greek wife, which adds a touch of class to a generally uninspired restaurant scene.

The *Paleokastro* restaurant outside Iraklio has terrific *axinous* (sea urchin roe) and *Balahoutis*, also outside Iraklio, is a working class taverna that specializes in snails.

Other resort areas have discos that are mobbed with international merrymakers during the height of the season. Some of the established ones are *Cosmos* and *Flash* in **Malia**, *Zorba's* outside **Matala** and the *Paleohora Club* in **Paleohora**.

223

BYZANTINE CHURCHES

It has been estimated that there are over 600 beautifully painted Byzantine churches on Crete. In the course of traveling through the island, the search for them provides fascinating diversions and actually finding them is at times quite difficult. Many of them are hidden in out-of-the-way places on the edge of villages, in fields, groves of olive or plane trees and on occasion on craggy ridges.

Most of these churches have never been restored. They are usually locked, and keys must be searched for among the villagers. They are badly lit by small, narrow slits of windows and to make things worse, candle soot, layers of accumulated oils and resins from incense and calcification blur in some cases completely obscure the images. It is always a good idea to take a powerful and wide-angled flashlight when visiting one of these churches.

Above: The Panagia i Kera Church in Kritsa.
Right: A fresco from its interior.

Architecturally, the churches of Crete fall roughly into four categories. The first of these includes large, three-aisled basilicas that show strong influences of Syro-Palestine style. There are the remains of over 40 of these basilicas, many of them domed and decorated with mosaic floors that date from prior to the ninth century when, in 825, the Arab Emirate was established on the island. It would appear that most of these churches were destroyed before and (or) during the Arab occupation. Yet, at Sougia, Hersonissos, and Panormos (18 km east of Rethimno along the coast) the basilica remains date from the fifth century and have rich mosaic floors. At Gortys, the surviving upper courses of the **Agios-Titos-Basilica** provide some idea as to the former majesty of these buildings.

The second category of churches are single-, double- or triple-aisled basilicas, long constructions with a surelevated middle nave. These are the most prevalent and are usually quite small, with vaulted roofs covered with tiles. A few of these churches are domed like the one in Kritsa, which has a high central vault over which the dome rests on a blind drum. Most of these churches are painted and appear all over the island. All can be dated to after the tenth century when the Byzantines re-took Crete from the Arabs. An especially beautiful example that has recently been restored can be seen in the Church of the Panagia in the village of Kournas. It has frescoes from the late eleventh or early twelfth century.

Domed cruciform churches make up the third category and are usually datable to the 14th century and after. These churches are roughly square in shape with two naves of different length (in some cases they are symmetric), crossed under the cupola. A variant is found in churches that have equal-length arms, over the central crossing of which a dome is built. The drums of these domes are usually quite high and are characteristic of Byzantine architecture as it evolved in the course of the 13th – 14th centuries in Macedonia and the southern Balkans. The Panagia at Lambini near Mirthios (around 1350) and the Panagia Gouvernitissa at Potamies near Kastelli Piedades, also 14th century, are good examples.

Finally, there are the churches that have a transverse arch that is higher than the nave, giving the building a cross shape – either externally or internally. These buildings are also dated to the 14th century. Good examples of these can be found in Agios Nikolaos in Males (in the Dikti Mountains 20 km northwest of Ierapetra) and the Church of the Saviour in Stamni (5 km inland from Amnissos, on the coast near Iraklio). The interior decoration of Byzantine churches follows traditions that are faithfully maintained and consistent. Variations are determined by specific architectural forms or their absence.

The dome is the most sacred area and is always reserved for an image of Christ as the Pantocrator. The apse with its half

dome is reserved for an image of the Virgin as *theotokos* or God-bearer. All vaulted areas are decorated with scenes from the *Dodekaorton* or Twelve Festivals, i.e. the cycle of events marking out the drama of the Redemption.

If a church does not have a dome, the Pantocrator image is set in the dome of the apse and the Theotokos image takes second place to it elsewhere. Images of the great saints are usually portrayed in the lower part of the apse. The following three recur often: St. John Hrisostomos, St. Basil and St. Gregory the Theologian. The fourth saint is often St. Nikolaos. On the lower walls of a church, a number of saints can be depicted, or cycles from the life of Christ, the Virgin or saints.

Even if your time is limited, you should try to visit at least one church that displays several schools and techniques. The Church of St. Mary at Kritsa (14th-15th century), which has recently been restored and had its paintings cleaned, is one of the finest and most characteristic churches on the island.

GRAPES AND OLIVES

Only a stone's throw away from a sandy beach lined with hotels near Iraklio, the scene that greets the visitor willing to walk off the beaten track could be straight out of *Zorba the Greek* by Nikos Kazantzakis. Beginning August 16, after the feast day of Panagia, under a scorching sun, it is time to harvest the grapes. Whole communities go out to the vineyards where they work hard all day long, talking and laughing as they gather the fruit that will end up as table grapes, raisins or wine.

Harvest time has changed little since dried raisins were sealed inside bulky clay amphorae, loaded onto sleek sailboats and shipped around the Mediterranean. Now the raisins are sifted and packed into burlap sacks, carried off in new Japanese four-wheel drive trucks and bought by the European Community.

Above: These pitless white grapes lie out in the sun to dry as raisins.

Entry into the EC has literally saved the lives of farmers and their families who can now sell their Cretan quality raisins on better terms.

Growing grapes is a labor-intensive process. It begins in the fall, with the cutting of ditches and rain drains near the roots. In January, when the vines are dormant, they are pruned, the dead branches cut off at the main shoots. In spring, the vineyard is sprayed against disease such as mildew and other fungi that could ruin a whole year's work. This spraying continues until the last minute when the dreaded month of August arrives. At the height of the summer heat the harvest begins. Families gather children, grandparents and even relatives from far off cities such as Athens and workers from Poland. In ten to twenty days the grapes are cut and sent to market or laid out to dry as raisins.

Producing raisins, or rather sultanas, named after the small *soultanina* grape, is a long and tedious process. First of all the grapes are hung on frames or laid out on the floor to dry in the sun. Sudden rain fall is always feared at this point, for it can diminish the quality of the raisins or even ruin an entire crop. The dried grapes are then pulled off the stem, sieved, cleaned and bagged.

The raising factories in Iraklio clean them again, dry them in ovens, sulphurize and oil them, and finally sort them out according to quality (a job that is done by hand), and repack them for export. The tourist boom in Crete is competing hard against grape production as a livelihood for the Cretans.

Olives

No one knows exactly where olives came from, but it is assumed that they originated somewhere in the eastern Mediterranean. They have been cultivated in Greece for several millenia already; on Crete alone the number of olive trees has been estimated at ten million.

The olive tree was holy to the goddess Athena and the winners at the Olympic games were crowned with an olive branch. For Jews and Christians it was a symbol of peace. The Phoenecians traded olive oil and thus contributed to spreading the tree.

For Cretans, the olive tree and its produce are an indispensable part of life. Virtually every family owns at least one or even several olive groves.

The oil from the fruit is used mainly in cooking. In earlier times it also fed oil lamps. Oil that has already been used is cleaned and worked into soap. Olives are also cleaned and either pickled or salted and form one of the basic foods of Cretans. Once all that appeared on the table or was carried to the fields was "bread, olives and wine." Olive wood is particularly hard and provides good firewood in winter.

Olive trees can grow for up to a thousand years and are 10 – 16 m high. Their almost grotesque, gnarled shape never

ceases to amaze. The olives ripen between December and February. During this period the olive harvest leaves villages deserted but the groves are alive with pickers. All you need is a few dozen olive trees to be busy for several months from dawn to dusk. Most of the olives serve to make oil. To reap the fruit a fine-mesh net is placed around the tree and the branches are struck with long poles. The work is arduous, especially if the trees stand on a slope and the heavy sacks have to be carried away by a donkey. Some of the less accessible trees are not even harvested for precisely that reason.

In past decades, heavy machinery allowed terraces to be cut into the slopes. A new Italian hybrid has been cultivated, a smaller tree that already yields after five years and is easier to harvest. To speed up the harvest on older trees someone came up with an ingenious idea: Blowing the olives off the branches using compressed air.

The best olive oil comes from the first light pressing (virgin). Further pressing produces a lower quality edible oil. The "lees" and the seeds yield a low quality oil that can be used in making soap.

Young foreigners who spend their winters on Crete frequently form the rank and file of olive pickers. One either agrees on a percentage of the oil produced from the crop or on a daily rate equivalent to about 20 US dollars.

Those who have sampled fresh olives will know that their bitterness makes them impossible to eat. To make them edible they have to be placed in water for several weeks and the water has to be changed daily. To speed up the process the olives are either crushed or nicked with a sharp knife. Once the bitterness is gone they are pickled in brine. Edible olives are generally larger and produce little oil. The most famous are the Kalamata olives. In order to avoid any damage to the fruit they are hand-picked from the tree.

TOURISM ON CRETE

In the last 25 years, Crete has undergone an explosive transformation into one of Europe's most popular destinations for mass tourism, accommodating tens of thousands of tourists every year. Testimony to this are the new blocks of hotels that litter some parts of the north coast, which are impossible to ignore. Examples of these complexes are particularly in evidence east of Iraklio, in the area around Hersonisos and over to Malia, around the bays of Agios Nikolaos or around Rethimno.

The reasons for this boom are easy to see. Crete is the southernmost holiday region in Greece and – together with the southern coast of Andalusia – the very southernmost part of Europe. The summer heat, which begins in early spring and holds on until the end of autumn, is reason enough for most residents of Cen-

Above: Hardy hikers carry their rucksacks.
Right: The less hardy go by car.

tral Europe to take advantage of it as a vacation spot – that is to say, to hit the beaches. In addition to these, furthermore, the island presents an attractive touch of exoticism: ancient ruins and monuments; splendid landscapes; and the local residents with their unusual, quaint customs.

At the beginning of the 1960s, only 2 out of every 100 hotel beds in Greece was located on Crete. You could only find hotels and pensions in large cities. Until 1970, for example, along a bathing beach such as that near the little village of Malia, the only accommodation for visitors was a single pension, the Pension Grammatikalis. Today, the one-time farmlands around the beach of Malia have been transformed, sporting some 70 hotel complexes.

Today, about one-sixth of Greece's total guest accommodations are located on Crete; and in the Greek tourist boom of recent years, this island has overtaken and outdone the former top destinations of Corfu and Rhodes. Crete has some

125,000 beds registered with the Greek tourist organization EOT; and official estimates have it that there are some 50,000 private, non-registered beds in addition to these.

It's impossible to get exact figures for the total number of visitors who come to Crete each year; the only figure available is the number of charter flight arrivals from abroad. But this alone recently amounted to 1.5 million (in 1971, it was all of 15,000). An additional million or so vacationers come to the island every year by boat.

Despite its rapid touristic development, however, Crete today occupies only a "normal" ranking in the list of favorite travel destinations in the Mediterranean. The island is midway between two extremes: while it's far from unspoiled, it's still not completely overrun. Furthermore, the majority of the visiting hordes keep to a relatively small area along the coasts, and usually come between the end of July and the middle of September. In the off-season, Crete still shows much of its original, distinctive face; outside of the beach communities, this is true all year round. For this island remains a land of peasant farmers and shepherds, who preserve their own special brand of stoical endurance. Crete, with its few, poor harbors along its unprotected and often inaccessible coastline, remains a land of the interior rather than of the coast. And in spite of the superficial changes that have taken place in recent years, the some 1,500 hamlets, villages and markets of this interior have managed, tough and sturdy, to preserve the traditional Cretan lifestyle. And here, even given the conditions of modern tourism, visitors today can still make plenty of discoveries. Here, too, the traditional Cretan hospitality, rightly renowned, is still in evidence.

In this area, unfortunately, some things were spoilt forever in the early years of tourism on Crete; some island residents

had cause to regret their generosity. Some of the first "alternative" travel guidebooks used to give as an insider tip the idea that you could get free meals, drinks, and a place to stay. Soon enough, Cretan villages were filled with people looking for a free ride. It's thus that backpacking to Crete began to get something of a bad reputation. Anyone today who seeks out a place to sleep somewhere in the open air on a Cretan beach (as hundreds of thousands of travelers do and have done) should be aware that many of the locals will join the State in regarding the presence of visitors with something less than unmitigated delight.

In the end, of course, it doesn't matter if you're traveling with a backpack or a Samsonite, if you visit Crete alone or on a package tour. Friendliness and tact, openness and genuine interest will always open doors for you. And if you do actually enter a Cretan house and experience some of the warmth of the local spirit, you'll understand just why it is that Crete is an incomparable country to visit.

ZORBA'S DANCE

Another time when my child died, I got up and danced. The others said "Zorba's gone mad." But I knew that if I didn't dance at that moment, I would go mad.

From *Zorba The Greek*

Dancing is not considered effeminate in Crete. In fact, as Zorba demonstrated, being a good dancer is a prerequisite for being a "real man." Many Cretan dances are lively and complex, with the leader performing athletic leaps and turns.

Known since Mycenaean times, the main instrument of Cretan music is the *lira*, usually carved from mulberry wood or occasionally walnut, with three metal strings. A *lira* is placed on the musician's thigh and played with a bow that sometimes has *gerakokoudouna* (hawk bells) attached, instead of resting on the player's shoulder like a violin. The strings are

Above: The lyre, Crete's folk instrument.
Right: The flutist from Festos.

stopped by the fingernails rather than the finger pads.

The *lira* produces a haunting primitive sound that is usually accompanied by one or two *laoutas* (lutes) which are larger and deeper in pitch. The violin used to predominate in eastern Crete but the *lira's* popularity spread from Rethimno and largely replaced it. Ironically, it is difficult to find *lira* music in Rethimno today. The *askomandoura* (goatskin bagpipe), guitar, *bouzouki* and *diouli* (small hand drum), can also accompany the *lira* nowadays.

The most popular Greek film coproduction is Michalis Cacoyannis' adaptation of Nikos Kazantzakis' *Zorba the Greek* (1965), starring Anthony Quinn as a quixotic drifter who pairs up with a proper Englishman (Alan Bates), in an attempt to reopen a mine in Crete.

The movie was responsible for the influx of thousands of tourists attracted by the stunning scenery and the popularity of the "Zorba Dance." The dance however, is not Cretan (Zorba is Macedonian), it's not even Greek: This *sirtaki* is a cinematic choreography of the fast *hasapikos*, which has its origins as a dance performed by the Butchers' Guild in Constantinople at the time of the Byzantine Empire.

Crete's three great mountain ranges divide the island into three parts and each one has developed a dance which is now pan-Cretan. From Hania comes the stately line dance *haniotis*, from Iraklio and Sitia the leaping *pidiktos,* and from Rethimno the jig-like *pentozalis* and the *sousta,* the springy coupling dance.

Many of Crete's finest lyra players perform in and around Iraklio in the summer and spend the winter playing in *kentra* (night spots) in Athens. The town of Anogia, 35 km southwest of Iraklio, is the home of some of the greatest *lira* players including the famed Xilouris family. Anogia has tavernas which offer typical Cretan music and cuisine and it holds a festival with a *lira* competition during the summer.

The *lira* players Antonis Peristeris and his son Manolis play in the summer at *Adelphi Tziblo Stephanki* in their home town of Gergeri, nestling in the mountains south of Iraklio, and at their own popular club *To Kastro* in Hymettos in Athens during the cooler months. Other notable *lira* players such as Giannis Sopasis, Tassoula Mamalakis and Yiorgos Papadakis play in the Athens area.

One fine musician in self-imposed exile is an Irishman, Ross Daley, a longtime resident of Hania. Daley plays a variety of instruments including the lyra, now mainly in concerts in Athens or in festival on the islands because he refuses to "plug in" and become amplified. The electrification of instruments is so popular that it is virtually impossible to hear accoustic-style music in the clubs.

To experience authentic Cretan traditions in music and dance, try to catch the festivities during the holidays, especially Easter, at village weddings, baptisms and

name days. Another Cretan tradition is the singing of *mandinades,* rhymed couplets mostly about love, with similies drawn from the Cretan countryside. At local celebrations, one can still hear *mandinades*, originally serenades performed under the window of a loved one in the early morning. Most *mandinades* sung today come from the vast repertoire of oral tradition, some with words in Cretan dialect that date back to the Middle Ages, and are often accompanied by dancers doing the Cretan version of the *sta tria,* the dignified *siganos*.

The epic romantic poem *Erotokritos*, laced with nationalistic overtones, was written by Vintsentzos Kornaros around 1645. It has over 10,000 lines, providing inexhaustible sources for *mandinades*.

Unfortunately, improvised *mandinades*, the most exciting form, are rarely heard these days. Composed on the spot by high-spirited minstrels, usually fueled by wine or raki, participants match wits as they fire off responses to one another's witty, and sometimes naughty verses.

A TASTE FOR WEAPONS

"There are people who call God by prayer and tears, others by patience and resignation and others by – blaspheming. Cretans call Him with gun shots."
      Live Free or Die, N. Kazantzakis

The Cretans are warriors and have felt to be for centuries. Maybe it is not obvious in Iraklio, Rethimno or Hania, where the Western costume, especially among the young, tends more and more to replace the traditional clothes of the Cretan men.

But as soon as you go deep in the countryside, to small villages such as Sfakia or Agios Mironas, many Cretans still wear the traditional garments: Riding breeches, high Cretan boots, called *stivania*, the cummerbund, the waistcoat and the little black turban with a fringe of small black beads.

Above: These traditional hand guns are more than just a souvenir for Cretans.

Such a costume is fit for war or, these days, the hunting of *kri-kri*, the wild goat that climbs up and down the Cretan mountains. The head scarf and the shirt are black, as a sign of mourning, and the large belt holds a knife.

A Silver Knife

Because they feel to be warriors, the Cretans have a taste for weapons. Treated with care and love, they are passed on from one generation to another, from grandfather to father and to grandson, in the same way as the name or the dowry of girls.

After the German occupation, the Cretans were supposed to give back any gun they possessed. But most of them did not. Today, there is a good gun in many Cretan houses. It is used for hunting, especially in the mountains, but it also comes in handy in case of a fight against another man.

Maybe not everybody has a gun in Crete, but every man at least has a knife.

The knife is still today a prominent object in the shop windows of Rethimno or Hania beside the steel water bottles on leather straps, the binoculars, the boots and the shotguns, everything needed to live in the mountainside.

With its handle in the shape of a goat's leg and its folding blade, the Cretan knife is an inseparable part of the manly Cretan costume. Slipped in the waist band, the handle to the right, the sheath to the left, it was a symbol of youth and virility, and useful too.

"He wore at the waist a silver knife
A knife such as that one
Nowhere will be found...",
says a popular song.

Such hand-made knives can be found in Hania at Stilianos Bonatos on Vasileas Georgiou Street.

From Minoan times to the present day, at work, during festivals, or in the struggle for freedom, the Cretan knife was part of life. By engraving the sheath, craftsmen tried to make it a work of art. One of the best artists was Grigoris Karidakis, who died in 1958.

Pallikari and Filotimo

The tradition of the *kapetanei* and the *pallikari* arises from the century-old struggle against oppression by the Turks. The "captain" was the best fighting man, chosen by common consent by the other men in the village to guide them in combat. The *pallikari* is a hero, ready at any time to defy death in the struggle for the freedom of the island.

A lot of words in the Cretan language express the glory of the fight, explains Jacques Lacarrière, a French author and Greek specialist. *Pallikari* means beauty and courage, physical as well as moral. *Filotimo*, on the other hand, means the unrestricted fidelity of a man to his beliefs, his family and to his people.

Two episodes of Cretan history can testify to this. The first is the attack on the monastery of Arkadi, which the Cretan guerillas used as a stronghold against the Turkish occupation. It took two days for the Turkish army to enter the monastery, and then the besieged set fire to the powder magazine, blowing up both themselves and the enemy. Another is the strange Battle of Crete, the first full-scale paratroop invasion in the history of mankind. On May 20, 1941, according to Hitler's directive 28, the seventh airborne division of German paratroopers invaded the airdrome of Maleme at precisely 7 a.m. Code-named "Mercury," it was to be the first and last of the airborne invasions by parachutists.

Max Schmeling, former world heavyweight boxing champion, told Berlin Radio after landing as a paratrooper that, "The fighting was hard but if the enemy had any heavy arms we could not have beaten them."

The Vendetta

Today, Cretans are considered as the best soldiers in Greece and often chosen to be included in the elitist divisions of the Greek army.

But a more controversial aspect of this tradition of fighting, freedom and proudness is the practice of the *vendetta*, still alive today. The Cretans often do not trust social justice and want personal revenge for any crime or wrong done to a member of their family.

It is possible today to see in remote parts of the island, on the door or the walls of a house where somebody has been killed, crosses drawn with the victim's blood. Some families treasure a shirt that is stained with the blood of the dead person, and this is handed from father to son until the crime is revenged. Sometimes years go by and it seems that the vendetta is over, before the opposite side hits back.

HUMAN SACRIFICE

During the summer of 1979, two excavations with sight of each other produced the first archaeological evidence to suggest that there was a dark side to the otherwise peaceful Minoans. These were the Greek excavations directed by Giannis and Efi Sakellarakis at Anemospilia near Arhanes and the British excavations directed by Peter Warren in the town of Knossos.

The recent excavations at Anemospilia cleared what remained of a small building placed on the northern slopes of Mount Iouhtas. The building had been destroyed by an earthquake at the end of the Old Palace period, about 1700 BC, trapping four occupants apparently engaged in a sacrificial ritual, not of a bull or goat, but a young man. The grisly

Above: Dr. Sakellarakis in Anemospilia.
Right: Is research casting a new light on Minoan cannibalism?

scene was uncovered in the westernmost of three rooms connected by a long corridor leading from the building's entrance in the east. The collapsed masonry lay over the skeletons of the three people: A woman in her late twenties, a man in his late thirties – already beyond the average life expectancy of a prehistoric Cretan –, and a young man of about eighteen. The young man had been bound and lay on a raised stone platform or altar. The excavators suggest that he had just been killed by the old man who slit his throat with a bronze hunting knife left on the spot when the building was destroyed. The woman may have been a priestess, and a fourth skeleton, found in the corridor near a fine vase decorated with a bull, may have been a temple attendant in the process of taking the victim's blood to offer it to the god. He never made it. The full force of the quake brought down the small remote temple trapping its occupants in a scene that caused much disquiet among archaeologists brought up in the tradition of peace-loving Minoans.

At Knossos, excavations behind the Stratigraphical Museum, about 1 km to the west of the palace, revealed a building destroyed by fire at the end of the New Palace period, about 1500 BC. The presence of ritual libation vases alerted the team to the possibility that they were entering some sort of shrine, but did not prepare them for the macabre deposits that lay beneath the thick layer of burnt building debris.

In the west room of the building they found the semi-articulated, unburned bones of at least two children, eight and eleven years of age, who seem to have been in good health at the time of death. The bones bore traces of cut marks showing that the children had been butchered in much the same way the Minoans butchered animals. Fine cuts, most likely made with obsidian blades, on the arms, legs and collar bones show that the flesh was deliberately stripped from the bones: The only explanation being that it was meant to be eaten. The skulls had been prised off the necks and the jaws forced open, perhaps to extract their tongues. One of the skulls had been cut open with a circular incision apparently to dig out the brain, again for what other reason than to eat it?

Both excavations have forced archaeologists to take a fresh look at Minoan religious practices and to consider more seriously the primitive aspects of Greek mythology. We know from Minoan iconography that bulls were sacrificed, and it is possible that in extreme circumstances a human may have been offered to the gods. It may also have been part of a rite like the later Dionysian rituals that we suspect had their origins in the cult of Cretan Zeus. Mythology recalls that the young Zeus was captured by the Titans, who lured him away from the Curetes with toys, and then tore him to pieces and devoured him. Scholars have long suspected a Cretan origin for the oldest of the Greek myths. The evidence from Anemospilia and Knossos goes a long way to supporting their theories, unsavory as it may seem.

MINOAN ART

The art of the Cretan Bronze Age must be viewed in the wider context of the contemporary eastern Mediterranean. The techniques and even many of the materials of the Minoan craftsman were borrowed and imported from Egypt, the Near East and Mesopotamia, but the result is always distinctively Minoan.

As Early Minoan settlements evolved from family dwellings to villages, and crafts such as metallurgy, stone carving, pottery making and wall-painting came to require technical skills and knowledge beyond the ability of the average agrarian, society found a need for specialized craftsmen. These individuals devoted their time to making products for everyday village consumption, but at the same time were responsible for keeping up with the technical advances being made in their craft in the East. When the Old Palaces at Knossos, Festos and Malia were established, shortly after 1900 BC, the finest of the craftsmen were called in to work on the first great public monuments in Crete, and the first true Minoan art appeared.

The most important fact the modern viewer must bear in mind is that Minoan art was created for religious purposes; there are no scenes of everyday life. Even the wonderful wall-paintings, with delicate lifelike renderings of flowers and birds, were probably executed to give the viewer a feeling of the season during which a particular festival or rite took place. No works are signed or attributed to an individual artist. The only artist's name that survives in later Greek mythology is that of Dedalus, the architect for the palace at Knossos.

The most distinctive products of the Old Palaces are the fine polychrome ceramics called Kamaresware after the Ka-

Right: A Minoan pitcher from the Kamares era.

mares Cave where they were first found toward the end of the last century. With the introduction of the potter's wheel around 1900 BC and the establishment of permanent pottery kilns that could reach temperatures of over 1000 degrees Celsius, the vase-makers in Crete where able to take the high quality neogene clays that abound on the lower slopes of Mount Iouhtas, south of Knossos, and create the finest ceramics in the prehistoric Mediterranean. Using designs adapted from nature and white, red, yellow, orange and violet pigments applied on a dark ground, they created masterpieces of uniform design based on the spiral, loop and flower petal, occasionally adding fish and animal motifs and, very rarely, humans. The liveliness and beauty of Kamaresware appealed to the Minoans' contemporaries and examples of the ware are found throughout the Greek islands, the Levant and Egypt where they were no doubt treasured. But Kamaresware makes up only a small percentage of the mass of domestic and utilitarian ceramics of the period, which, along with its fragility, has led specialists to suggest that it was produced for ceremonial purposes.

The finest art of the Aegean Bronze Age was produced during the period of the New Palaces, 1700 to 1500 BC, and is best represented by the wall-paintings that adorned the palace and surrounding houses at Knossos. Not true frescoes, the wall-paintings were applied to a thin layer of very fine white lime plaster. The scenes were organized in advance with indications of undulating landscapes usually painted as seen from above. The main figures and natural elements were then placed within the landscape or an architectural setting. Specialists regard the Knossos frescoes as being part of pictorial programmes in the palaces, perhaps commemorating ceremonies dealing with spring festivals, sacred marriage and initiation rites that took place at different times of the year.

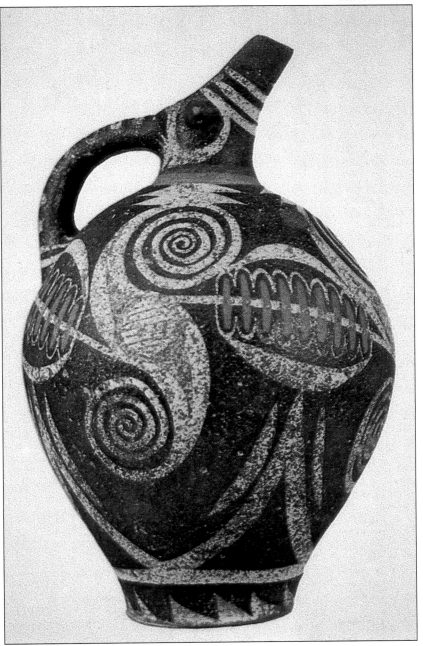

Nelles Maps

... get you going.

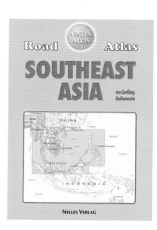

- Afghanistan
- Australia
- Bangkok
- Burma
- Caribbean Islands 1/
  Bermuda, Bahamas,
  Greater Antilles
- Caribbean Islands 2/
  Lesser Antilles
- Central America
- China 1/
  North-Eastern China
- China 2/
  Northern China
- China 3/
  Central China
- China 4/
  Southern China
- Crete
- Egypt
- Hawaiian Islands
- Hawaiian Islands 1/ Kauai

Nelles Maps

- Hawaiian Islands 2/
  Honolulu, Oahu
- Hawaiian Islands 3/
  Maui, Molokai, Lanai
- Hawaiian Islands 4/ Hawaii
- Himalaya
- Hong Kong
- Indian Subcontinent
- India 1/ Northern India
- India 2/ Western India
- India 3/ Eastern India
- India 4/ Southern India
- India 5/ North-Eastern India
- Indonesia
- Indonesia 1/ Sumatra
- Indonesia 2/
  Java + Nusa Tenggara
- Indonesia 3/ Bali
- Indonesia 4/ Kalimantan

- Indonesia 5/ Java + Bali
- Indonesia 6/ Sulawesi
- Indonesia 7/
  Irian Jaya + Maluku
- Jakarta
- Japan
- Kenya
- Korea
- Malaysia
- West Malaysia
- Manila
- Mexico
- Nepal
- New Zealand
- Pakistan
- Philippines
- Singapore
- South East Asia
- Sri Lanka
- Taiwan
- Thailand
- Vietnam, Laos, Cambodia

TABLE OF CONTENTS

PREPARATION

This section provides general information for the traveler to Crete. For more detailed and up to date information the traveler should contact the Greek National Tourist Organization in Athens and in Crete (GNTO), known as EOT in Greece, or abroad (for addresses see below).

Climate

The climate in Crete conforms to the traditional Mediterranean image of sunny and warm weather between mid-April and mid-October. Late spring and fall are the best times to visit – wild flowers in the spring, mellow evenings in the fall. Avoid, if you can, July and August – it is hot and crowded. Winters in Crete can be humid and cold, though, with a temperature ranging from 5 to 18 degrees C in coastal regions, and 0 to 15 degrees C inland. During the summer months, temperatures can reach 27 to 35 degrees C, although cool winds often save the day.

Clothing

If you visit Crete in the summer months bring very light clothing, avoiding synthetics and favoring cotton. Sandals are ideal but bring also a pair of hiking shoes – especially if you plan to walk through the Gorge of Samaria. A hat will protect you from the midday sun and a sweater will help you for the night breezes. Shorts are allowed everywhere except when visiting churches and monasteries. In fancier restaurants and hotels you will need a somewhat more formal dress and jacket. Take a couple of bathing suits. Nude bathing is allowed only in certain secluded beaches. Topless bathing is allowed in hotel (private) beaches and some public beaches.

Entry Regulations

You need a valid ID card if you are a citizen of Western Europe, including Switzerland and Austria. You need your passport if your are from the USA, Canada, Australia and New Zealand. No visa is necessary. However, if you want to stay longer than three months you must obtain a permit from the Bureau of Aliens in Athens (9 Halkokondili St.). Citizens of other countries should consult a Greek Embassy or consulate regarding the need for a visa before leaving their country. Crete does not have any diseases, so you do not need any health immunizations to enter the island.

Customs

Since the EU laws came into effect on January 1, 1993, all citizens of EU countries are allowed to transport objects falling into the vague category of "objects for personal use for the period of your stay." Among these objects are counted cameras and video cameras, radios, and similar travel gear; other import goods are limited to 200 cigarettes (Greeks are heavy smokers), up to 2 liters of wine, 1 liter of spirits, half a kilo of coffee (for adults over 18). Note that these restrictions even apply to goods from duty-free shops. When leaving the country, note that it's strictly forbidden, punishable by fine, to export any kind of antiquity (icons, archaeological finds, etc.).

Currency and Exchange

You can bring an unlimited amount of foreign currency and traveler's checks into Crete but you can take out only US$ 500 unless you have declared it upon entry. You can import or export only 3000 Greek drachmas. The official exchange rate is fixed by the Bank of Greece daily. Banks and most hotels can buy foreign currency.

TRAVELING TO CRETE

By car: If you plan to stay for a longer period on Crete then it is worth coming by car. There are two main roads from central Europe. The old road over (ex-)

Yugoslavia is as good as closed, and the trip through Hungary, Rumania and Bulgaria is very complicated.

The second, more pleasant, possibility is to travel through Italy. There are several car ferries a day from Ancona and Brindisi to the Greek mainland harbors of Igoumenitsa and Patras (Ancona to Igoumenitsa or Patras: 24-36 hours; from Brindisi 11-20 hours). From Bari, there are several ships a week to Igoumenitsa (13-20 hours; Otranto to Igoumenitsa, 8 hours. In the summer season, there are direct ship connections to Iraklio, once a week from Venice (March-October; 60 hours) and several times a week from Ancona (June-September, 55 hours).

By air: By charter flights from all major cities in Europe to Iraklio and Hania. Via **Olympic Airways** (the national airline of Greece) 4-5 daily flights from Athens to Iraklio and from Athens to Hania. Approximate flying time: 1/2 hour. For summer travel, early reservations recommended.

By ship: From Piraeus, the port of Athens, daily to Iraklio and Hania and vice versa (12 hours, each way). Several times a week, there's service to Iraklio from Paros / Naxos / Santorini. Boats run twice a week to Agios Nikolaos and Sintia (and on to Kapathos / Rhodes); once a week via Githio / Monemvasia (Peloponnese) / Kithira to Kastelli Kissamou.

TRAVELING IN CRETE

By bus: Regularly scheduled buses serve an extensive network of good roads city-wide, from the capital of each district to the other district capitals, and between the various towns and villages in each district.

By rented car: Rent-a-car offices can be found in most towns. The principal companies have branches at the airports. Speed limits: 100 km/h on the national network, 70 km/h on provincial roads, and 50 km/h in residential areas.

By organized tour: Travel agencies operate organized tours to the sights of the island of 1 or 2 day duration, for example from:

Iraklio to: Knossos, Gortina, Festos, Agia Triada, Matala, Fodele, Tilissos, Malia.

Hania to: Akrotiri, Agia Triada Monastery, Gonia Monastery, Kastelli, Samaria Gorge, Agia Roumeli, Sfakia, Paleohora.

Rethimno to: Arkadi Monastery and Anogia.

Agios Nikolaos to: Gournia, Lassithi Plain, Kritsa, Sitia, Vai, Zakros.

By yacht: Ports of entry are at Iraklio, Tel. 081/226073 and Hania, Tel. 0821/28 888. These ports have harbor, customs and health officials as well as a passport and foreign exchange control service. Fuel, water and provisions can be obtained here and transit logs must be stamped upon entry and departure. There is a yacht repair and maintenance workshop at Iraklio.

Hitchhiking

On the main stretches one is better off using public transportation instead of hitchhiking. On the byroads one can always give it a try. Locals are aware of the unreliability of the public system and often give hikers a ride. This sometimes means a bumpy ride on the back of a pick-up truck in the company of a dog or a goat. For the sake of politeness one should offer the driver a small obolus which he will either refuse in no uncertain terms or use it to invite you to a cup of coffee or an *ouzo*.

PRACTICAL TIPS

Accomodation

One can find all kinds of accommodation in Crete, from luxury hotels to pensions and rooms. The GNTO has published a list of hotels, but for more information inquire at the local police stations.

For reservations, write: XENEPEL, 24 Stadiou Street, 10561 Athens, Greece, fax: (0030)1/3225449, or call: (0030) 1/3237193.

The best known hotels in the big cities are: The **Xenia** hotels in Hania (B class) and Iraklio (A class); the **Doma** in Hania (B class), a converted neo-classic house with strong Cretan character; the **Atlantis** in Iraklio (A class), and other luxury hotels in Hersonisou Elounda and Agios Nikolaos. For all hotels you need prior booking, especially during the tourist season (June/September).

Banks

Banks are open daily except on weekends and holidays, Monday through Thursday from 8 am to 2 pm, Fridays from 8 am to 1:30 pm. You can also cash eurochecks on Saturdays in post offices. Many travel agencies also change money at the official rate. The fastest way to transfer money to Crete from abroad is to have it wired to a Cretan bank.

Business Hours

Business and shop hours are very complicated in Crete and vary according to the day of the week and the type of business. In general, though, schedules are more flexible in small towns and villages and more set in the big cities. Generally, businesses are open at 8 am and close on Monday, Wednesday and Saturday at 2:30 pm while on Tuesday, Thursday and Friday they close at 1:00 pm and reopen from 5 pm to 8:30 pm.

Credit Cards

The better hotels, restaurants and shops accept major credit cards; smaller establishments don't, though. Inquire before making purchases.

Eating and Drinking

Eating out in Crete is popular and affordable whether you use a formal restaurant or the more popular tavernas. The best way to choose your meal is by walking into the kitchen and pointing out your choice. You can eat your main meal at midday between 1:30 and 2:30 pm, or in the evening between 9 and 11 pm.

Start always with snacks – *mezes* – accompanied by an aperitif like the anise-flavored *ouzo*, and follow it up with the main dish and fresh fruit. The *meze* in Crete may be: *kohlí* = snails fired in oil, *gigantes* = large beans, *koukiá* = horse beans or fava beans, *melitsanosalata* = eggplant dip, *tzatzíki* = yoghurt with garlic and cucumbers, *dolmadákia* = stuffed vine leaves, *kalamarákia* = fried squid.

For a main meal, besides the Greek specialties of *moussaka* = eggplant and ground lamb with white sauce, and *pastitsio* = maccaroni casserole, Cretans are very good at preparing delicious *gemista* = stuffed tomatoes and peppers, *stifado* = stewed meat, *giouvarlákia* = meat-and-rice balls, *oktapódi* = fried octopus and, if you are lucky and want to go native, try *patsas* = tripe stew, offered early in the morning in certain restaurants, instead of breakfast!

As dessert, try the famous *bougatsa*, a sweet or cheesy custard pie, done to perfection at Kir Kor, the Armenian café at the Morosini Square of Iraklio, and *skaltsounia* (sweet tarts). If you are in Hania, try the sea urchin salad = *akinosalata* and *staka* = a butter dip, a gift from the Gods, offered on top of the Malaxa mountains overlooking Souda Bay.

Crete is known worldwide for its good wines, especially red ones and its throat-scorching *raki*, a spirit made of distilled lees from the wine press.

For all the above, try Balahoutis taverna (C category) on the road to Knossos, Iraklio and Birais on the main beach of Rethimno.

Electricity

A 220 volts AC, 50 cycle system operates. This means that appliances from the United States need converters. You also need an adapter, since Greek outlets and plugs are often three-pronged, different from those of many other countries.

Festivals and Holidays

Official public holidays are: January 1, January 6, March 25, Good Friday, Easter, May 1, Whitsun, August 15, October 28 and Christmas.

The festival calendar:

Sylvester/New Year: Greeks spend the turn of the new year playing cards and other games of chance. Shortly before midnight all doors and windows are opened in order to sweep out the old year and let in the new. Afterwards a new year's cake is served into which a coin has been baked. The person who finds the coin is supposed to have good luck in the new year.

January 6: On the feast of Epiphany, there are processions to the harbor in all major coastal towns to commemorate Christ's baptism. After blessing the water, the priest throws a cross into the sea, and young swimmers dive in to retrieve it.

Carnival: A week before Ash Wednesday. Some masquerading takes place in Hania, Rethimno, Iraklio and Ierapetra. On the final day of Carnival, all offices and stores stay closed. The day after Carnival, the forty-day fasting period begins. During this period, particularly in villages, no one eats meat, fish or milk products.

March 25: National holiday. Festivities with military parades in the cities to commemorate the beginning of the uprising against the Turks in 1821.

Good Friday: Church services and processions in most towns.

Easter Saturday: Midnight services after which the priest gives the new light in the form of a candle flame to the congregation, which uses it to light its own candles and then passes it on. The standard greeting at Easter is *Christos anesti* (Christ is risen). On town squares, large piles of brush are set alight and Judas is burned *in effigio*.

Easter Sunday: The most important holiday in the Orthodox creed. After the church service, the Easter lamb is served (often it is the baker who roasts it in a wood-fired oven). Easter in Greece is celebrated at a different date than in the Latin creed: April 23 (1995), April 14 (1996), April 27 (1997).

First Sunday after Easter: Agios Thomas; celebrations in those cities where the churches are consecrated to that saint and in eponymous villages.

April 23: Agios Georgios; festivities in the villages by that name.

May 1: Mainly a day for excursions. May garlands are hung on doors and on the hoods of cars.

May 8: Celebrations for Saint Ioannis in the Preveli monastery.

May 20-27: Commemoration of the Cretan resistance in Hania during World War II.

May 21: Agios Konstantinos in Pirgos.

Ascension of Christ *(Analips is):* Church services, e.g. in the church of Almiros near Agios Nikolaos.

Whitsun: Religious celebrations: these usually take place a little later, in accordance with the Greek church calendar.

June 24: Feast day of John the Baptist and midsummer festivities in the villages, brave young men jump through bonfires.

June 29: Petros and Pavlos. Celebrations in churches and villages to honor these two saints.

July 17: Agia Marina in Voni.

Second half of July: Wine festival in the city park of Rethimno.

July 26: Agia Paraskevi; festival near the Skotino caves in the district of Pediada.

July 27: Agios Panteleimonas: festivities take place in Fournes near Hania, Kounavi (Iraklion), Pigi (Pedhiadas).

August 6: *Metamorfosis tou Sotiros* (transfiguration of Christ). Processions on Mount Iouhtas near Arhanes, festivities in Skines (Hania), Armeni, Anogia, Arkalohori.

August 8: Agios Mironas in the village of Agios Mironas.

August 15: The Ascension of Mary is celebrated all over, in particular, however, in the monastery of Moni Chrisoskalitissa, Gonia near Kolimvari, Alikambos, Apokoronou (Hania), Faneromeni near Gournia. Festivities also in Neapoli, Mochos (Iraklio).

August 25: Agios Titos. Patron saint of Crete and Iraklio. Procession in Iraklio.

August 29: Decapitation of John the Baptist. Pilgrimage to the Rodopou peninsula from August 27 onward, celebrations in Platanias/Kalyves (Hania) and Moni Kapsas (southern shore).

August 31: Festivities in the Lassithi plain.

September 14: Pilgrimages to the chapels on the Psiloritis peaks, the Afendis Stavromenos and on the Kofinas. Festivities in Iraklio and Alikianos (Hania).

September 15: Pilgrimage to the cave church west of the Koudoumas monastery in the Asteroussia mountains.

October 7: John the Hermit. Festivities and processions at the Gouverneto monastery (Akrotiri).

October 28: National holiday commemorating the " No," the answer the dictator Metaxas gave Mussolini in 1940 when the latter wanted Italian faschist troops to have free entry to the country.

November 7-9: National holiday on Crete; commemoration of the resistance in the Arkadi monastery, festivities in Rethimno and Arkadi.

November 11: Agios Minas with processions in Iraklio to the cathedral by the same name.

December 4: Agia Varvara (Saint Barbara). Celebration in Agia Varvara.

December 5: Festivities in the monastery of Savathianon (Iraklio).

December 6: Agios Nikolaos. Celebration in Agios Nikolaos and villages and churches with the same name.

Christmas: The most important celebration in the Orthodox Church after Easter and the Ascension of Mary. Festive activities on village streets and in tavernas.

Health Care

Crete is an island with a "fetish" for pharmacies. You can find one on every corner of the big cities. Consult your local newspaper for the 24-hour pharmacies. In case of a medical emergency, call the local tourist police. These are the local numbers:

Agios Nikolaos (E. Crete) (0841) 28156
Hania (W. Crete) . . . . (0821) 24477
Iraklio (capital) . . . . . (081) 283190
Rethimno (center) . . . . (0831) 28156

The drinking water is safe but many tourists prefer to buy bottled water.

Hiking and Mountain Climbing

The Greek Mountaineering Association operates refuges (16 to 40 persons) in the White Mountains (at Kallergi and Volika) and on Psiloritis (Prino and Asites). Tel. Hania (0821) 24647 and Iraklio (081) 267110. Crete is a paradise for hikers and, especially, for mountain climbers, with extensive trails and mountains untouched by tourists.

Newspapers and Magazines

During the tourist season from May to September newspapers and magazines in German, English, French and Italian are sold in almost all tourist resorts. During the rest of the year foreign publications can be found in Hania, Iraklio, Rethimno and Agios Nikolaos. Furthermore, book stores, souvenir shops and the larger hotels usually carry publications on Crete in English, German and French.

Photographing

It is advisable to bring sufficient film material with you for your stay on Crete, as it is generally much more expensive on the island. Photographing (but not with video) in museums and archeological sites is free of charge as long as you do not use a flash and a tripod. When photographing people it is wise to ask their permission first. It is prohibited to photograph military bases and other installations. Signs indicating this are frequent in the bay of Soudia and on the Akrotiri peninsula. Disobeying these orders, including merely looking into your camera, can result in arrest and interrogation.

Postal Services

Although officially the post office is open Monday to Friday from 7.30 am to 6 pm, and on Saturday until 1 pm, certain services, like registered letters or parcel post, close earlier. So, better do your business in the morning.

Avoid sending packages home – too many restrictions are involved (inspection before closing the package, bringing your own material to wrap it, etc.). To send a telegram or to make a phone call, use the OTE, the state phone company. For local calls, you can also use the many kiosks on each corner, phone booths, telephones in hotels and restaurants. For long distance calls, you will need a metered phone. Inquire.

Shopping

Try to find old hand-woven fabrics and embroideries – rather rare today – woodcarvings, and jewelry (old Minoan replicas). Buy *vouryies,* old stones. When shopping in Iraklio, you can find old maps and rare books in some antique shops.

Sports / Recreation / Beaches

The extend of Crete's coastline makes it possible for bathers to enjoy different places to swim, mostly with clean and warm water. The best beaches are:

On the north coast, west of Hania – from the town of Hania to Kolimvari. On the west coast of the Hania district, the sandy beach of Phalassarna and, further south, Elafonissi. At Akrotiri: Stavros,

near Souda Bay; Almirida; from Georgioupolis all the way to Rethimno, the long sandy coast with Panormos, Bali, and Agia Pelagia.

On the eastern part of the north coast: near Agios Nikolaos is the beach at Sitia; the beaches east of Vai, with the famous palm trees; Kato Zakros, where you can combine swimming with sightseeing.

On the south side, the beaches of Paleohora, Loutro and Frangokastello in the district of Hania; Preveli and Agia Galini in the district of Rethimno. The famous or infamous (discovered by the hippies of the 60s) Matala beach and Kali Limenes in the district of Iraklio; Ierapetra and Agia Fotia in the district of Lassithi.

For water skiing use the bigger resort areas which have the equipment and instructors.

Tennis

Tennis anyone? Use the tennis clubs of Hania and Iraklio and the facilities of most big hotels.

Time Zone

Greek time is two hours ahead of Greenwich Mean Time. When it is 3 pm in Greece, it is 1 pm in London, 8 am in New York, and 5 am in Sidney. The clock is advanced one hour in the summer to give more daylight hours.

Tips

Service charges are included in all bills of hotels and restaurants. Customarily, customers leave an additional 5% tip.

Youth Hostels

Although Greek youth hostels belong to the Greek union of youth hostels and even carry the international insignia, they are nevertheless in private hands. Possession of a youth hostel pass does not necessarily guarantee lodgings. Furnishings and cleanliness often leave much to be desired and do not reflect international standards. The price for a night is about Dr. 1000 per person.

Iraklio: 24 Handakos Str.; Rethimno: 7 Pavlou-Vlastou St.; Agios Nikolaos: 5 Stratigou-Koraka St.; Sitia: 4 Therissou St.; Hania: 33 Drakanianou St.. Malia, Mirtos, Plakias and Mirthios also have youth hostels.

ADDRESSES

Offices of the GNTO Abroad

Australia and New Zealand: 51-57, Pitt Street, Sydney, N.S.W. 2000, Tel. 241-1663/4, Telex: 25209.

Belgium: 173, Avenue Louise, 1050, Bruxelles, Tel. 6475770, 6475944, Telex: 24044.

Canada: a) 68, Scollard St., Toronto, Ontario, Lower Level Unit E M5R 1g2, Tel. 9582220, Telex: 218604; b) 1233, Rue de la Montagne, Montreal, Quebec H3G, 1Z2, Tel. 8711535, Telex: 60021.

France: 3, Avenue de l' Opéra, Paris 75001, Tel. 42606575, Telex: 680345.

Great Britain and Ireland: a) 195-197, Regent St., London W1R 8DL, Tel. 7345997, Telex: 21122; b) (Office for planning congresses in Greece): Coworth Park House Ascot, Berkshire SL 5 UK, Tel. (99) 087-2440, Telex: 846962.

Holland: Leidsestraat 13, NS 1017, Amsterdam, Tel. 254212/3/4, Telex: 15465.

USA: a) 645, Fifth Avenue, Olympic Tower, New York, N.Y. 10022, Tel. 4215777, Telex: 66489; b) 611, West Sixth St., Suite 2198, Los Angeles, California 90017, Tel. 6266969, Telex: 686441; c) 168, North Michigan Ave., National Bank of Greece Building, Chicago, Illinois 60601, Tel. 7921084, Telex: 283468.

Embassies and Consulates

Australia: 37 D. Soutsou St, Athens, Tel. 6447303. **Austria**: 26 Alexandras Ave, Athens, Tel. 8211036. **Belgium**: 3 Sekeri St, Athens, Tel. 3617886. **Canada**: 4 I. Genadiou St, Athens, Tel. 7239511. **Cyprus**: 16 Irodotou St, Athens, Tel. 7237883. **Denmark**: 15 Filikis Eterias Sq, Kolonaki, Tel. 7249315. **Finland**: 1 Eratosthonous St & Vass. Konstantinou Ave, Athens, Tel. 7515064. **France**: 7 Vass. Sophias Ave, Athens, Tel. 7290151-6. **Germany**: 10 Vass. Sophias, Maroussi, Tel. 36941; Consulate, Iraklio, 7 Grafou St, P.O. Box 1083, Tel. (081) 226288. **Great Britain**: 1 Ploutarhou St, Athens, Tel. 7236211; Vice Consulate, Iraklion, 16 Papalexandrou, Tel. (081) 224012. **Hong Kong**: 2 Vass. Alexandrou Ave, Athens, Tel. 7242666. **Ireland**: 7 Vass. Konstantinou Ave, Athens, Tel. 7232771. **Israel**: 1 Marathonodromon St, Paleo Psihiko, Tel. 6719530. **Italy**: 2 Sekeri St, Athens, Tel. 3611722. **Japan**: 2-4 Messogion Ave, Athens, Tel. 7758101. **Luxembourg**: 11 Stissihorou St, Athens, Tel. 7217948. **Malta**: 2 Efplias St, Piraeus, Tel. 4181501. **Netherlands**: 5-7 Vass. Konstantinou Ave, Athens, Tel. 7239701. **New Zealand:** 15-17 Tsoha St, Athens, Tel. 6410311. **Norway**: 7 Vass. Konstantinou Ave, Athens, Tel. 7246173. **Sweden**: 7 Vass. Konstantinou Ave, Athens, Tel. 7290421. **Switzerland**: 2 Iassiou St, Athens, Tel. 7230364/6. **USA**: 91 Vass. Sophias Ave, Athens, Tel. 7212951.

On Arrival

Detailed information about your stay in Greece and your tours through the country is available at:

1. The inland agencies of the GNTO: **Hania**: a) Pantheon building, Kriari St. 40, Tel. (0821) 26426; b) Akti Tombazi 6, Tel. 43300. **Iraklio**: Xanthoudidou St. 1, Tel. (081) 228203/225.

2. The information offices of the towns and communities: **Agios Nikolaos**: Akti I. Koundourou 20, Tel. (0841) 22357.

Ierapetra: City hall, Tel. (0842) 28658.
Rethimno: El. Venizelou St., Tel. (0831) 29148. **Sitia**: Iroon Politehniou, Tel. (0843) 24955.

Automobile Club
Breakdown Service

ADAC Emergency Station, Athens, Mesogion 2-4, Tel. (91) 7775644.
Greek Automobile Club (ELPA), Athens, Mesogion 2, Tel. (01) 7791615.

Useful Telephone Numbers

	Hania	Rethimno
Area Code	0821	0831
Hospital	27231	27491
GNTO/Town Hall	26426	29148
Harbor Master	89240	22276
Olympic Airways	27701/3	22257
Bus terminal/City	23024	22212
Long distance	23052	
Road Assistance	26059	29950
Police	24477	28156

	Iraklio	Ag.Nikol.
Area Code	081	0841
Hospital	231931	22369
GNTO/Town Hall	228203	22357
Harbor Master	226073	22312
Olympic Airways	229191	22034
Bus terminal/City	283925	22234
Long distance	288544	
Road Assistance	289440	22620
Police	283190	22251

GREEK ALPHABET

A	α	alfa . . . . a
B	β	wita (beta) . . . . w
Γ	γ	gamma . . . . g (before a,o,u)
		j (before e,i)
Δ	δ	delta . . . . . . th (engl. the)
E	ε	epsilon . . . . e
Z	ζ	sita (zeta) . . . . z
H	η	ita (eta) i
Θ	θ	thita (theta) . . th (engl. thing)
I	ι	jota i
K	κ	kapa . . . . k
Λ	λ	lambda l
M	μ	mi . . . . m
N	ν	ni . . . . n
Ξ	ξ	xi . . . . ks
O	o	omikron . . . . o
Π	π	pi . . . . p
P	ρ	ro . . . . r
Σ	σ	sigma . . . . s, ß
T	τ	taf (tau) . . . . t
Y	υ	ipsilon i
Φ	φ	phi . . . . f
X	χ	chi . . . . ch
Ψ	ψ	psi . . . . ps
Ω	ω	omega . . . . o

Diphthongs

| α ι . . . . e |
| ε ι . . . . i |
| ο ι . . . . i |
| α υ . . . . af/aw |
| ε υ . . . . ef/ew |
| ο υ . . . . u |
| γ γ . . . . ng |
| μ π . . . . b/mb |
| ν τ . . . . d/nd |

USEFUL GREEK PHRASES

Hello/Goodbye . . . . *herete*
What is your name . . . . . *pos se lene*
My name is... . . . . *me lene...*
My home is in... . . . .
. . . . *to spiti mou einai sto...*
Where is the... . . . . *pou einai...*
How far is the... . . *poso makria einai...*
How do I get to...? . . . . *pos pao sto...?*
How much does this cost? . *poso kanei?*
This is expensive . . *afto einai akrivo*
I want something to drink . . . .
. . . . *thelo kati na pio*
May I have the bill? . . . .
. . . . *boro na eho to logariasmo?*
Where do you live? . . *pou zeis/menis?*
What is this? . . . . *ti einai afto?*
How are you? . . . . *pos eisai?*
What time is it? . . . . . . *ti ora einai?*
We'd like a room . . . . . *theloume*

for two	domatio yia dio
please	parakalo
thank you	efharisto
yes	ne
no	oikhi
okay	endaksi
come	ela
sorry	signomi
today	simera
tomorrow	avrio
yesterday	hthes
evening	wradi
water	nero
good	kalos
milk	gala
yogurt	yaourti
sugar	zahari
raisins	stafides
olive	elia
oil	ladi
meat	kreas
fish	psari
beach	paralia
cave	spilia
church	ekleesia
ship	plio/vapori
sea	thalassa
village	horio
hot	zesto
cold	krio
food	fai
pharmacy	farmakio
medicine	farmako
hospital	nosokomio
room	domatio
clean	katharo
dirty	vromiko
harbor	limani
shower	dousch
work	doulia
left	aristera
right	dexia
straight	isia
doctor	iatros
time	ora
city	poli
street	tdhromos
river	potamos
far	makria

near	konta
high	psila
low	hamila
down	kato
above	pano
dog	skilos
help	voithia
bus	leoforio
plate	piato
glass	potiri
knife	macheri
fork	piruni
spoon	kutali
cheap	ftino
expensive	akriwo
morning	to proi
noon	to messimeri
afternoon	to apojewma

Sunday	kiriaki
Monday	dheftera
Tuesday	triti
Wednesday	tetarti
Thursday	pempti
Friday	paraskewi
Saturday	sawato

1	ena
2	dhio
3	tria
4	tessera
5	pende
6	eksi
7	efta
8	okto
9	enea
10	dheka
20	ikosi
30	trianda
40	saranda
50	peninda
60	eksinda
70	evdominda
80	ogdonda
90	eneninda
100	ekato
1000	hilia
2000	dio hilliades
1,000,000	ena ekatomirio

AUTHORS

Michèle Macrakis, a graduate of Rhode Island School of Design and Project Editor of this book was awarded the I.T.T. (Fulbright) fellowship to photograph time in Crete in 1981. Of Cretan ancestry, she now lives in Athens continuing her work on Crete, while working as a professional photographer for many magazines and agencies.

Lily Macrakis, a graduate of the University of Athens, with a PhD from Radcliffe, is a Peloponnesian married to a Cretan residing in Belmont, Mass. She is Chairman of the History Department and Director of The Greek Studies Program at Regis College, Weston. She received the Academy of Athens Prize in 1988.

Nikos Stavroulakis owns a *pirgos* (tower) in Hania and is the director of the Jewish Museum of Greece in Athens.

Tom Stone has lived in Greece for the past 22 years, three of them in Rethimno. He has published several books and articles about the country.

Kerin Hope, an erstwhile archaeologist, is the Athens correspondent for the *Financial Times*.

Costas Paris works for *Vis-News* and *REUTERS* in Athens.

Samantha Stenzel was born in Chicago and educated at the University of Illinois and Northeastern University. She became intrigued with Crete after seeing Cacoyannis' film *Zorba The Greek*. She moved to Athens over a decade go and works as a correspondent for *Variety of New York* and *Hollywood,* the cinema columnist for *The Athenian,* and teaches cinema appreciation at the Hellenic-American Union.

Jean Pierre Altier is the bureau chief of Agence France Presse in Athens.

Sandy MacGillivray is Assistant Professor of Archaeology at Columbia University in New York. He studied Classics at McGill University and received his PhD from the University of Edinburgh. He has served as Knossos Curator and Assistant Director of the British School at Athens, and is currently co-director of the British excavations at Palekastro.

Wolfgang Josing, who studied Medieval and New Greek philology and ancient history, has been intimately connected with Greece for over 30 years. He lived on Crete for many years and revised the 2nd edition of *Nelles Guide Crete*. He was also the Project Editor and aothor of the *Nelles-Guide to Grecce - Mainland.*

PHOTOGRAPHERS